W9-AUA-817

The Bad and the Lonely

The Bad and the Lonely

Seven stories of the best – and worst – Canadian outlaws

Martin Robin

James Lorimer & Company, Publishers
Toronto   1976

Copyright © 1976 by Martin Robin. All rights reserved. No part of this book may be reproduced or transmitted in any form or by any means, electronic or mechanical, including photocopying, or by any information storage or retrieval system, without permission in writing from the publishers.

ISBN 0-88862-122-1 paper
ISBN 0-88862-121-3 cloth
Design: Don Fernley
Printed and bound in Canada

Canadian Cataloguing in Publication Data

Robin, Martin, 1936-
  The bad and the lonely

ISBN 0-88862-121-3

1. Outlaws. 2. Brigands and robbers - Canada.
I. Title.

HV6453.C3R62   364.1'55'0971   C76-017134-3

Photo credits:

Provincial Archives, Victoria, B.C.: 1, 2, 3, 4, 14, 15, 16, 17, 18, 22, 23, 24, 25, 26 and cover photograph

Oscar Dhu's *Donald Morrison, The Canadian Outlaw*, reprinted by Page-Sangster Co. Ltd., 1965: 5, 6, 7

Saskatchewan Provincial Archives: 8, 9

The *Globe*, Toronto: 10, 11, 12, 13

Royal Canadian Mounted Police: 19, 20, 21

James Lorimer & Company, Publishers
35 Britain Street
Toronto, Ontario

To my daughter Freda

Contents

Preface

It occurred to me a while ago that it might be a good idea to write a book on an impoverished species – Canadian heroes. But I soon gave up the task as nearly hopeless and instead turned to the more sensible endeavour of conjuring Canadian villains. What follows is a collection of stories, drawn from the actual historical record, of poor and simple men who, for one reason or another, collided with the law.

In the eyes of the authorities, these men were villains who received their just deserts – after considerable time and expense in apprehending them. They had committed awful deeds against civil society, and were forced to pay for them, sometimes with their lives. Not all, however, were judged so harshly by their contemporary peers, who often perceived something just in the outlaw's cause, and felt for their sad plight. Hopefully, the reader will forgive me if I too, for reasons obscure, occasionally desert the side of the law's majesty, and empathize with the pursued.

There were many people – librarians, colleagues, my publisher and editors – who helped me to bring these stories to light, and I thank them. I owe a special debt of gratitude to my wife Grace who typed the manuscript and supported me in my work with unfailing encouragement.

Martin Robin
Vancouver, Canada

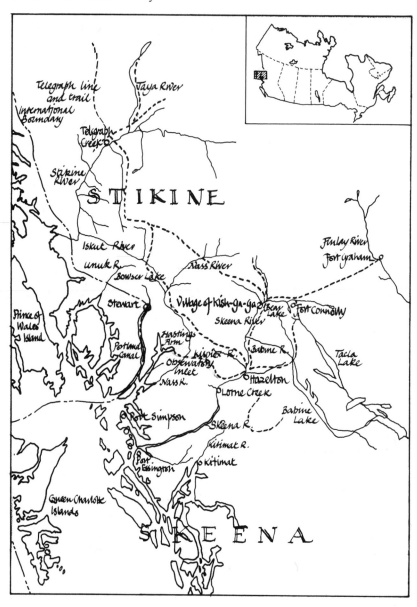

Simple Simon

Near the doorway of British Columbia's provincial museum, in the early years of the present century, there stood guard a large and threatening grizzly. It was a fierce beast, of immense size, with a smug, ferocious countenance ornamented with shining white teeth. But the bear had long since ceased growling. Nicely dressed and mounted, the grizzly had been presented by provincial Auditor-General J. A. Anderson as a gift to the people of British Columbia, who were reminded of the donor's prowess and munificence in an accompanying plaque.

Mr. Anderson donated the bear; but he did not shoot it. The task of killing the animal fell to a Kispiox Indian named Simon Gun-a-noot, sometimes called Simon Johnson, who lived in a small village several miles north of the town of Hazelton, in north-central British Columbia. For Mr. Anderson, the bear's killing was an exciting event; to Gun-a-noot, it was routine. An expert, powerfully built hunter in his early thirties, Gun-a-noot owned many trophies. Among his own people, in the wild country stretching north from Hazelton to the junction of the Kispiox and Skeena rivers, Simon Gun-a-noot was known for his strength, endurance, marksmanship and mastery of the hard terrain of the northern wilderness. Among the whites of Hazelton, he was known as a pretty good Indian.

Hazelton was a tough place in the century's early years. A supply centre perched at the head of navigation of the Skeena River, servicing the Babine region and the great forested area north between the Skeena and Stikine Rivers, the frontier town attracted swarms of trappers, packers, prospectors and adventurers who wandered in and out of the surrounding wilderness. Hazelton counted around 200 settlers, a few untidy rows of log shacks, a Hudson's Bay store, a church, an infirmary, a tiny police constabulary, and an unruly populace of nomad bushmen. Among its busiest institutions was the jail, a small wooden shack adjoined by a stockade which entertained, for varying periods of time, an assortment of bearded and sodden guests – white, Indian, and half-breed – who had run afoul of his Majesty the King.

Being a sensible man, Gun-a-noot avoided the prison. "For an Indian," local Constable James Kirby later confessed, Simon Gun-a-noot was nicely behaved. He hunted and trapped, winter and summer, and sometimes travelled as far as Victoria and Vancouver, where he sold his furs and bought supplies for the small store he ran outside of Kispiox village. Gun-a-noot lived with his wife Sarah and a single child several miles from the village, in a log house on a small ranch where he kept a few cows, several horses and a large team of dogs employed, during the winter months, to haul sleds on hunting expeditions along the Skeena River.

Gun-a-noot did not divide all of his time between field and home. He sometimes visited with family in the neighbouring village, or drank with friends in their homes, at unofficial beverage places, or at roadhouses favoured with licenses by the province's attorney-general and his political friends. One such place at Two

Mile Creek, owned by James Cameron, known as the "Geezer," had only recently received a license when, in the evening of June 18, 1906, Gun-a-noot and several friends dropped by for a drink and a chat. Among the Geezer's other guests that evening was a bearded packer and prospector, Alex McIntosh, the son of a former Hudson's Bay Company employee and an Indian woman, who drank often and heavily: in the bushes, at roadhouses and dives, and in prison, which he often visited. Simon Gun-a-noot had arrived to celebrate a successful hunt. McIntosh, a rough brawler, was there in honour of his release from jail, where he had served several months for illegally peddling alcohol. Alex McIntosh would have stayed in jail a few days longer, but for the intervention of a Mr. Charles Barrett, who needed the convict's services for a pack train due to depart shortly for the North.

It was a usual evening at the Geezer's. The drinking began early and extended into the morning hours when a quarrel developed between McIntosh and Gun-a-noot. Since a heavy alcoholic vapour hung over the house, enshrouding its dreary occupants, accounts differed as to the quarrel's origin and progress. Most located the trouble in a remark made by McIntosh about Gun-a-noot's wife. In any event, a fight ensued, resulting in facial injuries and assorted bruises to both parties. Gun-a-noot staggered upstairs, into the room of a Charles Fulmore who, on an extended drunk, had risen after midnight to cook himself a meal. Here the Indian washed his bloodied face and muttered a brief warning about "fixing" McIntosh, which he repeated later, before departing home on the back of his horse. McIntosh, his face red and swollen and nursing a badly-injured finger, rode away to the packers' camp where he rounded up some horses for the next day's train and consulted the local cook about his wounds. He then departed for the Hazelton hospital to get his injured finger dressed.

Alex McIntosh never reached Hazelton. Early the next morning, a group of Babine Lake Indians found him dead on his back, along a narrow trail, bounded on both sides by heavy underbrush, a mile from Hazelton. When Coroner Edward Hicks Beach and Doctor H. C. Wrinch arrived in the early morning, they found the body still warm. McIntosh had been killed, the coroner discovered, by a bullet which entered his body several inches to the right of his lower spine and exited through the collar-bone. It had been fired, the coroner surmised, by an assailant who hid close to the ground and trained his gun upwards as his victim rode by. McIntosh had been dragged several feet and abandoned to the flies.

Constable James Kirby had scarcely arranged for the disposition of the body, which was loaded into a cart for delivery to Hazelton, when news arrived, carried by Gus Sampan, a local trapper, that a second body had been discovered along the trail leading from Hazelton to the Kispiox Indian village. The new victim, Max Leclair, had not attended the Geezer's reception the night before, barely knew McIntosh and Gun-a-noot, and had quarreled, so it appeared, with nobody. Leclair, originally from Victoria and recently from Kamloops, was a guide, packer, hunter and author of occasional wild-life stories in the local newspapers, the last of which appeared in the *Kamloops Sentinel* in the edition announcing his death. He had arrived at Hazelton in April to prepare for a hunting expedition in the company of a man named Cowan and the honourable G. R. Maxwell, who had projected an extended trip northeast of Hazelton during the summer months. The circumstances of Max Leclair's death resembled McIntosh's. Leclair had been felled from his horse, which was never recovered, by a bullet fired upward by an unknown marksman into his lower back. He was found, on his back, in the middle of the trail.

The news of the twin deaths spread quickly through the local white community and Constable James Kirby, charged with the investigation, began an eager search. It was no easy job and Kirby's early inquiries yielded few results. There were no hard clues at the scene of either crime nor any eyewitnesses to the shootings. Interviews with local residents evoked few intelligible responses. The trail inevitably led to Cameron's Two Mile Inn whose guests from the previous night scratched their beards and muttered insensibly when asked to recall events and persons. After a hard morning's look, the constable came to a singular and profound conclusion. "I arrived at Two Mile," he reported to the Victoria superintendent, "and after going over the ground around the hotel and also the up and down stairs and taking in the faces and talk from the Indians there, came to the conclusion that there had been a genuine drinking bout going on."

The constable and coroner fared no better at the inquest where a dreary parade of hung-over and intoxicated witnesses staggered through the inquiry dazedly volunteering a string of "don't knows" and "can't remembers." Some hotel participants, like Mr. Charles Fulmore, on a three-day bender, passed out along the way and failed to make the inquest. Others, like Mr. Ike Moore, were so coarse and abusive that they had to be ejected. The Geezer did show, with an aching head, and volunteered very little information. The following day, before his scheduled appearance in court on a charge of selling alcohol to Indians, he disappeared altogether and was never heard from. The alcoholic vapour and the clouded recollections of a vague altercation, did not, however, prevent the jurors from coming to a firm and sensible verdict. "We, having heard all the evidence relating to the above case, have come to conclusion that Alex McIntosh was killed by a gunshot wound on the morning of the 19th instant between Two Mile Creek and the hospital, and are agreed that it was a case of wilfull murder by a person of the name of Simon Gun-a-noot (Indian) of Kispiox Village." Since no one among the bleary witnesses could recall any previous dispute between Gun-a-noot and Max Leclair or, for that matter, the presence of Leclair at the Geezer's, the verdict on the Leclair death was less certain and emphatic. The same jurors "very strongly" suspected "an Indian named Simon Gun-a-noot and an Indian named Peter Hi-ma-dan, as the murderer, or murderers." The second suspect, Gun-a-noot's brother-in-law, had been seen in his company during the previous evening.

Constable James Kirby now had a direction and, in the company of five constables sworn in and armed after consultation with Victoria Provincial Police Superintendent F. S. Hussey, set out for the ranch of Gun-a-noot. The Indian was not home, and his wife professed ignorance of his location.[1] In the corral nearby

---

1 Years later, in a death bed statement, Hi-ma-dan's wife is reported to have confessed to the killing of Leclair who she alleged had made sexual advances towards her. Gun-a-noot, she claimed, appeared at the death scene soon after and agreed to take the blame.

the constables found four dead horses. Three had been shot, and the fourth rendered senseless by a sharp instrument later identified as an ice pick. Constable Kirby concluded the Indian had murdered the horses to forestall their use by a pursuing party. But the presence nearby of several brothers of Alex McIntosh suggested they may have been killed by the dead man's kin as an act of revenge.

Continuing their search, the police rode to Hi-ma-dan's home where the wanted man's wife also pleaded ignorance of her husband's location. When the officers reached Gun-a-noot's small store, they found its goods, valued at $200, intact. As they left the store, they noticed a single occupant in a canoe crossing a nearby river. When the canoeman reached the shore, he hurriedly disembarked and disappeared into the bushes. The constables gave chase and, at neighbouring Glen Vowell, stumbled upon Gun-a-noot's father Nah-Gun, a fractious Indian who had served several terms in the local jail, and had little faith in the fabled justice of white men.

Nah-Gun's cynicism was well-placed, for he was immediately arrested and lodged in the local jail where he brooded for several days and mulled over ways of gaining his freedom. The old man soon hit on a sensible plan. Observing the happy location of the outhouse, whose rear wall extended outside of the adjoining stockade, Nah-Gun complained of stomach cramps. His attendant, a loquacious gentleman known as "Windy" Johnson, proved sympathetic to the old man's ailment and kept a relaxed watch outside while the Indian did his duty. On one occasion, however, Windy found Nah-Gun's stay indoors inordinately long. When several raps on the door yielded no response, Windy pried it open and found the Indian gone, through a large opening in the back wall occasioned by the removal of several planks. Needless to say, Windy was severely reprimanded for his lax performance and soon lost his job. He was subsequently known as "Silent" Johnson.

Old Nah-Gun did not go home. Instead he collected his wife and joined his fugitive son who, while Kirby's posse raced madly up and down the local trails, remained close to home. In the several days following the drunken inquest, Gun-a-noot carefully collected his kin including his wife and child, and his sister-in-law, Hi-ma-dan's wife, who was no mean acquisition. "Peter's wife is a Stikene (sic) woman and a hard case when roused," Officer Kirby later reported, "and also the best shot in the party."

Their forces intact, the outlaw band quickly vacated the Hazelton district. They headed north into the thickly-wooded and mountainous country between the Skeena and Stikine Rivers where Gun-a-noot had fished and hunted for decades. The band first made for Kisgegas, a tiny settlement east of the junction of the Babine and Skeena Rivers. From Kisgegas they continued north to Fort Connelly and Bear Lake and briefly visited with the Bear Lake Indians. The trek, by foot, continued north and east to the head of the Nass River where Gun-a-noot had stored a large cache in preparation for the next winter's hunt. The cache yielded ammunition, fish nets, traps, knives, hatchets and three canoes, which were soon transported to the nearby tributaries of the Nass. Fortified with supplies, in the midst of the vast and desolate region between Hazelton and Telegraph Creek, the nomad outlaw band prepared for the approaching winter, which proved one of the coldest on record. "Old-timers still recall the early marshalling of the steel-grey clouds heralding the approach of the winter of that year," a local paper recalled, "followed by month upon month of cold, the severity of which had never been known before, and has never since been experienced in this north country."

While the Indians retreated into a wilderness domain which few white men had dared to penetrate, the local constabulary probed the countryside around Hazelton. The police desperately wanted their Indians and frowned at the bad moral effect the fugitives' freedom might have on the local natives who were restless over land claims and fishing rights. Constable Kirby's pleas for help brought willing responses. A North West Mounted Police officer came by and offered sage advice and several volunteers. There was brief talk of sending a Mounted Police search unit from Edmonton. Sergeant F. R. Murray, a Provincial Constable, remained in the Hazelton district gathering clues the entire summer. Superintendent Hussey wired authority to Kirby to recruit and arm a half dozen special constables who were duly sworn in, supplied with rifles and horses, and sent off on a hunt. A reward of $300 was offered by Superintendent Hussey and posted by Indian Agent Loring in all of the nearby villages, whose residents professed a universal ignorance of the outlaws' location. As an aid in loosening their tongues, the reward was doubled in August to $600 and, several months later, raised to $1,000.

The police were not without some good early clues. Several days after Gun-a-noot's departure, a patrol came upon fifteen dogs tied up on the river-bank, opposite the village of Kispiox. Surmising they were Gun-a-noot's, and placed there as a sentinel system, the police shot the entire lot. In the process of execution, they noticed fresh tracks leading into the nearby bushes. They followed the trail for an entire day, until a fortuitous rainstorm destroyed the scent.

After a full summer of searching, the police realized they had taken on a formidable task. By taking their families with them into the woods, the fugitives forestalled their use as decoys and hostages. And by deserting the Hazelton district, the outlaw band drew the police into a country so wild and expansive that a concentrated search, without vast resources, was nearly impossible. Gun-a-noot fled to a cruel, virgin region whose contours were barely mapped, where supplies could be transported only with great difficulty, where bitter cold winters alternated with steaming insect-ridden summers, where narrow trails wound crazily through dense forests, ravines and freezing lakes. As the *Kamloops Standard* observed, the outlaw band had retreated into "a howling wilderness for hundreds of miles totally uninhabited except for the Yukon Telegraph service-staff which the Indians will have no difficulty avoiding."

The Indians did avoid the telegraph people as well as the gasping search parties which stumbled through the bushes chasing evanescent rumours. In August, it was heard that Gun-a-noot's party had been to the Kisgegas settlement on the Bear Lake trail. Indian Agent John Flawin, from Fort Simpson, outfitted a party of five, led by Government Agent Berryman from Aldermere, in Bulkey Vally. Berryman, equipped with pack-horses and enough supplies to last the autumn, twice visited the village where he learned nothing except that Gun-a-noot had been seen at Bear

Lake.

When the Berryman party returned to Hazelton early and exhausted, a further expedition was outfitted under the generalship of Constable Otway Wilkie, an old trailblazer sent to Hazelton by Superintendent Hussey. Wilkie's mission to Bear Lake, in the company of three special constables, in late September, had a special urgency, since the fugitive's continued defiance was having a noticeable bad effect on the Babine Lake Indians who were then engaged in a bitter quarrel with government officials and the canneries over fishing rights. When local officials tore down barriers which had been thrown across several streams, the Indians raised them again and assaulted the special constable sent to interfere with their work. "Because of the non-capture of the murderers Simon Gun-a-noot and Peter Hi-ma-dan," the *Kamloops Standard* complained, "the Indians in this district are becoming very cheeky and defying the law." The Skeena River canners sent a request for aid "to suppress the Indians" to Mr. Campbell Sweeney, member of the Canadian Fisheries Commission in Ottawa.

Simon Gun-a-noot had nothing directly to do with the Babine troubles. He was too busy running for his life. But his evasion of the search parties was a source of strength to the Indians and a growing concern to Otway Wilkie who wearily made his way along the Bear Lake trail towards Fort Connelly. Wilkie discovered there was substance to the rumours Gun-a-noot had visited the fort on the shores of Bear Lake; but he had arrived too late. According to the Bear Lake Indians, the fugitives had lingered there for two days before departing west along the trails running north from Telegraph Creek.

Otway Wilkie rested a few days at Fort Connelly, where he gathered further intelligence about his elusive quarry, awaited the arrival from the hunt of a trader named Plug Hat Tom, and informed the local Indians about the rewards for the capture of Gun-a-noot and Hi-ma-dan. In a letter to a Victoria superior, Wilkie claimed the Bear Lake Indians were hostile to Gun-a-noot, considered him a trespasser on their hunting grounds and were prepared to arrest or kill him if he returned. The constable also interviewed a man named McPhail, who claimed he recently met and spoke with Gun-a-noot. According to McPhail, the Indian wept when he told his story and protested he had nothing to do with the white men's deaths in Hazelton.

Aside from these faint gleanings, Wilkie had few clues of Gun-a-noot's whereabouts before his departure west in early October, across the mountains towards Telegraph Trail. Wilkie's journey was difficult and it took him over eleven days to cover the distance to number four cabin where the exhausted party rested before leaving for a Skeena tributary where Gun-a-noot was known to have a cache. The search party did locate several caches, which were thought to be Gun-a-noot's, none of which had been touched. When they came across a log-cabin favoured by the Indian, they found the fireplace green. Starved for provisions, and clues of their quarry's location, the party returned to cabins four and five along Telegraph Trail, wired a report, ate several hearty meals, and began the long trek home. "Up here there are no roads only trails and no feed this time of year," Wilkie wrote to Hussey, "It is a very hard country to travel in, very mountainous and at present impossible to use either horses or dogs. It will not be fit for horses till next summer and not fit for dogs until early spring . . . at present it is impossible to get food anywhere north from here only on a man's back (sic)." Upon returning to Hazelton Wilkie advised a temporary abandonment of the search. "I am convinced not only from my own observation but from the opinion of old trappers in the country, that it is impossible to continue the hunt at present." The constable's advice was followed and, in the late autumn of 1907, the three special constables who shared his Bear Lake sojourn were paid and laid off.

During the cruel winter of 1906-7, which witnessed temperatures as low as fifty-three-below-zero, officers Wilkie and Kirby, augmented by local Indian Department officials, sought further clues of Gun-a-noot's location. Indians returning from the hunt for Christmas shopping in Hazelton were interrogated. Posters were scattered again in the local villages advertising rewards, and punishments for aiding and abetting. Gun-a-noot's aunt and uncle were brought before a local magistrate where they testified that the cache they shared with Simon, at the source of the Nass, had been looted of its contents. The constables heard a bewildering variety of stories. One account had him at Bear Lake, another at the head-waters of the Nass. He was seen at Kisgegas, at Fort Connelly and at Blackwater, a tributary of the Nass. Strange hunters were spied along the mountain ridges near the eighth and ninth cabins of Telegraph Trail.

What excited the officers most were rumours which filtered in during the spring, that the outlaws were destitute and hard-pressed during the depth of winter. A Kisgegas Indian, Peter Jackson, informed Indian Agent Loring that he heard the outlaws had died from exposure near the shores of Bear Lake and was prepared to bring in their bodies for a proper reward. Loring bought Jackson's story. "Mr. Loring was under the impression the party had perished," Wilkie wrote Hussey, "He told me today that Simon and his father are both subject to inflammatory rheumatism and that having such a long, severe winter 53-below-zero they could not stand it." Jackson was sent to fetch the bodies or, if he located the fugitive party alive, to convey to them the message they could count, in the event of their surrender, on free government legal aid. Other Indians, and Métis, were offered or took bribes from the constables and returned little valuable information. After an entire winter and spring of interrogation, of Indians and half-breeds, prospectors and bushmen, the constables were starved for "reliable information." The major problem was with their informants who showed a peculiar reluctance to co-operate with either police or Indian Department officials. Officer Wilkie complained, "The Indians all seem to be afraid to talk of them." Agent Hankin discerned a similar reticence and weak civic spirit. "The Indians are not making the slightest effort to locate Simon," he wrote the police superintendent, "They are going their usual rounds and keeping away from any place where they think Simon might be." One Indian, however, named Solo-man Dick, a relative of Gun-a-noot, did firmly promise to find the outlaws, after informing everyone within earshot of his purpose: to aid and succour the fugitives by providing them with clothing and supplies.

Having tried a waiting strategy, and finding it wanting, Constable Wilkie returned to the chase. In the early summer of 1907, he returned to Victoria and impressed on Superintendent Hussey the need for an elaborate search-and-capture expedition. Hussey agreed and, on August 10, Wilkie left for Fort Simpson on the *S.S. Camosun* in the company of Sergeant F. Murray of the Vancouver Provincial Police, and Mr. Bert Glassey, a New Westminster bushwacker. Several guides and packers were recruited together with a group of special constables with the unlikely names of Huntley, Tyner, Murgatroyd and Jealous – the latter two ex-NWMP men – retained at salaries of $75 a month. Near Port Simpson, the search party split into two groups. One, led by Constable Huggard headed north via the Portland Canal to the Stikine River which was followed, with no results, to Telegraph Creek. The second, commanded by Otway Wilkie, ascended the Skeena River to Hazelton, where a new assault on the Bear Lake country was launched.

The second Wilkie expedition in search of the Indian Gun-a-noot was inflicted with an unending series of frustrations and reversals. A Métis named Paquette, recruited by Sergeant Murray as a guide after admitting to knowledge of the outlaws' whereabouts, deserted the cause around Driftwood River. A voyage on Bear Lake resulted in an overturned raft and the loss of supplies of rice, tea and sugar. When the Wilkie party attempted to steal quietly into the local Indian village, their presence was discovered and ignored. The constable was plagued with deep snow-falls and a blizzard of evanescent rumours. Mr. Paquette's replacement guide, Jack Graham, succeeded in losing himself along Telegraph Trail. When Graham failed to appear at their cabin, Wilkie and Huntley searched for him and wandered confusedly for eight days in the ice and snow around the Sustut River, before retreating in a blinding snowstorm to their rented Bear Lake cabin. Several days later, Graham arrived in a frozen and exhausted state, his snowshoes worn to pieces after twelve days of trudging through three foot drifts of snow.

While Jack Graham warmed his chilled feet, a halfbreed guide, Thomas Charles, joined the payroll and led Wilkie and Huntley on a fishing expedition through the Bear Lake mountains towards the Omineca River. The going was slow and the party made two trips daily: the first to blaze the trail, the second to claim and carry their supplies. Leaving the Omineca River, they hiked through White Wolf Pass where their food supply ran so low that starvation seemed a distinct possibility. Fortunately they stumbled on a pair of cabins, occupied by two gold prospectors, Bates and Olson, who volunteered food and shelter. It was decided, at this juncture, to dismiss Mr. Charles, and send him back to forage for Graham, by then in a lonely and semi-starved state. With Charles gone, Wilkie recruited Bates and Olson and, by his later account, explored the Sustut and Ingenika districts. Wilkie found blazes on trees and heard occasional stories of wanderings to Kisgegas and Bear Lake. Although the constable nowhere sighted the outlaw party, he did succeed in effecting an arrest. For two years, the police had been seeking an Indian named Skookum-House-Tom – alias Sam Brown – who had allegedly stolen some furs from a house in Kispiox and ignored a summons to account for his actions. "Skookum-House had been to a place by the name of Kisargar," Wilkie later disclosed, "which is situated between Bear Lake and Hazelton, at the head of the Bear Lake mountains. Here he drove the Indians into the church with a loaded revolver. After he had done this he escaped. But before he went away he shouted, 'I am going to join Simon and Peter, the bad men'." Whether Skookum ever located Gun-a-noot is problematic, but he did have the misfortune of meeting Constable Wilkie who removed his furs and a cash amount of $100 as a security deposit for a court appearance at the Bear Lake Spring Session. "When I arrested him he was in a dark room," Wilkie informed a *Daily Times* reporter, "but he did not make any resistance although he was armed, and from the time of his arrest onward he neither showed fight nor did he give us any trouble of any kind."

With Skookum quietly in hand, Otway Wilkie thought seriously of returning home, a prospect enhanced by a meeting with a band of Omineca Indians who told Wilkie of their discovery, in July, 1906, of the head of a white man "quite fresh" and only recently severed from the body. After hearing from the same people a further account of the mysterious disappearance of a white trapper named Fisher, headed for Fort Grahame with a pack-horse laden with furs, the idea of departure gained a new urgency. "After we had met these Indians," he recounted, "I began to realize that the search was useless, and we started on our return journey." So Otway Wilkie, employing Thomas Charles as a guide and Bates as an aid with the dogs, trailed on snowshoes, over the mountains and down the Nilkitkwa and Babine Rivers which eventually brought him to Hazelton. On February 14, he descended the ice of the Skeena to the Copper River, followed the trail to Kitimat and boarded the *S.S. Amur* to Victoria, which he reached on March 12. Wilkie did not return to Hazelton for a third expedition. Instead, he entered a claim for $500 extra allowance as partial compensation for "the most difficult task ever undertaken by the British Columbia Police in my memory of thirty years in British Columbia."

To Superintendent F. S. Hussey, Otway Wilkie's monetary claims were a secondary matter. What troubled the Superintendent more were the outlaw Indian's continued evasions which invited extensive critical accounts from the opposition press, including the *Vancouver Daily World,* whose special northern correspondent claimed that Wilkie, despite his protestations, had barely left his cabin at Bear Lake, succeeded in losing himself at Sustut Lake – where he was rescued by Bates and Olson – and never reached the Ingenika country where Gun-a-noot had been seen by several prospectors as well as by the reporter himself.

The Victoria constabulary pondered these claims and, in midwinter of 1908-09, decided to act. Their emissary on this occasion was a garrulous prospector named Frank Watson, a sometime resident of Vancouver's Commercial Hotel, who claimed to have encountered Peter Hi-ma-dan during the summer months of 1908 on the shores of Thutadie Lake. Being unarmed, Watson made no attempt to arrest the fugitive who made him several gifts of caribou meat.

Frank Watson's chance came in early December 1908 when he prepared to return to the north as F. S. Hussey's special constable. The prospector left Vancouver December 2 for Kitsalas Canyon where he picked up a guide and companion, Joe Belleway, who knew the location of the outlaw's hunting-grounds. After securing provisions, and arming themselves with prospectors' outfits to allay suspicions, they travelled by snowshoe up the

Kitsumkalum River, a tributary of the Skeena, towards Kitsumkalum Lake. They had barely gained the lake, about forty miles
from the Skeena, when the fresh tracks of a large party of people
were located leading north. They followed the trail and on January 8, after a full day's travel in forty-below-zero weather,
Watson and Belleway struck an Indian encampment consisting of
a dozen men, a half dozen women and several babies in
papooses. "We were received hospitably enough," Watson later
recounted, "but it was apparent from the start that we were
regarded with suspicion. One of the first Indians I spotted was
Peter ... whom I had encountered with a band of Indians while
prospecting last summer near Thutadie Lake in the Ingenika district ... Peter had little to say, although the other Indians plied us
with questions as to our mission in such a region in the depth of
mid-winter. They were armed with Winchester repeating rifles
and their cartridge belts were fairly bulging. We told them we
were on a prospecting expedition to the head of the Nass River
and inquired about the most direct route. This reply was received
with derision especially by the squaws. 'It is queer that you
should be hunting for gold in the depth of mid-winter. We don't
believe your story,' remarked one of the young bucks around the
campfire the evening of our arrival as he gently handled his
rifle."

Frank Watson had come to cashier Gun-a-noot and Hi-ma-
dan. But he soon realized a more likely prospect was his own
capture, and possibly murder. Watson lingered for two days
vainly hoping that the Indians would scatter on returning to the
hunt and thereby expose Hi-ma-dan, who seemed to regard the
Watson visit "with more indifference than his companions," to an
easy capture. On the third day, however, when the weather mod-
erated, Watson was disabused of the notion: "The Indians, armed
with rifles, waited on us in a body and told us that they did not
want our company any longer and asked us to return the way we
had come. Their threats were covert ones. Not once were we
threatened with harm, but the Indian is too smooth a customer to
act that way. One of the Indians, acting as a spokesman, once
more assured us that they did not believe our story, and with no
little eloquence said that white men had been known to penetrate

that region and never return alive. All the while the other Indians fondled their rifles in a manner to indicate that we would receive summary treatment if we persisted in remaining any longer. So we saw their argument, and, packing our outfit, said good-bye and started south, while the Indians with their tents already packed, struck off in the direction of the Nass River." When Watson returned to Vancouver, he announced he was finished with trailing Indian murderers "where the odds are so unfair" and offered the view it would take "a very considerable force" to capture the outlaws who had "numerous friendly allies ready to risk their time and if necessary their lives to prevent a capture."

Superintendent Hussey was not yet prepared to follow Watson's advice and risk a large expedition in search of a pair of phantoms lurking in the depths of a land forlorn. A grand expedition would have been too costly, too prone to excite the Indians already angry over land claims and fishing rights and too easy to ridicule for critics already nicely feasting on Wrongway Wilkie's trek. So the government persisted with more modest probes and gentler tactics. The reward for the outlaws' capture was more than doubled to $2300. Since the provincial constables made no progress, Victoria decided to try international sleuths. Mr. P. K. Ahern, General Superintendent of the Pinkerton National Detective Agency in Seattle was contacted and several Pinkerton men, which cost the provincial government $11,000, wandered in and out of Hazelton during the early months of 1910. Ahern sent crack trackers and bushmen, but they fared no better than the local people. When Mr. Bennett, a Pinkerton man, returned to Seattle via Victoria, he complained bitterly that one of the constables under Chief Maitland-Dougall, head of the Hazelton detachment, "was too fond of whisky and other things and that in consequence he was not a good constable."

With the Pinkertons gone, Chief James Maitland-Dougall and his Atlin counterpart, Walter Owen, continued their probes. Abjuring the bleak prospect of chasing Gun-a-noot in the bush, they chose to wait for the Indian, or for men who knew him, to come to them. The constables continued to bribe and quiz guides and hunters, and collected a nice file of guesses about the outlaws' movements. Charles Starrit, an Indian Hazelton resident in the pay of Maitland-Dougall, claimed Gun-a-noot sometimes camped in the Caribou Mountains, ten miles north of Hazelton, paid night visits to his relatives in town and, on one occasion, Winchester in hand, visited with Mr. Starrit in his tent at night.

Harry W. Dodd, a Telegraph Creek provincial constable heard reports of similar sightings and prowlings. During the summer months of 1910, the outlaws were seen three times. Bob Abesta, an Indian guide employed by the American Botanical Survey, led by L. Mixter of Boston, reported seeing Gun-a-noot armed with a 30/40 rifle and two automatic revolvers across the river from Telegraph Creek on July 23. After asking Abesta the identity and destination of the Mixter party, Gun-a-noot disappeared into the bush. Five days later, when the Mixter party approached the second south fork of the Stikine, they spotted a man on the trail fifty yards distant who, on eyeing the Botanical explorers, disappeared among the flora. Abesta identified him as Gun-a-noot and later offered, for a fee of $2300, to lure the outlaw to Telegraph Creek. "Abesta asked me what the government offered for Simon," Harry Dodd reported to Hussey, "and said that if the government would give $2300 for Simon alone, he would try and arrange to hunt with Simon this winter, and bring him into Telegraph in the spring, to sell his furs . . ." In early August, Joe Williams, a prospector, and an Indian named Leon, sighted a heavily laden man with three dogs near the Klappan River, who inquired about the location of the Mixter party. Leon identified the stranger as Hi-ma-dan.

The sightings and meetings continued in later months and years. J. P. Thorkerson, a Salvation Army missionary at Glen Vowell, one summer evening was led into a hut in the Babine Lake country by Soloman Dick, and there met Gun-a-noot who expressed an intention to give himself up. In March, 1912, a prospector, Frank Chettleburgh, was busy locating claims along the Pebble River, 150 miles north of Hazelton, when he noticed a curl of smoke across the valley. When Chettleburgh asked his Indian guide about the neighbouring camper, the guide replied, "Just another Indian" and later, "He doesn't like white men." Chettleburgh's neighbour turned out to be friendly. The Indian asked him about a cache down the river and, upon hearing it was

Chettleburgh's, asked whether he could have a jar of jam. Chettleburgh concurred. A week later, the prospector found a chip of wood at the cache bearing the penciled legend, "I take one jam." Several days later, on a wet afternoon, Chettleburgh was accosted by the same Indian while in his tent. The Indian, identified by his guide as Gun-a-noot, gave him a hind quarter of caribou to "pay for the jam" and disappeared into the rain.

The Indian was not long gone before he encountered, in late spring of 1913, another white man R. T. Hankin, an employee of the Yukon Telegraph line. Hankin was enjoying the warmth of an evening campfire when he was approached by a pair of Indians – Gun-a-noot and Hi-ma-dan – who glided in on sleds. The Indians shared a meal with Hankin who heard from his guests a surprisingly accurate account of his recent movements. A year later, when camped near his cabin on Level Mountain, Hankin was paid another night visit in his tent. The Indian brought a supply of caribou meat which he traded for beans and bacon. And he spoke, in the dead of night, of his sorrows and intentions. It seemed that after eight years of flight the outlaw was tired, contemplated surrender, and wanted to hear about his chances of escaping jail. Gun-a-noot disclaimed any interest in accepting a government-appointed lawyer to prosecute his case and spoke instead of earning enough money – which he reckoned at $2,000 – to hire his own legal counsel. The Indian was depressed about deaths in his family and wanted to spare its remaining members further hardships in exile.

Gun-a-noot, in fact, in the slow stretch of years following his precipitous flight, had done a remarkable job in confounding his pursuers. A master of the woods, the outlaw moved stealthily in a wild hunting preserve whose intricate contours he had long known. Gun-a-noot was peripatetic, a restless nomad who camped at favoured places but never stayed long enough to invite detection or capture. His home was everywhere; near the village of Kisgegas or Fort Connelly on Bear Lake; at Meziadin Lake near Stewart or by Kitwanga west of Kispiox; at the Nass's head or on the shores of Kinaskan Lake near the Klappan Flats; throughout the bleak, uninhabited Groundhog region which, save for an occasional prospector or a Yukon Telegraph worker, white men generally avoided. It was, for the uninitiated, a cruel land, heavily wooded and mountainous, stretching south from Telegraph Creek to Hazelton, and east from Fort Grahame on the Finlay River to the town of Stewart nestled by a glacier on the Portland Canal. There were few districts in this vast domain, which included the Skeena, Stikine, Kispiox, Nass and Iskut Rivers and their numerous tributaries, which the Indian avoided, or failed to hunt.

The first winter had been the hardest. The weather had been bitterly cold and the fugitives fed briefly on groundhogs and edible roots. But they soon turned seriously to hunting, fishing and trapping, using supplies lifted from the winter cache at the Nass River. Their allies marketed their mink and marten furs at Telegraph, Hazelton and Stewart, returning in the spring with the profits, in the form of canned foods, blankets, clothing and ammunition. The cash surplus was kept by Gun-a-noot in a legal aid fund.

Unlike poor Crusoe, who endured too long without companionship – and nearly went mad trying to stay sane – Gun-a-noot was not, during his self-imposed exile, alone. The Indian fled with his own family and Hi-ma-dan's, who remained perpetual sources of aid and comfort. But there was a bitter attrition over the years. Hi-ma-dan's wife died after returning to Hazelton in the early war years, while Sarah Gun-a-noot lost three of the four children she bore in the wilderness. Simon's mother passed away after a long illness. During most of his exile, Simon was deprived of the strength and companionship of his father, Nah-gun, who died within a year of their departure. It was said that Nah-gun, when his health failed, expressed a wish to be buried by a beautiful emerald-green lake where he had often hunted, and his son carried him forty miles by sled and on his back to a place of rest near the water's edge.

Gun-a-noot's family was precious; but he would not have evaded his captors without the aid, tacit and active, of Indian allies. The police were fond of describing the outlaw as an outcast, certain to be killed by the Indians at Fort Grahame, at Babine Lake, in the Stikine country or elsewhere, if he dared to trespass into their hunting preserve. Gun-a-noot did trespass, everywhere, but no Indian dared arrest, or kill him. Those who took bribes, or were temporarily employed as special constables, supplied the authorities little information.

Instead of turning him in and collecting a handsome and inflating reward, the Indians either protected him or joined in a conspiracy of silence. Gun-a-noot had his active friends and collaborators like Solomon Dick and Dan Skewill who sold his furs, brought him supplies, and reported on police movements. And he had family in Hazelton and Kispiox who sheltered him during nocturnal visits. But he enjoyed, as well, a larger constituency of tacit allies throughout the Skeena and Stikine regions who abjured co-operation with the government or police. A brave woodsman who chose outlawry in the forest over the uncertain fate of white man's justice, Gun-a-noot enjoyed a wide sympathy among the poor hunters and fishermen who shared his fears and suspicions and admired his remarkable courage. When Bob Abesta, the Indian guide for the American Biological Survey Party, discussed with Chief Constable Dodd of Telegraph Creek, the prospect of luring Gun-a-noot to captivity, he set a price of $3,000 for his labour. "He would not try for less," Dodd wrote Hussey, "as he knows that if he succeeds, he will never be able to hunt to the south of here again, and he wants to be fully recompensed."

Bob Abesta never did collect a reward for the capture of an outlaw who, in June 1916, began a second decade of stubborn evasion. Gun-a-noot's strategy, faultlessly pursued, was entirely defensive. His only concern, in his years of wandering, was with survival. He had no interest in killing people and sensibly realized that a single dead policeman would invite hundreds into the bush. The Indian had his chances and temptations. On several occasions, the police followed him so closely they were easy targets for his and Hi-ma-dan's rifles. Gun-a-noot sometimes stole provisions from their campsite at night or, in a jovial vein, appended his initials to trees blazed by the search parties. He spied his pursuers from mountain ridges, followed their activities with field-glasses furnished by his supply agents and gathered intelligence of their movements from friendly guides. But he continued, through the long stretch of the war years, a peaceful and patient outlaw, waiting for the right time and opportunity to emerge from the forest.

By pursuing a purely defensive strategy, Gun-a-noot bought years of time. The police continued to dispatch occasional and desultory search parties, and they persisted with their interrogations of guides, prospectors and Indians. But the empty years took their toll. The headquarters of the Hazelton district was moved to Smithers. New men arrived who had barely heard of the case while the ardour of the veterans was cooled by a decade of frustration. It was common knowledge, in Hazelton, Stewart and Telegraph Creek during the war that the outlaw was about, and visiting in town. And it was equally well-advertised, that he was contemplating surrender. By leaking news of his imminent surrender Gun-a-noot invited the police to lay back and wait, which they gladly did.

By the spring of 1919, their vigil was approaching a welcome conclusion. Gun-a-noot had long thought of surrendering and, from his early years in exile, he often broached the subject with friends and strangers. By the war's conclusion, however, the wish to quit the forest became an obsession. The Indian was tired. His father and mother had died. Three children perished in the forest. His two remaining children had no schooling and none of the benefits of civil society. His wife was ill and showed no prospect of improvement. In his mid-forties, Simon Gun-a-noot was sick of running and hiding.

Gun-a-noot would have quit the forest earlier had he faith in white man's justice. But the Indian was no believer and had no contacts with lawyers or others who could disabuse him of his skeptical notions and raise his hopes for aquittal. His meeting, sometime in the year 1917, with an old prospector and supply contractor for the Yukon Telegraph line named George Beirnes, changed all this. Beirnes and the outlaw became friends and during several meetings discussed the prospects of surrender. Beirnes was reassuring and told Gun-a-noot he knew a lawyer who could successfully fight his case.

The lawyer was from Victoria and his name was Stewart Henderson. A graduate of the University of Toronto, Henderson worked briefly in the Federal Justice Department, and served as

an Ottawa alderman, before striking west for the Yukon gold
fields. Henderson sat for several terms as a Liberal M.L.A. for
Yale, practised law in Ashcroft before moving to Victoria in
1913, and established a reputation as a brilliant and successful
criminal lawyer. Among his favourite clients were Chinese and
Indians who came to view him as a staunch defender. Henderson
was tough, combative, acid-tongued, and, when approached by
George Beirnes about Simon Gun-a-noot, he was firmly convinced there would be no trouble winning an aquittal. Henderson's assessment and willingness to act were conveyed to Gun-a-
noot, who met with the Victoria lawyer several times in the
woods outside of Hazelton. Besides being interested in the law,
Henderson valued money and agreed to accept, as a fee for
defending his client, a large sum which Gun-a-noot had carefully
saved during his years of trapping. Their deal concluded, Henderson and Gun-a-noot, accompanied by George Beirnes, on June
24, 1919, at four o'clock in the afternoon, presented themselves at
Hazelton's jailhouse where Beirnes announced, to an incredulous
Constable James Kelly, that the Indian with him – greying,
slightly stooped and worn – was the wanted outlaw.

Gun-a-noot stayed only briefly in the Hazelton jail where he
slept on a feather bed lent by George Beirnes, ate food prepared
outside the jail and, according to Constable Sperry Cline, was
supplied with plenty of fresh air through a jail door usually left
open to relieve the accused's claustrophobia. While the outlaw
languished in prison, ancient witnesses were contacted and yel-
lowed and dusted documents removed from their Victoria
pigeon-hole. The preliminary hearing before Government Agent
and Stipendary Magistrate James Hoskins was held in Smithers
where an application was made to change the trial's venue. It was
granted and the outlaw was transported to New Westminster's
Oakalla Prison where, besides huddling with his lawyer, he met
with the chief geographer of the Surveyor-General's Department
and passed on valuable information on the province's Bear Lake,
Babine and Groundhog districts.

The verdict of the October 1919 trial of a man described by the
Daily Province as a "picturesque super Indian," was a foregone
conclusion. The crown prosecutor, Alex Henderson, did his best

to revive the faded recollections of several witnesses and disabuse the minds of the jurors of romantic notions of Gun-a-noot's wilderness feat, or of his kinship to the fabled Robin Hood and Rob Roy. But Stewart Henderson had little trouble disposing of the major crown witnesses, including Constable James Kirby, who stumbled through an inept testimony. Henderson tore into the inquest following the murder of McIntosh, shredded the testimony of witnesses Thorkerson and McPhail – who vaguely recollected hearing confessions from Gun-a-noot while a fugitive from justice – reminded the jurors of the absence of both eye-witnesses and hard clues including the murder weapon, and suggested that Constable Kirby and his superiors had chased, for thirteen years, the wrong man. Henderson made sense and the jurors took only fifteen minutes to render a verdict of acquittal on the McIntosh killing.

Simon Gun-a-noot was a free man. But before returning to Kispiox, he rested several days in a Vancouver hospital. A three-day trial in a stuffy Vancouver courtroom, it appears, had strained him more than thirteen years in the forest. When released from the hospital, Gun-a-noot returned quietly home, spoke little of his trial, in either Vancouver or the northern wilderness, and awaited the arrival of Peter Hi-ma-dan who early in 1920 surrendered himself. Defended by Henderson, Hi-ma-dan was freed following a Hazelton preliminary hearing.

The return of the outlaws was welcome news to the whites of the Hazelton district as well as to the Indians who celebrated, and framed in legend, Gun-a-noot's heroic evasion. For the local board of trade, it augured well for development and the tourist business. "Hundreds of tourists every year have been kept out of the country," George Beirnes announced following Gun-a-noot's acquittal "owing to exaggerated reports that the woods are full of dangerous outlaws. Women especially became alarmed at the possibility of encountering a real-life outlaw. Even settlers have been influenced to keep away for the same cause." Although Gun-a-noot and Hi-ma-dan were back, the woods had not yet been cleared. Their example, it appeared, had inspired several other Indian fugitives wanted on various minor charges to take to the forest north of Hazelton.

Notes

A large part of the Gun-a-noot story has been pieced together from newspaper accounts in the *Vancouver Province, Victoria Daily Times, Kamloops Inland Sentinel, Kamloops Standard* and the *Interior News.* The correspondence between Provincial Police Superintendent F. S. Hussey and various constables, in the *Attorney-General's Papers,* British Columbia Provincial Police Records, Public Archives of British Columbia, contains valuable information on the chase and capture of Gun-a-noot. There has been, over the decades, a steady stream of periodical articles on Gun-a-noot, the most useful being: Morton L. Bennet (Cecil Clark), "The Story of Gun-a-noot," *The Shoulder Strap,* Winter, 1940; N. De Bertrand Lugrin, "Gun-a-noot," *Maclean's,* July 15, 1936; R. S. Somerville, "The Saga of Gun-a-noot," *Saturday Night,* Vol., 33, No. 3; Howard O'Hagan, "The Man Who Stayed Invisible for Thirteen Years," *Maclean's,* July 5, 1958. Thomas P. Kelley's *Run Indian Run,* Paperjacks, 1972, is inaccurate and overdrawn.

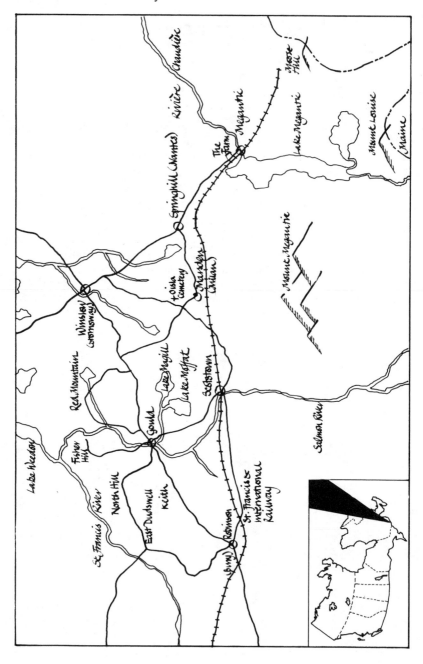

Poor Donald

The farm at issue included over a hundred acres of cleared land, a rude house on a hill and a pair of small barns. The owner, in the year 1885, was a gnarled Scottish immigrant from the Island of Lewis. Murdo Morrison would likely have stayed at home, in a shanty somewhere on the bleak, wind-swept island in the Outer Hebrides, had he been able to make a living there. But Lewis, in the middle years of the nineteenth century, was a crowded place, where the poor crofters and fishermen desperately struggled for space with the sheep and, later, deer favoured by the local lords.

The lucrative animals won and the crofters made the long ocean voyage from Glasgow to the New World, where several found themselves in the wild country east of Sherbrooke, Quebec. Among these early arrivals were Murdo Morrison and his wife

Sophie whose voyage to the Eastern Townships was sponsored by the British American Land Company, a colonizing firm which owned huge tracts of land stretching south and east from Montreal to the borders of Maine and New Hampshire. The Morrisons first settled on a small plot in the township of Lingwick where they cleared the rocks and trees, built a small cabin with a cedar roof and stone fireplace, gossiped in Gaelic with their Highland neighbours and raised a horde of children who, at judicious intervals, were married off. The youngest were Norman, born around 1848, and Donald, a stubborn, athletic boy who first glimpsed the Red Mountains towering over his father's farm a decade later.

By the time Murdo Morrison moved east, to take up a land parcel in the township of Whitton, only the youngest boys remained. The new farm was larger than the old, comprising almost two hundred acres in two parcels separated by a road connecting the largely French-Canadian village of Megantic (which adjoined the lake with the same name) and Springhill. The Morrison log house, like similar habitations occupied by Scottish settlers throughout the townships of Whitton, Winslow, Marsden, Hampden and Lingwick, rested on a hill overlooking the beautiful Lake Megantic.

The Morrisons worked hard to improve their land. They cleared the rocks, extracted stumps and built a pair of barns, which housed their hay and animals, and a snug log house from the cedar and maple which abounded in the vicinity. The children aided in the improvement, spending months and years fashioning a rough estate from the Quebec wilderness.

It was doubtless a sad blow to the father when Donald departed for the United States in 1879. At the time of his leaving, he was tall, about six feet, strongly built and desperate for a respite from the drudgery of home. He had blue eyes, high cheek bones, tawny hair, a full moustache and a strong jaw suggesting a certain stubbornness and determination, not unlike his father's. Morrison drifted south to Texas and the neighbouring cattle states where he worked as a ranch hand and cowboy. During the next four years he drove cattle in the American southwest and Canadian northwest, where he developed a facility with horses and guns.

Donald Morrison's adventures as a cowboy ended in 1883 when he returned to Megantic, at his father's request, to help manage the farm. The youngest son soon found, however, that the father, a domineering, inflexible man lately afflicted by bouts of senility, was not easily moved to recompense his younger progeny for their labour. Quarrels, some of long duration, developed over wages and the disposition of the land. Donald and his older brother became active suitors for compensation from the father, who soon sought the aid of a local Scottish capitalist, Major Malcolm B. McAulay. A native of Rosshire, McAulay had attained the rank of lieutenant-colonel in the Unionist Army during the American Civil War before settling in the Megantic region. The major was no dirt farmer. Well-connected through marriage with the Bailey and Pope families of Compton County, he had earned considerable wealth in construction, lumber and money-lending. Though basically a blunt and forthright man with excellent political connections and a ruthless facility for making money, the major suffered from a certain minor conceit: he thought himself an ordinary, impoverished settler like his neighbours and felt his usurious dealings with them were simple exercises in human cooperation. "I am simply a poor man," he once stated, "when I lend some spare money, I do it to help people out of difficulties, and I never had trouble with anyone."

The major might have maintained his unblemished social service record had he avoided any dealings with the Morrison family. But the truth of the matter is that McAulay snooped where money could be made, and he soon found the Morrison quarrel and the father's gullible senility a good chance for gain. Donald and his older brother Norman each pressed for a cash compensation, which Donald calculated in his case to exceed $900, a figure arrived at by adding the $700 he contributed towards setting aside the first mortgage to the $200 he felt due to him for his labour on the farm for almost two years, beginning with his return in late 1883. Norman had claims of his own, competitive with Donald's, which sent him and the old man, who favoured the elder son's claim, into the willing arms of McAulay. When the complicated transaction had finished, Norman had received a minor compensation for his work and the father had gained $400 in cash and a promissory note of $400 "to be applied against the mortgage when due." Major McAulay emerged with a $1,100 mortgage on the land and buildings, earning 9% per annum, while Donald discovered he had received nothing.

The youngest son was a simple man, with an elementary conception of the rights of labour. Deprived of his just reward, he sought remedies. He badgered his father, who had no money to give him, and argued with Major McAulay who remained adamant. He then sought the advice of lawyers in Sherbrooke and, later, Montreal, who wrote letters on his behalf demanding payment. When these failed, Donald, on the advice of a lawyer named B. C. MacLean, sued his father and in May 1876 obtained a judgement of $900. MacLean then advised his client to force the farm to a sheriff's sale, purchase it and move to set aside the McAulay mortgage as fraudulent. Donald confusedly concurred and, on September 18, 1886, in Cookshire, Quebec, the property of Murdo Morrison was offered for sale. Among the bidders were Donald Morrison and Major McAulay, who offered $1,000 for the land. Donald Morrison, it appears, did not have the ready cash necessary to effect the purchase; the major did, and the farm went to him.

What began as a simple claim for back pay became, in the autumn of 1886, a primal battle for the possession of the family homestead. The Morrison family, now apparently reconciled, stayed at the farm while Donald scurried to lawyers to find ways to set aside McAulay's claims and ownership. Donald consulted eminent counsel in Sherbrooke and when he failed to obtain satisfaction, he sought equally eminent advice in Montreal, including the opinion of Mr. R. E. Greenshields, of the firm of Greenshields, Guerin and Greenshields, who found his Megantic client somewhat paranoid and unlikely to effect any higher court decision upsetting the McAulay claim. "I remember Morrison very well," R. E. Greenshields later reported, "He came into my office several times about the spring and summer of 1887. He was a well-dressed, respectable-looking man, but I had not long spoken to him when I became convinced that he was a monomaniac on the farm question. He was under the illusion that everyone was against him. When I had fully examined the record in the case, I became convinced that he had not sufficient reasons to warrant the belief that the Court of Review would overrule the decision of the Superior Court at Sherbrooke. Morrison seemed to be a very determined man."

Donald could not be faulted for his lack of effort. He brought the McAulay purchase before a local adjudication, and lost. The mortgage was contested before the district court, and McAulay won. When McAulay finally initiated proceedings for the eviction of the Morrison squatters, Donald's lawyer failed to make an appearance, since his client had defaulted on payment of fees.

The Morrisons were evicted in mid-March 1887 and the parents relocated in a shack on several scrub acres near the village of Marsden (later Milan), a small railway station west of Megantic Village. For Donald, however, the fight had just begun and he reappeared at the abandoned farm and took up residence. Soon after his return, he noticed several peeled logs on the property which Major McAulay had prepared for delivery as telegraph poles. Donald took out his saw and cut up the poles into pieces of firewood size. McAulay ran to the local justice and demanded Morrison's arrest. A warrant was issued, and Donald was taken into custody by Constable William Edwards and subsequently fined $50 for willful destruction of property. On returning home, he discovered that his furniture and personal effects had been removed from the house at McAulay's instigation. He tried to have McAulay arrested for forceable entry, but had trouble finding witnesses and a lawyer to represent him. "I tried to get him arrested for taking the things from the trunk," he later complained, "but no lawyer in Sherbrooke would take the case. That was burning me to the very heart, that this man got off scot free no matter what he did while I was punished for every little thing."

Donald stubbornly moved back into the house in June of 1887, and was again ejected, by High Constable Moe of the Sherbrooke Police Force. By now Major McAulay had drunk his fill of Donald's maniacal persistence and he began looking around for a way of ridding himself of the cursed property. The Major found few interested buyers among the local Scottish residents who closely followed the dispute and sympathized with young Donald's plight. But he did find a purchaser among the French-Canadians, in the person of M. Auguste Duquette who obtained the property from McAulay in July 1887 for the sum of $1,500. M. Duquette was not looking for trouble. He was merely seeking a roof over his head and a piece of land to farm, and he was assured by Major McAulay that the trouble with the land was over and done with. But he received a contrary assurance from Morrison who advised the new owners that they remained on the land at their peril, a threat subsequently conveyed by the poor, confused M. Duquette to McAulay who told him that Morrison could easily be arrested for intimidation.

The Duquettes moved in and Donald Morrison continued his harassment which escalated into a peculiar guerilla war when Mrs. Duquette, dressed in a flowing nightgown and cotton bonnet, advanced one evening into her living room towards a large grandfather clock which she usually wound before retiring for the night. Mrs. Duquette had barely begun the operation when a bullet, fired from the window, shattered the clock's face. The Duquettes never saw the culprit but they had strong suspicions who he might be. They continued worrying about the lurking Morrison and gathering brief intelligence about his movements. But they persisted in their nervous residency and, by the early spring of 1888, had even begun to entertain relaxing thoughts that the Megantic maniac was relenting in his battle. They did not long entertain this illusion. One evening they discovered their barn burning and bitterly watched it levelled to the ground. Not long after, in May, a worse calamity befell them when, during a brief absence in town, someone set fire to their farmhouse.

The Morrison-Duquette homestead drama soon became an exciting topic in the surrounding Scottish farm settlements, in the neighbouring villages of Megantic, Springhill and Stornoway, and further west, in the city of Sherbrooke where news of incendiarism in the back woods crept into the local press. Few people believed the burnings were accidents, and among the Gaelic-speaking Scots word circulated that Donald Morrison, old Murdo's poorest and youngest son, the young woodsman with the chip on his shoulder, was seeking his just revenge. Among the persons absolutely convinced of Morrison's guilt and of the threats to the community posed by his free passage was Major Malcolm McAulay who nourished, in addition, a wholesome suspicion that his own life might be in danger.

Major McAulay and his high-placed friends did not have any hard evidence that Morrison had set the blazes. No one had seen him do it, and Morrison insisted he was in Springhill during the burning of the barn, and in Hampton when the house was levelled. But the major knew, without a doubt, that the burnings were no accident and no one else beside Murdo's crazy son could be interested in harming the unhappy Duquettes. So he prevailed upon Mr. Joseph H. Morin, a farmer from Sweetsburgh, Missisquoi, who served as a justice of the peace in the St. Francis district, to issue a warrant for the arrest of Morrison on a charge of arson and assault. Charged with executing the warrant was Donald's old friend Bailiff William Edwards who had earlier taken him in for interfering with McAulay's telephone poles.

Bailiff Edwards proved a reluctant agent and sought help in apprehending a rebel whose accelerating defiance of the law was inspired by the deep conviction about its unjust application. Edwards had long known Morrison and appreciated his anger and desperation. The bailiff was a prudent man who knew that Donald was not only obsessed with his rights but intent on enforcing them with a gun which he was known to carry with him. For these reasons, Bailiff Edwards raised no objection when a large gruff American named Lucius (Jack) Warren appeared at Mr. Morin's door to offer assistance in securing the Megantic maverick.

Jack Warren was not a favourite among the local highlanders; nor did he care to be. A sometime resident of the local "American" hotel, run by a man called Nelson Leet, Warren had lived in Megantic for about four years, during which time he fished, hunted, guided and took frequent trips across the border into Maine on what several of his neighbours thought were whisky-smuggling excursions. But his questionable reputation among the local highlanders was less crucial to Justice Morin than his willingness to undertake the hard task of securing Morrison. In late May, Morin swore Warren in as a special constable before his clerk and notary Mr. Joseph Napoleon Thibaudeau, who also witnessed the burly American's declaration of an oath of allegiance to the British Crown.

Having armed himself with a warrant in his coat pocket and a revolver in a holster at his side, Jack Warren lurked and wandered around Megantic Village. Warren was not a quiet retiring sort and made no effort to hide his intention of arresting Morrison, whom he had never met, by force if necessary. The American based himself in the American Hotel where he boarded, drank beer and bragged to his mates about his menacing purpose. From the vantage of a seat on the hotel's veranda, he scoured the main street of Megantic, where he daily expected the outlaw to make an appearance.

Morrison did not disappoint him and what ensued from their meeting was more fitting to Tombstone, Arizona than Megantic, Quebec. On June 22, 1888, in the early afternoon of a warm and sunny day, Donald Morrison, late an invisible resident of the nearby countryside, appeared on the main street of the village. Morrison knew Warren hung around the local hotel and held a warrant for his arrest, but he suspected that its term had run out. He came to town, he later declared, to buy some groceries, and his slow walk along the sidewalk towards the American Hotel drew nervous glances from the local blacksmiths, merchants and shopkeepers who stepped indoors when the outlaw appeared. Morrison was near the hotel veranda when Jack Warren, who had been sitting there awhile, asked the proprietor whether the man with the cane in his right hand was the wanted outlaw. When Mr. Leet replied in the affirmative, the special constable rose, entered the hotel, quickly reappeared and descended into the street where he placed himself several yards from his quarry, blocking his way. Morrison told Warren to "stand clear," and moved off the sidewalk. Warren replied that he was looking for him, asked him not to worry and, stepping off the sidewalk, blocked his way again. Similar verbal exchanges and logistic manoeuvres ensued for a brief minute until both men went for their guns. Morrison was quicker and put a bullet through Warren's neck, killing him instantly. Morrison then coolly withdrew, before a frightened audience of local residents, leaving the body to be claimed by Mr. George C. Mayo, the collector of customs in Maine, who found Jack Warren flat on his back with a neatly folded warrant in his coat pocket and his gun in the dirt.

Jack Warren's funeral, held a few days later, was meagerly attended by a clergyman, who said several kind words, a few hotel cronies and a long figure dressed in a black overcoat and wide brim hat who remained at the rear, head bowed and perfectly still, throughout the brief ceremony. The man in black was Donald Morrison who, in the days following the Warren killing, behaved as if nothing had really happened. There were, it is true, two warrants out for him: one for arson and the other, issued following a coroner's inquest, for murder. But there seemed nobody around to serve them. Constable Edwards knew better and no volunteers rushed forward to take Jack Warren's place in the village of Megantic or in any of the neighbouring towns where there existed among the Scottish settlers a sympathy for the outlaw who, it was agreed, had been badly wronged and fired at Warren in self-defence. There was, in addition, a marked respect for Morrison's proven prowess with a gun and for his determination to use it to resist arrest. It was said he could cut a clothesline with a gun in either hand, or uncork an ink bottle at forty yards.

Enjoying a brief immunity, Morrison freely wandered in the streets of Megantic and neighbouring environs without incident. He bought supplies at the local store, chatted and supped with friends, drank beer at the Prince of Wales Hotel and on Sundays, being a God-fearing man, attended church. News of his free movement, however, soon reached Sherbrooke and Quebec City, where the authorities heard of his defiance from the local peace officers and read of his exploits in the local papers.

It was not long before several provincial constables descended on the Megantic area determined to seek out and arrest the suspect who had earned the classification "extremely dangerous." But Morrison was forewarned of their visit and when the officers began making discreet inquiries, they found that reports of the outlaw's high visibility had been greatly exaggerated. The officers boarded at the local hotel and began peeking and looking everywhere in the vicinity of Megantic. But they learned nothing in the ensuing weeks except the difficulty of apprehending, with a few men, one wanted man in the land of the Scottish settlement stretching from Megantic north and west to Winslow and further west to Gould in the township of Lingwick: eight hundred square miles of forests and lakes where the outlaw, a hardened frontiersman, had spent most of his life. The policemen were new to the district and found it impossible to penetrate its hidden spaces, its hills, woods, lakes and lonely homesteads connected by dirt roads known only to the local residents.

The physical obstacles were bad enough. What troubled the police as much were the social barriers. Like other groups in the checkered Canadian quilt, the Scottish in the settlements east of Sherbrooke tended to stick together, a disposition towards closure which earned them the familiar description "clannish." In this instance, however, there was more than a customary affinity deriving from a physical proximity and common culture. Most of the local people were poor, like the wanted man, and many had suffered at the hands of moneylenders and lawyers whom Morrison had cursed and defied. "To understand the state of affairs," a *Montreal Star* correspondent wrote, "it must be stated that the people of the Scotch settlements declare that they have suffered for years and years the greatest injustice at the hands of unscrupulous money-lenders. Till the Morrison outbreak, the hostility of the people did not show itself. He was the first to openly declare his enmity, and his friends and countrymen, who claimed to have suffered as much as he has, consider it their duty to stand by him." Like Morrison, the local people were hardy pioneers who had wrested a simple living from the brutal Quebec wilderness. Poor Donald may have been stubborn, and even demented, but his fight was theirs, a primal battle for the homestead against swindlers and usurers feeding off the men of the soil. There was also, in Donald's mad assertion, a certain minor heroism which recalled the days of folk heroes of larger dimension like Bonnie Prince Charlie, Sir William Wallace and the fabled Rob Roy. The rural Quebec Scottish, like their forebearers, carried their folk heroes close to their hearts. Some even found, in their local rebel cowboy, a Scottish answer to Riel whose tragic cause lived among the French in Quebec. "This man is on the highway to become a hero," wrote a correspondent to the *Sherbrooke Pio-*

neer, "Thanks to the ever increasing sympathy that his numerous fellow countrymen of the district entertain for him, the greater number of them say that Morrison – and this is what encourages him – acted in self-defense when he killed Warren . . . a great number of Scotchmen reason as follows: 'Why blame us if we take sides with a fellow-countryman who had or felt that he had serious grievances and who killed a person whom he took to be a murderer while thousands of French Canadians defend Riel who, in 1870, killed Thomas Scott?' "[1]

The Quebec police, during the summer months of 1888, snooped and wandered, but they soon realized that, given their scarce resources and the negative attitude of the local citizenry, their task was hopeless. The police, in a small traditional community, were conspicuous, and the officers had a distinct feeling that their movements in Megantic and without, along the roads and in the villages, in the hotels and streets, were scrutinized and, perhaps, reported to the hunted man. They found the local people singularly uncommunicative. The police were English or French and sensibly understood that Canada was a bilingual place where men spoke either one or the other of the languages of the founding races. They discovered, however, that many of the local people spoke neither, communicating instead in a strange gibberish they were told was Gaelic. The Quebec policemen, like their Sherbrooke predecessors, encountered either a wall of silence or a flood of Gaelic.

When the men did gather some brief intelligence, it was usu-

---

1 Morrison's exploits soon unleashed a local bard who eventually composed an artless tome chronicling the tribulations of the Megantic's Rob Roy. A sample will suffice:

> Ten cadgers, and the bold Dugas
> Can't take our Riel and man awa'
> No, e'n their bagpipes when they blaw
>
> For Morrison.

> We'll gang to jail, e're ye shall ken
> Whether he's in the town or glen.
> We'll let you see we're Hell and men
>
> Like Morrison.

The writer called himself Roderick Dhu. *Montreal Daily Star,* April 6, 1889.

ally to the effect that Morrison was desperate, prepared to sell his life dearly and could count on his many friends to protect and defend him in a pinch. The officers, however, sometimes found it difficult to identify and place their informants. Adding to the confusion of Gaelic parlance was the profusion of common names. There were so many McLaulays, McLeans, Mathesons, McLeods and Morrisons around, including several Donald Morrisons – of a more pacific sort – that the police could scarcely separate the men from their neighbours. Their confusion was multiplied by the local custom of using nicknames in place of the original designations.

After six weeks the detectives and police from Sherbrooke and Quebec had not yet glimpsed the Megantic outlaw whose easy movements drew harsh editorial comments in the Sherbrooke press. The police looked clumsy in their pursuit of a man whose "experience as a cowboy in Texas . . . evidently made him reckless and indifferent to ordinary forms of law." But their paper bluster and Morrison's cause enjoyed only a local notoriety, until an eager young reporter from Montreal's large English daily the *Star* got hold of the story in early August and enlarged it to uncomfortable dimensions. Peter Spanjaardt and Donald Morrison needed each other. Morrison felt misunderstood and persecuted by the Sherbrooke press which, he was convinced, failed to appreciate the justness of his cause. He was, it was rumoured, prepared to surrender himself only after his case had been fairly ventilated and brought to the attention of the public and the officials who might then give him a fair trial. Peter Spanjaardt, for his part, was bored with the police beat and with a recent assignment to cover a murder case in Sherbrooke. He needed a good story to make his name and he found it in the Morrison case.

Spanjaardt soon had his assignment transferred forty miles east to Megantic where he began reporting events of the chase. "Things at Lake Megantic are not half as bad as painted," he announced upon arrival. "Instead of a place where murder and incendiarism run riot, and where every man parades the railway platform with a shotgun to see whether there are any detectives on the incoming train, a stranger arriving at the village finds a quiet little settlement beautifully located right at the foot of Lake

Megantic, inhabited by an apparently law-abiding people." But Spanjaardt soon located behind Megantic's idyllic summer face a powerful and general antipathy towards the visiting detectives, who were constantly watched and denied information, and a corresponding sympathy for the outlaw, who was widely defended as a good settler driven to violence by the force of circumstances. "All, old and young, high and low, male and female, Scotch and French, have nothing but good to say of Morrison," Spanjaardt concluded, "The general verdict is that he was one of the best, the most gentlemanly and kindhearted boys in the Township." Spanjaardt won friends and confidantes throughout Morrison's domain, which he described in a series of dispatches to his home newspaper. Among the places he visited was the abandoned farm where the burnt foundations of the barn and house warmed in the summer sun and the hay in the fields stood uncut, several feet high. Morrison, it seems, had warned the unhappy Duquette about removing the hay and the latter, already sick with care, stayed away from the fields.

Spanjaardt's cultivation of the local residents and sympathetic reports of their cause brought results and, soon after his arrival, arrangements were made for an interview with the outlaw. The meeting was organized by a group of Morrison's friends, later designated by Spanjaardt as "The Megantic Outlaw Protective Association," who first cleared the matter and checked the reporter's credentials with Mr. Hugh Graham, the owner of the *Star*. Mr. Graham spoke well of Spanjaardt who was directed, over a quiet breakfast in the local hotel, to board the train for Sherbrooke and get off at the first stop outside of Megantic. The reporter was met here by a guide who led him through the dense woods to a clearing where he was greeted by an armed Scotsman in a horse and buggy. The journey's second stage covered twenty-eight miles through heavy bush, numerous hills and gullies and occasional homesteads, whose residents, when asked about the Morrison affair, volunteered their affirmation of the outlaw's just cause. At points along the way, Spanjaardt noted the presence of armed sentinels who told the driver, in Gaelic, that the way was clear.

It was not until late afternoon, after lunch at a wayside hotel and a long wait at the local blacksmith's, that Spanjaardt and his guide travelled down a winding side road to a grey farmhouse. A young boy who was waiting in front vanished through the front door. The reporter waited in the carriage until summoned into the parlor where, seated at the corner of the sofa, was "the modern Rob Roy, the Megantic desperado, or whatever people have chosen to call the slayer of Jack Warren."

When Spanjaardt entered, Morrison rose quickly, blushed and offered his hand in a warm greeting. The outlaw, who wore a grey checked suit with a brown flannel shirt, quickly dispensed with the preliminary etiquette. He was anxious to explain his troubles and talked freely about the family quarrels, the unfair mortgage, McAulay's machinations, the unhappy sheriff's sale, the fight over the eviction, the sad loss of the homestead, the costly dealings with firms of lawyers, the endless frustrations. Morrison denied burning Duquette's barn and house and gave a detailed rendering of his duel with Warren who, he alleged, spoke openly of killing him, practiced target shooting and drew his revolver first during the fatal confrontation. When Spanjaardt asked Morrison about his future plans, the outlaw replied he planned to keep clear until his case had a fair public airing. "I am trying to keep out of the way," he stated, "but if I am cornered they will never take me alive, for I know and have known before that there is no justice for me in Sherbrooke. The Sherbrooke papers will not even publish anything for me." Morrison closed with a declaration that he intended to shoot no one, but would not hesitate to sell his life "as dear as possible" if cornered. "When the matter goes through the press," he continued, "so that the people can see what the trouble is, I will know better what to do."

Spanjaardt had his story; and Morrison, his publicity. The reporter shook the outlaw's hand, accepted a cold glass of milk and boarded the carriage for a farmhouse nearby where a late supper was eaten. Spanjaardt travelled all night through an ugly blowing rain to the village of Megantic, where he arrived before noon the next day. A full and lurid account of the adventure soon appeared in the *Montreal Star,* written by a "War Correspondent" who had interviewed "the Rob Roy of the Region." The piece was decorated with bold headlines, including "a rebellion in Megantic," "Morrison the Murderer defended by the Yeomanry" and "the Clan in Arms."

Among the interested students of Spanjaardt's hyperbolic reportage was the attorney-general of the province of Quebec, the Honourable Arthur Turcotte who, by early September, became desperately angry at Morrison's evasions. Throughout the month of August, Turcotte continued dispatching search parties into the Megantic region but the results were again meager. The detectives met the same silence, surveillance and gibberish as their predecessors and they reported back to Mr. Turcotte of a vast local conspiracy to protect the outlaw. Turcotte decided to augment his forces and enlisted the aid of Chief Hughes of the Montreal Police Force. "My connection with this business", Chief Hughes later disclosed, "commenced on September 8, when I received a letter from the Honourable M. Turcotte, asking me if it was true that I was willing to undertake the capture of Morrison if the government was prepared to give me $1,000, and stating that if such was the case they would back me to the fullest extent, as they were intent on bringing him to justice. I answered that such was not the case, but at the request of my friends I decided to help the government as far as I could in the matter."

Chief Hughes went to Quebec City, met with Turcotte and returned to Montreal with a promise of aid. A batch of Montreal policemen soon arrived at Megantic, but after a few weeks of fruitless searching, they reported to Chief Hughes that something like an expedition would be needed. "From reports made to me," the chief stated, "I came to the conclusion that the only way to secure Morrison was by a coup de main. My plan consisted in picking twenty good men from the force and to surround the district in which Morrison was secreted and then to effect the arrest . . . in spite of the fact that he is in a most difficult country with mountains and woods everywhere and horrible roads. I am informed that lately Morrison has taken to drinking hard together with a cowboy of the West, and that he will now accept no compromise of any kind, and that he is prepared to sell his life as dearly as possible if an attempt is made to arrest him."

At no time during the autumn of 1888, and through the winter of the new year, did the Megantic outlaw need to sell himself, dearly or otherwise. The Quebec detectives continued searching, along main and side roads, at farmhouses and nearby villages and in the lobbies of hotels. The Montreal police joined the search and found the fugitive as invisible as had their Quebec colleagues. The local citizens were threatened and warned of arrest on suspicion of harbouring and aiding the outlaw. The entire region, from Megantic to Gould, was placarded with signs warning of the consequences of co-operation with the outlaw. The homes of his friends, or suspected friends, were invigilated and searched. A reward of $1,200 and later $3,000 was advertised for information leading to his capture. Negotiations were commenced, now and then, with "certain private citizens" to hand over the outlaw, in return for the reward and the gratitude of officialdom. And, while the police searched and negotiated, they sometimes quarreled, in full public view. The attorney-general published in the government organ in Quebec City a full record of his correspondence with Chief Hughes of Montreal, who replied with his own account of the fruitless events in the Montreal English daily.

What the police stumbled against was a firm wall of sympathy for the fugitive given effect through the informal network known as The Megantic Outlaw Protective Association. The sympathy was spread wide among the shopkeepers and artisans of Megantic Village, Springhill, Stornoway and Gould; the farmers and settlers throughout the townships of Whitton, Winslow and Lingwick; the working-men in the lumber camps, pulp mills and on the railway lines stretching from Bury to Megantic. Morrison had key friends everywhere. Malcolm MacLean, the postmaster, and Findlay MacLeod, the hotel keeper, helped him in Springhill. Mr. Hugh Leonard, the village mayor, and his brother, who ran the local hotel, were available in Stornoway, as was William Matheson, the blacksmith. In Megantic, the storekeeper Malcolm Matheson kept a close watch on police movements and regularly shipped supplies to his hunted friend.

Morrison could have fled the district across the border into neighbouring Maine, but he chose to stay close around home. He ate irregularly at farmhouses, in homes in villages, sometimes at hotels. Food was left for him, nicely packaged, on back porches. He slept everywhere, including at his parents' cabin in Marsden which was irregularly scrutinized by the police. In winter, the outlaw moved across the snows easily on snowshoes, hitched rides on friendly sleighs and travelled, third class, in box cars on the local railway, in full knowledge of several workers and the station master. Morrison was often close to the police on remote roadways, at farmhouses where he hid in cellars and attics or escaped out the back door and near the local church, where he eavesdropped on the occasional sermon. It was rumoured he went to local dances. On one occasion he was said to have hidden under a lounge chair covered by the flowing skirts of local wallflowers. The outlaw occasionally let loose and went on drinking expeditions in town with friends at bars frequented by the police.

Throughout the winter months of 1889, the Megantic Outlaw Protective Association continued its aid program and moved to end the affair by contacting sympathetic outsiders and negotiating an honourable surrender. A lawyer named Lynch and another, F. X. Lemieux, who defended Riel, were consulted about prospects for a successful trial defense. Edward Blake was sent a full record of the affair, from the mortgage to the killing of Warren. The prestigious firm of Greenshields, Guerin and Greenshields was approached. The officers of the Associated Caledonian Societies were requested to intervene with the government and were said to favour a deal involving the use of reward money, granted in return for Morrison's surrender, as legal fees in the ensuing trial. It was rumoured, as well, that through friendly third parties, certain government officials made overtures to Morrison that, in the event of his quiet and permanent departure, they were prepared to prevent needless trouble and expense and drop the case altogether.

But Morrison stayed close to home and forced the government, by late March 1889, to pursue a new and severe course of action. The entire Megantic district was placed under martial law and an expedition outfitted for the purpose of breaking the Protective Association and capturing the outlaw. The chief of staff of the expedition was an iron judge, C. Aime Dugas, who later left his judicial mark in the Yukon where he served for many years. The judge's headquarters staff included High Constable Bissonette and Captain Leggatt of the Montreal Police Force, who served as the major lieutenants and a Dr. Tremblay of the Montreal Police Force, who acted as Chief Clerk. Among the three journalists attached to the headquarters staff as "war correspondents at the front" was the ubiquitous Mr. Spanjaardt who caused the irritable judge no end of trouble.

The foot soldiers of Judge Dugas' expedition numbered, at the peak of the campaign, over a hundred men drawn from a variety of places and occupations. Besides the local detectives and several Pinkerton imports, there were Montreal city policemen, Sherbrooke policemen, Quebec provincial constables, several jail guards from the capital and a small force of volunteers from the first company of the Ninth Battalion based in Quebec City. "There were grey-bearded veterans and beardless volunteers," Mr. Spanjaardt wrote, "some of them wearing the helmet of the provincials, others the cap of the gaol guards, and others again the forage cap or whatever hat they thought suited best. Some carried Snider rifles, some Martini-Henry guns and some Remington carbines, while the provincials were conspicuous by their monstrous .48 calibre revolver, a regular pocket cannon with interchangeable barrels. The provincials and gaol-guards are mostly well-formed, very heavily built men, but the volunteers are very little beyond the regular size. Most of them are French Canadians and several of them brought large valises, and in some cases vast trunks which, more than anything else, gave the other members of the expedition a forcible reminder of their own scanty wardrobes." Among the expedition's most prized members was Captain Clarke of the Montreal police force who came equipped with a bagpipe. One evening, Captain Clarke entertained a raft of curious hotel lobby loiterers in Stornoway in an attempt to prove that bagpipes and kilts were not the sole province of fugitives – or perhaps to lure the outlaw from his hole, like the piper of Hamlin.

Captain Clarke's doleful pipes were the least of Judge Dugas' weapons, which included arrest warrants distributed along the expedition's slow route from Megantic village to Springhill, Stornoway and later Gould. The judge and his cohorts arrived in the late spring's midst and had a hard time moving around. The lakes were still frozen over when the judge stepped from his train and a hard crust of snow covered the ground. They advanced towards Springhill by sleighs, grudgingly volunteered by the citizenry, and, on one occasion, Judge Dugas and his party were pitched into a snow drift. In the villages of Stornoway, Megantic and Springhill the field force crammed into tiny hotels where many slept on the floor in buffalo robes. At a Stornoway hostel, the entire floor space was covered with sweating and snoring men who were so pressed for room that they debated the prospect of using a piano as a bed. "It was finally decided not to use the piano," an account read, "for fear that the happy possessor of such a musical bunk might roll on the keys and disturb the rest of the others. The precaution, however, was of little use, for some of the men kept chattering away all night while the others got up at four o'clock and immediately commenced drawing a most varied assortment of known and unknown airs from the piano."

Such levity, however, did not interest Judge C. A. Dugas, a stern and serious man, who had come to do a job. Throughout his travels to Megantic, Springhill, Stornoway and Gould, where he later established his headquarters, the judge lectured and interviewed local citizens, distributed warnings of the grave consequences of collaborating with a criminal and left a trail of warrants for the arrest of some of Morrison's staunchest defenders, among them Malcolm Matheson, the Megantic shopkeeper, Finlay MacLeod, the hotelier, and Mr. D. K. McDonald, who had posted on the train ticket wicket in Springhill a picture of the outlaw with the appended statement, "a good man." The arrested men were taken to Sherbrooke and jailed for several days until their bail was posted by the local M.P.P. for Compton, John McIntosh.

The judge's assault on the local Protective Association was complemented by a fierce prosecution of the search, which spread to the far corners of the district. The men worked hard and long, often from six a.m. until midnight. Houses were entered and searched, including the Morrison cabin outside of Marsden, where a large trunk containing packs of the outlaw's letters and personal possessions was removed. Shanties, farmhouses, barns and churches were combed for clues. "We are obliged to keep our arms and a round of ammunition in hand continually," an officer reported from Gould, "I can assure you the Scotchmen who laugh at the Quebec police are putting on long faces now, and do not at all care to have our visit. Morrison was on the doorstep of the church here last Sunday morning at 11 o'clock. He left for the hill, about three miles from here, in the afternoon. The hill is inhabited entirely by friends or relations of Morrison." As the days passed, the search's arc extended wider, and deeper – down a mine shaft at the Excelsior copper mine, eight miles east of Broughton and more than sixty miles from any place Morrison had been seen. The source of the rumour of Morrison's descent was Mr. J. N. Greenshields, who had jokingly remarked to the local station agent at Broughton that "three men went down the Kent shaft and only two came up again and they say the third man must be Morrison." The news reached High Constable Bissonette who, with several colleagues, stormed the Kent shaft and the neighbouring Fanny Eliza, which ran 1600 feet underground.

The High Constable's mining venture merely added to Judge Dugas' malaise and fueled the mounting criticism of the Lake Megantic Fishing Expedition. Mayor Grenier and the Montreal City Council began wondering whether their own police, shipped in droves from the home beat into the back woods to hunt a demented Scotchman, were being usefully deployed by the Attorney General who, in a telegram to the council, warned that the Montreal contingent was "absolutely required to effect the arrest of Morrison." Back in the cities, the absence of police officers confounded proceedings of the Court of Queen's Bench and the Court of Special Sessions where, among others, a Madame Joly who had allegedly stolen $60 from one of her boarders, faced several consecutive adjournments. Opposition politicians laughed out loud while the city dailies, which at first applauded the expedition, claimed that Morrison's continued defiance of the law "would set people in other places wondering what sort of country this is and whether Texan ideas and Texan habits had been imported into it." As the momentum of the expedition slowed, the press turned sour and began speculating about whether a field battery would be needed to augment the search. The Megantic

Expedition became "The Police Picnic." "Morrison has not been arrested," the *Star* observed, "but nearly everyone else in the district has; whether for giving aid or comfort to the enemy or for laughing at the expedition is not quite clear. We hope it is not the latter, because if so the whole population of the Dominion will soon be languishing in gaol. The spectacle of fifty brass-buttoned warriors marching and counter-marching, with a piper at their head, through the back woods, in pursuit of Morrison, is not a fit subject for mirth . . . If the affair is to be regarded as a picnic got up for the physical and moral improvement of policemen, well and good, but let the whole force take it in turns."

The press fire continued while Judge Dugas pondered further ways of flushing the outlaw from his hideout. One stratagem, favoured by the mayors of Stornoway and Gould and by several J.P.'s, was to effect a meeting between the outlaw and the judge on neutral ground, where they could possibly resolve their differences. The idea of a summit conference in the woods first came from Morrison's friends who won Judge Dugas' reluctant approval. A lonely schoolhouse, several miles from Gould, where the expedition based its operation, was chosen as the locale of the meeting, which Dugas attended unarmed in the company of several local people. The meeting was brief, courteous and devoid of any results. Dugas had surmised that Morrison, whom he thought "a monomanic on the question of his rights," contemplated surrender, and he assured the outlaw of a fair trial. Morrison seemed less convinced of the benign prospects following surrender and, if he did earlier consider giving himself up, had evidently abandoned the thought before or during their meeting. "He made no conditions whatever," Dugas later reported, "he simply said to me: 'Well, if I give myself up I'll have to go to penitentiary, and that I do not want. I'll wait for an answer from Mr. Blake.' " In an interview with Peter Spanjaardt, on the eve of the Dugas meeting, Morrison reiterated his lack of faith in the courts of law: "My heart bleeds whenever I think of the wrongs that they have done me and, besides, I have lost all faith in justice through my bitter experience of days agone. Money can do anything, and in the case of the burning of the barn buildings alone, men enough can be bought near the Shadagee River at ten dollars apiece to convict me. I do not want to take my chances."

So Morrison melted into the woods and Dugas resumed the hard business of trying to flush him out. Soon after the judge's return to headquarters, negotiations began, at the instigation of the United Caledonian Societies, represented by a certain "high-placed educator" and certain government officials, equally high-placed, to effect another truce and Morrison surrender. But Dugas ignored the new initiatives and resumed the chase with renewed anger and vigour. He began with warrants, numbering forty-five, served on a wide range of suspects, some of whom, like the Megantic outlaw, disappeared into the woods. While the trains sped the other suspects to Sherbrooke, the judge redeployed his men. The police occasionally played cards, drank beer, listened to Captain Clarke's bagpipes or poured and consumed chunks of amber-coloured maple taffy hardened by the late spring snow. But they mostly plodded about in small groups of four or five stationed at key junctions: at St. Leon near Marsden, in the town of Springhill, at Weedon and Red Mountain Road, at Golson Road near Big Hill and in the vicinity of Gould. Special attention was given the home of Morrison's parents outside of Marsden where, under the cover of foliage, a careful surveillance was maintained for weeks by a small and stubborn group of men who sometimes slept in the spring frost, in a tent pitched on beds of pine branches.

The captain of the determined Marsden force was Silas H. Carpenter, the head of the Montreal Detective Bureau who, since the beginning of the new year, had paid half a dozen futile visits to the Megantic district. Accompanying Carpenter on his frigid vigil was a big and powerful detective named James McMahon who had recently assisted in the capture of the celebrated murderer McGrath and was known for his forceful ability to handle criminals and halt runaway horses. As a guide and native informant, the detectives recruited a tall wiry outdoorsman with shoulder-length black hair and a close knowledge of the woods around Megantic. His name was Pierre Leroyer, a native of Châteauroux, France, and a thrice-wounded casualty of the Franco-Prussian War. Leroyer hunted and trapped for years for the Hudson's Bay Company in the Canadian Northwest, before settling down in the Megantic area as a hunter, trapper and guide for the Megantic Fish and Game Club. Known locally as a Métis, Leroyer was a crack shot and local maverick who made his mark in Montreal at a winter carnival where he harnessed and drove a trained moose. His shanty near Lake Megantic doubled as a menagerie, holding at various times several bears, a pair of deer, a lone porcupine and, according to one writer, a pair of monkeys.

Pierre Leroyer added a certain flair and competence to the detective team which, on the evening of Saturday, April 20, 1889, began a new and intense vigil in the bushes near the Morrison house. It was Easter weekend and the recent arrival of a party of respectable Caledonians at Winslow, where Silas Carpenter had recently gone, ripened the possibility of a home visit by the outlaw for a meal or a change in clothes or some familial advice. The Caledonians, represented by a Dr. Graham and Reverend McLeod, had arrived to effect a truce and to this purpose had fortified themselves with blessings from the Honourable Premier Mercier and with a letter in hand from Edward Blake to Donald Morrison assuring him of a fair trial in the event of his surrender. The visiting gentlemen waxed busy upon arrival. They contacted High Constable Bissonette, who endorsed their peace efforts, and spoke with several notable locals including Mr. Leonard of Stornoway who conveyed their peaceful intentions, through third parties, to the outlaw in the woods. And they huddled with the local ministers who, from the pulpit on Easter Sunday, urged Donald Morrison to end his resistance.

This was probably the outlaw's intention when he arrived at the home of his parents mid-afternoon on Easter Sunday. Leroyer and McMahon were not certain it was Morrison who entered the house but their suspicions were aroused by the peculiar behaviour of the outlaw's mother who, at intervals throughout the late afternoon, stepped outdoors and carefully surveyed the surrounding area. When darkness fell, the detectives moved up to a window through which they spied, supping at the table with his back to them, a man so fair the scout thought him grey. "He looks kind of old," Leroyer whispered, to which McMahon replied, "We will wait a while." Their wait was short. Having supped nicely, the man rose and received from the old lady a bottle of milk, some biscuits and a handshake. Detective McMahon recognized Donald Morrison when he turned to leave and drew his Winchester as the outlaw stepped out the door. The detective told him to throw up his hands. The outlaw fired wildly into the dark and ran madly towards a short fence nearby, seeking the freedom of the woods. Both McMahon and Leroyer fired their Winchesters, and missed. They then dropped their rifles and McMahon fired his Colt revolver several times as he chased Morrison towards the fence. McMahon's first three shots misfired, but the final ones took effect, hitting Morrison in the hip just as he reached the fence. The outlaw fell over the fence and the burly detective landed on him, shouting to his face that his cowboy days had ended.

And they had. The detectives carried their man several yards to a knoll, where McMahon stayed with him while Leroyer fruitlessly searched for a team of horses. Instead, a group of policemen were brought from Marsden; they carried the wounded man, wrapped in a blanket and rugs, back to town and lodged him face down, to relieve the pain, at their local headquarters, where he was fed sugar and brandy. The wounded man was soon shipped out on the train to Sherbrooke and lodged at the local jail. Detective McMahon departed for Montreal where he was greeted at the station with an embrace and a shining new revolver by Chief Hughes, whose embarrassment had ended. The city council and Mayor Grenier were equally delighted and council members, at a special afternoon session, lauded the conduct of the city force in Megantic and offered a civic medal to brave Detective McMahon.

The Megantic expedition had ended and preparations for the Megantic trial began soon after the outlaw's jailing in Sherbrooke. The talk in and around Sherbrooke, the likely trial seat, was only of Morrison, his frantic resistance, his capture, his prospects of conviction or acquittal. In Quebec City, Judge Dugas and Premier Mercier consulted the Attorney General who engaged, for the prosecution, the services of Mr. Charles Fitzpatrick and Mr. L. C. Belanger, a prominent Sherbrooke attorney. Morrison's friends and the Caledonian Societies set up a defence fund headed by Dr. Graham, with Winslow Mayor Leonard as treasurer, and raised several thousand dollars mostly from the Megantic district where the Irish and French Canadians joined with the Scottish in a generous contribution. The defence recruited legal stars of their own: Mr. J. N. Greenshields of Montreal, one of the wealthiest and most prestigious members of the Montreal bar, and Mr. F. X. Lemieux of Quebec City, an equally established attorney. Both former members of Riel's defence team, they were joined by a young Sherbrooke barrister John Leonard, a brother of Winslow's mayor and friend of Morrison since childhood.

The trial was postponed several times while opinion hardened and the lawyers sparred over the venue. Sherbrooke finally became the seat of the hearing which began in early October under the direction of Justice Edward T. Brook, who succeeded A. T. Galt as the Sherbrooke representative to the House of Commons and later earned an appointment to the local Superior Court. From the outset, the trial attracted wide publicity and drew a full house: of lawyers, mayors, ministers, councillors and poor settlers from the Megantic district – with the exception of old Murdo Morrison, who stayed at home to dig potatoes. On the eve of its commencement, a strange thing happened outside of the village of Megantic, where a local resident had filled his barn with hay before departing for Sherbrooke. While Auguste Duquette was absent in town, and Donald Morrison tossed wildly in his cell, someone had lit a match and burned the barn to the ground.

For Mr. Fitzpatrick and Mr. Belanger the trial of Donald Morrison for the murder of Lucius Warren was an opportunity to purge the air of sympathy and romance which hung about the guilty head of the accused. "Thanks be to God," Mr. Belanger opened, "the sensational stories published during the past year, holding up Morrison as the 'modern Rob Roy,' and all the stories invented by newspapers about the case will now be set aright." The Crown attorney thought it simply a matter of murder, without provocation or justification, and they hung their case around this view. They argued that Morrison was twice a felon before Warren sought him, that Warren was a legitimate constable, duly sworn in, that he was merely doing his duty in trying to arrest

Morrison, that he did not threaten the accused or draw his gun, before Morrison fired without provocation and coldly left the scene without even examining the product of his evil work.

The defence lawyers were equally eloquent in their contrary assertion that Morrison's homicide was justifiable. Witnesses were brought forward to testify to the accused's exemplary youth and character and to the questionable person of Lucius Warren. The lawyers questioned the legitimacy of Warren's warrant, which they claimed had not been properly drawn, and they challenged the status of his appointment since he was an American citizen improperly sworn in. They saw the facts of the killing differently, drawing from several witnesses the assertion that Warren had threatened to kill Morrison and drew his gun first during the Megantic encounter. Mr. Greenshields argued that Morrison was a good settler who had killed only in the last resort, to save his own life. "The prisoner belongs to a fearless people, the Scotch," Greenshields expounded, "men who believe that when they have rights they are ready to fight for the preservation of these rights till their last drop of blood. In transferring the cane from one hand to another and taking his pistol to defend his own life he showed that he had the nerve and the courage of the people to whom he belonged."

For the jurors, it was a hard choice, and their lengthy deliberation raised brief hopes that a concensus would not be reached. But they eventually resolved their differences and brought in a verdict of manslaughter, tempered with a recommendation of mercy. Judge Brooks heard their recommendation and considered it during the several days preceding the sentencing. But the judge was a stern man, irked by the outlaw's extended freedom in the woods. "The court cannot be ignorant that for a . . . period of ten months," he lectured the accused, "you remained in a state of armed opposition to the constitutional authorities of the land . . . that previous to the time of your capture, you had been defying the law for nearly a year, and after a reward had been offered for your apprehension, that you still continued in a state of armed resistance to the law of the land." In defense of the law's majesty and supremacy, the judge arrived at a harsh sentence: eighteen years, at hard labour, in the provincial penitentiary of St. Vincent de Paul.

Donald Morrison was returned to his Sherbrooke prison cell, which he shared with the fratricide Remi Lamontagne. He remained there briefly, until his departure for the tomb of the living in the company of a fourteen-year-old boy named Crott, sentenced to four years in the reformatory for "carnal knowledge" of a girl under ten.

The outlaw did not, at first, take easily to a prison some thought was unfit even for the rats which plied its sewers. The prospects of an extended confinement unnerved him and he refused his meals. When he was too weak to resist his force-feeders, he spat up the morsels. Later, when the first symptoms of pulmonary consumption appeared, Morrison refused the drugs prescribed by the prison doctor.

The convict lingered sullenly in prison for almost five years; in June 1894 his condition had so worsened that a reporter found him in the prison hospital a virtual skeleton, consumed by a high fever and shaken by fierce fits of coughing. Morrison's end was close and the reports of the prison doctor together with outside representations from friends and officials who knew his desperate state, brought a release from the Minister of Justice: to a bed in the Royal Victoria Hospital where he died several days later. Services were held in the hospital theatre attended by several local Scottish residents, and by a number of convalescents dressed in hospital grey. The body was subsequently removed, in the Halifax Express, to Megantic where it was displayed in a glass-covered rosewood casket to friends and family and buried in a cemetery at Ghilsa near Marsden where, among others, old Murdo wept bitterly over his son's demise.

Notes

Several short books have been written on Morrison, including: Oscar Dhu, (Angus MacKay) *Donald Morrison, The Canadian Outlaw* (unlisted publisher), 1892, reprinted 1965 by Page-Sangster Co. Limited, Sherbrooke, Quebec; and Henry G. Kidd, *Donald Morrison, The Megantic Outlaw* (privately printed). The Dhu book is an artless romantic folk tale, written in blank verse, by a local bard. Kidd's is an unreliable hearsay piece. A recent account, based on the skeletal facts and ornamented with invented dialogue, is Bernard Epps, *The Outlaw of Megantic,* McClelland and Stewart Ltd., Toronto, 1973. A short treatment of the story can be found in Peter Span's article, "The Outlaw of Megantic," in *The Wide World Magazine,* Vol. 28, No. 167, March, 1912. L. S. Channell's *History of Compton County,* 1896, Cookshire, includes some useful material. J. Albert Gravel wrote a short, informative account called "Donald Morrison: du cow-boy au Outlaw à Lac Megantic en 1889", in *Mélanges Historiques dans et autour des Cantons de l'Est, III.* Detailed accounts of the hunt for Morrison, his capture, trial, and subsequent death can be found in the *Montreal Star. The Globe* carried several accounts of the Morrison hunt and trial.

Simon Gun-a-noot.

Peter Hi-ma-dan and Simon Gun-a-noot at the fourth cabin on Telegraph Trail.

Above: Simon Gun-a-noot *(second from left)* in Hazelton, after turning himself in. With him are *(left to right)* Chief Constable John Kelly, Constable Sperry Cline and Deputy-Inspector T.W. Parsons of the B.C. Police.

Below: Simon Gun-a-noot's grave at Bowser Lake.

Donald Morrison.

Above: An illustration from 1892 showing Donald Morrison shooting Jack Warren.

Below: The house of Murdo Morrison, Donald's father, Marsden, Quebec. 1. Where Donald was shot. 2. Where Donald fell. The old man is Donald's father.

Northwest Mounted Police guarding the bluff where Almighty Voice was hidden, 1897.

View of the terrain and operations concerning the siege of Almighty Voice. The Voice and his two companions were trapped in the clump of trees *(in the right of the photo).*

Judith Donnelly and old James Donnelly, parents of the ill-fated family.
They were in their mid-sixties when they were murdered.

The Donnelly homestead as it appeared before the murderers burned it down.

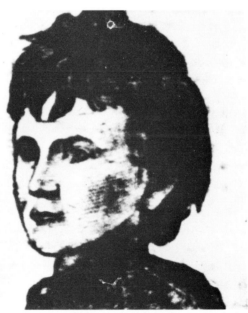

Johnny Connor, the eleven-year-old boy who was staying with the Donnelleys on the night of the murders. He hid under a bed and witnessed the killings. It was essentially on his testimony that the Crown built its case against the murderers.

The McLean brothers: Allan, *(above left)*, Archie *(right)*, and Charlie *(below left)*, and their companion Alexander Hare *(below right)*.

The cabin, near Ashcroft, B.C., where the McLeans were captured.

Uluksak *(left)* and Sinnisak.

Above: The prisoners, Uluksak and Sinnisak with Constable A. Lamont on the mainland opposite Herschel Island, July 1916. Outline of Herschel Island can be seen in the distance to the north.

Below: The Eskimo prisoners in Edmonton, where they were brought for trial. *(Back row, left to right)* Crown lawyer C.C. McCaul, Inspector C.D. La Nauze, defence lawyer J.F. Walbridge, and Constable J.E. Wight. *(Front row, left to right)* Special Constable Ilavinik, witness Koeha, Uluksak, Sinnisak, and translator Pat Klengenberg.

Above: The big rock about twenty-three miles east of Kamloops where the C.P.R. Transcontinental Express No. 97 was held up, now known as Bill Miner Rock.

$11,500.00
REWARD

The Canadian Pacific Railway Coy.

3: a reward of $5,000 (Five Thousand Dollars) for the capture, dead or alive, of the three robbers who held up train 97 between Ducks and Kamloops on the morning of the 9th inst., or $1,000 (One Thousand Dollars) for the capture, dead or alive, of any one of the robbers.

The Dominion Government

Also offers $5,000 (Five Thousand Dollars) on the same terms as the above.

The Provincial Government

Offers One Thousand Five Hundred Dollars (Five Hundred Dollars for each man) for capture and conviction.

DESCRIPTION.

LEADER: About 5 ft. 7 in. in height, slim build, about 50 years of age, wore a grey stubby moustache, face and hands very much sun burnt, eyes somewhat inflamed, wore glasses, tattoo mark on back of right hand, wore a black slouch hat and a blue-black overcoat.

SECOND MAN: About 5 ft. 7 in. in height, medium build, weight about 170 lbs, black hair, dark complexion, very clear and distinct voice, with slight Cockney accent, wore an old blue sweater.

THIRD MAN: Age about 40 years, about 5 ft. 10 in. in height, light or reddish moustache and thin face.

By Order.

Kamloops, B. C., May 12th, 1906.

Above: The "Bill Miner" party enroute to Kamloops following Miner's capture. Miner, Lewis Colquon and Shorty Dunn are in the wagon and wrapped in blankets.

Below: The Bill Miner preliminary trial under way in the old Court House at Kamloops. Addressing the court is Attorney-General F.J. Fulton, the prosecuting attorney. Bill Miner and Lewis Colquon are in the prisoner's box and William (Shorty) Dunn is seen on the left, leaning on the railing.

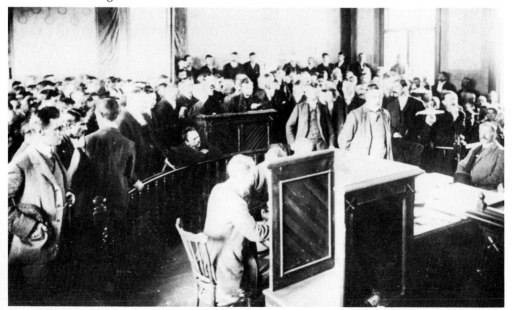

Bill Miner.

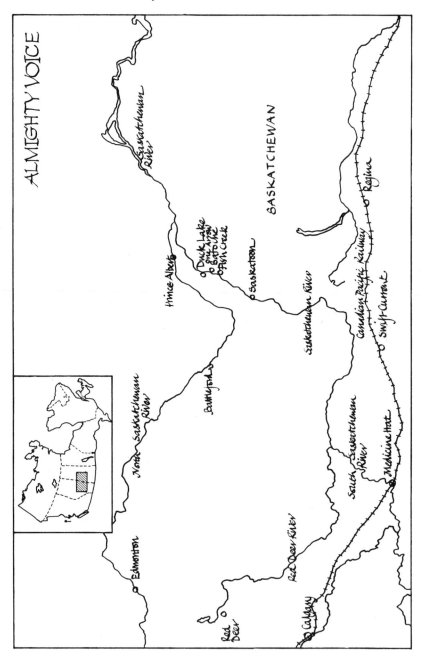

Private Warpaths

When Lieutenant-governor Alexander Morris undertook his civilizing trek through the central plains of Canada during the middle years of the 1870's, many of the Plains Indians little appreciated the true import of his mission. They were unaware that Morris, who moved with ease and assurance among the scattered tribes of the northern plains, was a trail blazer and a civilizer. He came to bring the word of the Great White Mother who wished her red children to give up the fruitless chase of the buffalo and retire instead to the tranquil squalor of land reserves. Morris came well-fortified. Behind him rested the Great White Mother's soft and ample bosom, the big money of eastern finance, the hardware of industrial capitalism and the men in scarlet coats of the North West Mounted Police. Behind the chiefs, who met with Morris along the way, lay a pile of bleached buffalo bones. So the chiefs of the Swampy Crees and the Bloods, the Wood Crees and the Piegans, took treaty and led their straggling remnant onto the rough lands set aside for their improvement.

Morris' promise of a new and better life for the Canadian Plains Indians, for which they traded their ancient hunting domain, was never fulfilled. Along with most of their brethren, the Cree of One Arrow's band, located near Batoche below the South Saskatchewan, and the Bloods from around MacLeod near the southwest border of the Territories, settled into reservation Indians. The Bloods hunted a bit, mowed and gathered hay, which they supplied to the local ranches, drank heavily, collected welfare pittances known as annuity payments, and hauled coal for the MacLeod detachment of the North West Mounted Police. "Very few blankets are now worn," a police commissioner reported, "and white men's clothes are used by the men." When the destitute Métis and their Cree allies rose in 1885, the Bloods were too anaemic, or prudent, to join. One Arrow's Cree were no better off. They grew some mixed vegetables and cereal crops, raised a few cattle with the aid of breeding stock supplied by the Indian Agents, and glumly lined up once a year for their meagre annuity payments. But they mostly starved and drank whisky and suffered from nutritional diseases which depleted their numbers until, by the year 1885, when the Métis made their last stand, they numbered 200 souls. Unlike the Bloods, One Arrow's Cree, including the warrior John Sounding Sky, took up arms during the Northwest Rebellion and fought hard and well at Fish Creek and Batoche, where Gabriel Dumont earned his fame. For his efforts, One Arrow, who had been loosely aligned with a maverick chief named Beardy, was deprived of his chieftainship and sent to prison for three years.

During the post-rebellion decade, One Arrow's people languished while the new white settler class put the plow to the sod. "For Canada, the great and unrealized factor was the industrialization of much of Europe and the United States," wrote W. G. Hardy, "Factory workers need bread and cities are parasites on the bounty of the soil." The cry for wheat was answered by Ontario immigrants and later by peasants from central and eastern Europe who rode the Canadian Pacific Railway west and took up the land vacated by the Plains Indians. Using the Oliver chilled-steel plow, and the McCormick and Massey Harris binders, the settlers transformed the land while the Indians lolled on their reserves under the watchful eyes of government agents and of the Mounted Police, charged with the task of maintaining British style law and equally British order. By 1895, when the Mounted Police celebrated the end of Canada's first post-rebellion decade, the civilizing task looked easy. "The Indians throughout this district, as a rule, show the greatest respect of authority," a NWMP report read in 1895, "and . . . no violence has been offered or any resistance made, to any member of this force while in the execution of his duty for a very long time." In the few years following Big Bear's little war, the Indians around the seat of the Northwest Rebellion had become, in the eyes of the settlers and mounties, apathetic drones too cowardly to either compete in or confront a world which promised their extinction.

To the Mounted Policemen stationed around Duck Lake, Almighty Voice, known in the agency records as Jean Baptiste, seemed no different from his Swampy Cree colleagues who lounged around Chief One Arrow's reserve, or at nearby Fort a la Corne. The Voice was not very imposing in appearance. His height was medium and build spare. Both his hands and feet were rather small and he gave, overall, an impression of femininity. The young Indian wore his hair long, down to his shoulders, and his large dark eyes were set under a broad flat forehead. The nose was sharply curved, like a parrot's, and flat at the tip. The sole taint on this pleasant face was a scar which began at the left corner of the mouth and ran diagonally upwards, covering most of the cheek, towards the ear.

Nor was the Voice in his youth a trouble-maker. He was, it is true, known for his physical prowess, his strength, speed of foot and ability to handle a rifle. But there were no real outlets other than hunting for his stealth and energies. So he gathered hay, hunted a bit, courted several women including the daughters of the Rump and Old Dust and picked up scraps of English and bits of food around the NWMP post at Batoche where he ran errands and occasionally washed dishes.

Almighty Voice might have continued in this mundane vein had he not had an unfortunate misadventure with a cow. Accounts differ about the animal's origin. Some say the poor beast belonged to a farmer whose land adjoined the reserve. Others insist that it was a mere stray, perhaps sent by the Divinity to confound the unhappy Indian. A more likely story is that the animal in question was one of several supplied to the Indians on loan, for breeding purposes, by the Department of Indian Affairs. Whatever its origin, the cow was fated to be prematurely eaten. Whether to supply a wedding feast or, more likely, to sustain his sick young wife who needed a portion of fresh meat, Almighty Voice killed and butchered the cow without the Department's permission and, with his family and friends, consumed the unfortunate beast.

Had the Voice's wife died, from illness or malnutrition, no stir in the Department of Indian Affairs or within the Duck Lake sanctum of the NWMP would have resulted. An Indian's death, after all, was providential and not accountable on the balance sheets carefully drawn up by the Indian Agent, who kept a strict record of hoes, stackers, rakes and other useful implements. The Voice's wife's death would never had made the annual report of the NWMP Commissioners which troubled itself with an Indian's crime, but never with his death. But an Indian had not died; a cow had been butchered. British law had been broken and one of the Queen's own beasts, which had replaced the buffalo as a Canadian prairie divinity, had suffered an early extinction. Accordingly, when Almighty Voice, in the company of his brother-in-law, Young Dust, presented himself for treaty payment on October 22, 1895, at Duck Lake, he was taken into custody by Sergeant Colin Campbell Colebrook of the Batoche NWMP detachment and removed to the small one-room log prison house at Duck Lake. Here the two Indians, who were jointly charged with the killing, were given a bunk and blanket each, in preparation for their trial before Indian Agent McKenzie, scheduled for the next day.

A good friend had preceded the Voice to prison. Three days previous to the cow's killing, his father John Sounding Sky had been arrested on a charge of theft. A neighbour's minor farm implement had disappeared or been mislaid, and Sounding Sky had been hauled before the local J.P. and given a six month sentence. The old man was dispatched to the guardhouse at Prince Albert and dignified with the task, twice a day, of loading and hauling a wagon carrying manure from the Mounted Police stable to a dump a short distance away.

Almighty Voice loved his father, and doubtless wished his company. But the impending circumstances of their fraternizing, likely to follow from his own summary trial, did not please him. Since the Voice was not known as a trouble-maker, and his crime, while serious, was not heinous, a slack guard was maintained. Neither he nor Young Dust were shackled and the guards outside snoozed comfortably. During a change of guard, in the middle of the night, the Voice saw his chance and slipped into the moonlit darkness. He jogged six miles to the western bank of the South Saskatchewan River and swam a half mile through the icy waters to the south shore. After a further fourteen miles he presented himself at the door of his mother, Spotted Calf. The Voice rested a day or two around the reserve, prepared his rifle, ammunition and pony, gathered his young wife, the daughter of Old Dust, and departed northeastward in the direction of John Smith's reserve fifty miles away. The mounties, meanwhile, were not slack. The Indian's flight from the Duck Lake jail was quickly discovered and a brief search made of his reserve. The man in charge of the operation was, again, Sergeant Colebrook, who had first arrested the Indian. Now, in the company of Métis guide Francis Dumont, an old student of scents, trails and the Cree language, he struck out in a light, falling snow which made tracking easy. The sergeant travelled in finer style than the Métis, preferring a team-drawn buckboard to the comfortless back of a horse. But the heavy snow impeded the cart's travel and, along the way, Colebrook exchanged his carriage for a horse, volunteered by interpreter and guide Joseph McKay, sent from Prince Albert to augment the trip. By nightfall the searchers had picked up the Voice's trail and were almost upon him.

The next morning they moved across the frozen prairie, broken here and there by clumps of willows, until they came to a slight rise a few miles northeast of Kinistino. Here they were stopped short by the blast of a rifle. Urging their horses forward, they suddenly came upon a young Indian girl, dismounted from her pony and standing at the trail's side. A few yards away was her companion, a lithe, sparely built young Indian, with a scar on his left cheek, carrying a prairie chicken he had just killed. Across his shoulder was a double-barreled muzzle-loading rifle, which he soon unslung and pointed towards the approaching party. The sergeant, an old hand at handling difficult Indians, moved his horse forward, asking the fugitive, in English, in a firm voice, to surrender himself. But the Indian was not ready to submit and instead of dropping his gun, he leveled it at the sergeant and shouted in Cree, to scout Dumont, to tell the mountie to go away. Dumont translated the message but Colebrook continued to move slowly forward, calling on Dumont to transmit his own demand to the Indian. The Voice held his ground and repeated his warning that he would shoot the policeman if he did not leave. Colebrook again took no heed and, dropping his reins, raised his right hand in a gesture of peace, while slipping his left into his overcoat pocket where he grasped a gun. With his legs, Colebrook urged the horse forward to a distance of twenty-five feet from the Indian, who fired a bullet into the sergeant's chest. Colebrook straightened momentarily and fell from his horse, dead. Dumont, who knew the Indian had meant business, but somehow could not get the message to Colebrook, swung his horse around and galloped madly away in the direction of the home of a nearby settler, to whom he related the morning's sad events. A Constable Tennant, stationed on fire-duty at nearby Flett's Springs, rode to the scene where the fallen sergeant's body lay, unmoved and untouched. Nearby was the Indian girl, toasting the prairie chicken shot for breakfast by her husband – who did not stay for the meal. The young Indian, who had graduated in a short week from a cattle to mountie-killer, had fled alone, into the merciless wind and cold of the prairie winter.

It was not long before the dead sergeant's body was removed to Prince Albert where he was buried several days later with police honours. The dead man was a dutiful policeman and an experienced Indian fighter. An Englishman by birth who emigrated to the Canadian Northwest in 1883, Colebrook enlisted in the Mounted Police and, two years after his arrival, found himself in the thick of the Northwest Rebellion. He served in General Strange's column, fought with Superintendent Sam Steele's scouts, and took part in the bitter engagement with Big Bear's warriors at Frenchman's Butte. At the Rebellion's close, he shared the distinction, with several of his colleagues, of maintaining custody of the notorious Indian chief before his commission to prison. A photograph of the sullen Bear, seated, wrapped in a blanket and staring glumly ahead, still survives. Standing behind him are four guards including Colebrook, second from the left, a keen young man of twenty-five, clutching his rifle-barrel and peering determinedly over the shoulder of the doomed prisoner.

Colebrook's own demise, a decade later, perpetrated by an impetuous young Indian whose father and chief had fought on the rebel side, sparked a flurry of activity at the local detachments and a cry for vengeance from the settler press. A party under J. Allan, known as Broncho Jack, was rushed to the scene from Duck Lake. A further contingent of men and horses arrived from Batoche. The trail was scented and followed through the light snow in the direction of the Fort a la Corne Reserve where it was lost, thanks to a providential thaw. In the weeks following, the police kept searching south and east of the reserve but there were no clues of the fugitive's whereabouts. The Indian was rumoured at Nut Lake and Quill Lake, where relatives were said to protect him; north of Prince Albert, hiding in the woods among the Wood Crees; south of the border, sheltered by American cousins; and at his home reserve, where he was said to hide in a specially constructed dug-out attached to his parents' root cellar by a tunnel.

"It is absolutely impossible to get any information from any of the Indians," reported Superintendent Moffatt, "Whether this is because they know nothing or because they are too loyal to one of their own race to tell, I cannot say, but I am inclined to think . . . that the Indian we want is not in the district." The search parties sent out in the dead of winter encountered numerous physical and social obstacles. "The difficulties in the way of tracing or capturing 'Almight Voice' are very great," the same officer continued. "The country through which he can roam covers a very large area, and is one which offers almost insurmountable obstacles to discovering him. It is practically limitless and is uninhabited except by roving bands of Indians who would naturally befriend him. A very large portion of it is hilly and densely wooded and the balance is what is known as 'bluffy'."

In the spring of 1896, a single clue appeared. About forty miles south of Batoche a Métis hunter, Philip Gardipi, came across an abandoned horse which answered to the description of the one used by Almighty Voice at the time of Colebrook's murder. The police immediately dispatched a search party and enlisted Gardipi as an aid, with an unofficial promise of a $100 reward in the event of the Indian's capture. The party scoured the countryside for over a month, until the melting of the snows which made tracking impossible. A few days before the search's end, John Sounding Sky was released from the Prince Albert Penitentiary, in the hope he would lead the police to his son. "A close watch has been kept on him," the Prince Albert superintendent reported, "but without the results desired."

The continuing meagre results did not, of course, buttress the Force's renown as proficient manhunters. Nor did it aid the reputation of its senior officers and government officials who, anxious to economize and confident in their ability to soon apprehend a lone Indian, persisted in refusing to post a reward for his capture. The longer the officials waited, the more strident were the warnings of the press who speculated about the true worth of a mounted policeman's life and the earned value of the Force's reputation. "Surely a constable who loses his life in nobly carrying out his duty is more to be regretted than a few stacks of hay," the *Manitoba Free Press* surmised, after the government announced a $500 reward leading to the arrest of a haystack arsonist, "If not, the government should let us know how many bales, or parts of a bale, one mounted policeman's life is worth." Similar views were advertised in the editorial columns of the territorial press until, on the 20th day of April 1896, a proclamation was issued, in the name of "Victoria, by the Grace of God . . . Defender of the Faith, etc." and signed by Charles Tupper, Secretary of State, offering $500 for any person or persons "who will give such information as will lead to the apprehension and conviction of an Indian known as Jean Baptiste or Almighty Voice." The proclamation, which advertised in bold letters a modest sum, noted, like all similar documents, that it was "highly important for the peace and safety of our subjects that such a crime should not remain unpunished." But, in the months following its issuance, there were no takers either among the destitute of One Arrow's reserve or any of its neighbouring enclaves. "From the time the leaves fell this autumn," Superintendent Moffatt concluded in his report for the year 1896, "parties have been scouring the country to the south, southwest and southeast of the reserve but not the slightest trace of the fugitive has been found to date."

Had Superintendent Moffatt's probing friends extended their search further south and west of the Voice's reserve, across several hundred miles of prairie into the grasslands of the border country, they would doubtless have been less plagued by the self-pity endemic to futile search operations. For here, in the blossoming ranch country bordering the Americans and the Rockies, in the farthest western corner of the territory occupied by the Black feet, Bloods and Piegans, the mounted policemen under Superintendent Sam Steele were being pitifully confounded by a chase so furious that it made its neighbouring equivalent appear like a Sunday park airing among Toronto burghers. The source of the perturbation was a Blood named Bad-Young-Man, or Dried Meat or, more commonly, Charcoal – as he was known by the clerks at the local Blood Indian Agency. Unable to place his trust in the justice of the Great White Mother, Charcoal had proceeded to declare a private personal war on her representatives, a fight so frenetically prosecuted that for an entire month the glazed eyes of the territorial settlers and the hysteria of their press were removed from the Voice's case entirely, and concentrated instead in the southwest, where search parties fell over each other chasing a lone, hungry Indian.

Charcoal had never been an obscure reservation Indian. An eminent warrior with an impeccable fighting record, he was highly esteemed by the Bloods and, apparently, by the NWMP whose superintendent Sam Steele wrote of him: "For some years

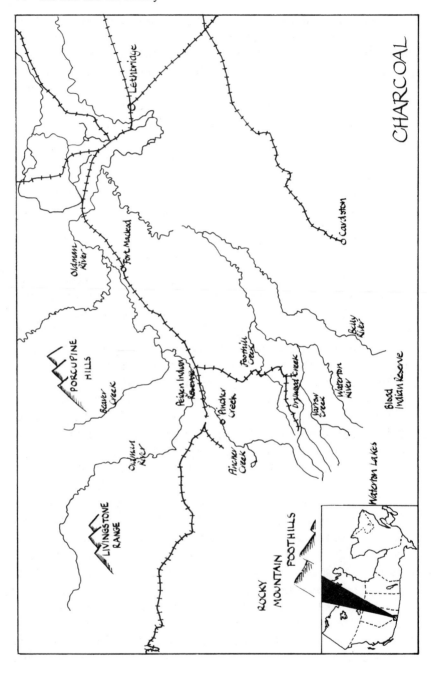

before we met the Blood, he was spoken of by (his tribesmen) as one of their most remarkable warriors, a hero in their eyes from every point of view. In those days he rarely slept in camp, was generally on the warpath or on horse-stealing expeditions against the hereditary enemies of his tribe, a restless brave who for a long time hated the whites. To many he seemed a myth, but when we came into the wilderness we found him only too much alive."

A rambunctious sort, Charcoal at the outset caused the Mounted Police many difficulties. But his relations with them improved over the years. "He had given us much trouble," Steele wrote, "but as time went on our just treatment had the effect of making him friendly and for several years he had been well-behaved."

Charcoal's good behaviour ended on October 12 or 13, 1896, when the body of a Blood Indian named Medicine Pipe Stem was found in the cattle-shed on the calf pasture of the Cochrane Company ranch near MacLeod. When a police inspector was sent the same day to the Blood reserve to investigate, he discovered a second casualty in the person of a farm instructor called McNeil, who had been shot at and wounded in the arm by an irate Indian. Indian Agent James Wilson soon volunteered the theory, on information presented by a Blood named Little Pine, who had been recently visited in his lodge by Charcoal, that the likely source of both assaults was Charcoal. Apparently he had admitted both the killing of Pipe Stem and the wounding of McNeil. Charcoal's sole expression of regret, according to Little Pine, was at his failure to dispose of Agent Wilson and Chief Red Crow, whom he held in scant regard.

Little Pine's intelligence was enough for the police, and several search parties were dispatched in pursuit of the fugitive who departed, according to their informer, in the company of four women and two sons. Two days later a warrant for Charcoal's arrest was issued following the findings of a coroner's jury at Stand-off. A new search was organized, pointed in the direction of the tortuous Kootenay and Belly Rivers which offered numerous shelters along their wooded banks.

The expeditions were barely outfitted when the first clues appeared of Charcoal's location. A settler named Henderson who had been busy loading timber on to a wagon at Big Bend fifteen miles from the NWMP detachment, and had removed his overcoat for that purpose, reported it stolen by an Indian who disappeared into the bushes. The thief was Charcoal who, feeling his need for warmth under the circumstances more pressing than Mr. Henderson's, had helped himself to that gentleman's garb. Now warmly attired, he and his family moved deeper into the woods and camped near the edge of a 500 acre pine forest, thick with underbrush standing as high as six feet, and surrounded by steep mountains. Two parties of police, reinforced by a contingent of Bloods, pursued to the timber's edge where they removed their hats and boots to facilitate their travel. After five miles they located in the valley below, amidst a forest of pine, the fugitive camp consisting of a teepee, several ponies and the women and children. The police approached cautiously but they soon cracked a few branches, alerting the fugitive to their advance. A brief shooting war occurred with Charcoal standing in front of the teepee firing into the bush. He soon decided that flight was more sensible and, with two women and a child, abandoned camp and fled deeper into the forest. When the mounties stormed the camp they discovered the ponies, two women and a child, and a cache of provisions sufficient to sustain the fugitive for a month, including the carcass of a recently-slaughtered steer.

When a new contingent of police under Inspector Davidson arrived, a cordon was arranged by police and Blood mercenaries who ringed the entire valley. By nightfall a plan had been hatched to close the circle foot by foot, beginning at the crack of day. Until then a close watch was organized; the sentries agreed not to fire unless certain of their quarry, lest a colleague be the victim of the bullet.

The night's vigilance and the next day's search brought nothing except confusion over the mysterious disappearance of the horses of Inspector Davidson's party which had been earlier installed at an abandoned ranch six miles distant. When a messenger was sent to feed the horses in the morning, he reported them missing. Subsequent riders who arrived at Bright's ranch to check on their whereabouts concluded from careful research that the horses had been returned to the timber. As Superintendent

Steele discovered later in the day, from a dispatch which referred to a strange Indian sighted near a ranch on the Old Man's River, the horses had not been returned but stolen and stampeded by the fugitive Indian. Charcoal had escaped the cordon, covered six miles on foot to Bright's ranch, released the horses, then galloped a further fifty miles to the ranch known as La Grandeur. Here he entered the kitchen in Mrs. La Grandeur's presence and, without a word of greeting or thanks, helped himself to a hurried meal. Mrs. La Grandeur, indignant at his incivility, conveyed her displeasure to the police, who later discovered several of their missing horses.

For Superintendent Sam Steele, the chase had just begun. A reward of $200 was posted and a dispatch carried by a lone messenger 120 miles to Major George Steel, the American Indian Agent at the Blackfoot Reservation, warning of a possible escape south. Groups of Piegan and Blood mercenaries, carefully screened by the Indian agents, were armed with repeater rifles, allocated a token supply of ammunition, placed under the tutelage of police officers and rewarded with food, warm underclothing, fodder for their horses and a living wage of fifty cents a day. When the Indians had been exhausted by the chase, they were replaced by new men. The use of Indian search parties created alarms in the territorial and eastern press, who reported as many as 250 employed at the same time. The papers wondered about the wisdom of placing trust and arms in the hands of red men hunting one of their own. The Indian recruits were augmented by packs of constables, commissioned and non-commissioned officers, special recruits, ex-members of the force and numerous ranchers and cowboys from around Calgary, MacLeod, Gleichen, Lethbridge and Pincher Creek.

Charcoal, though a man of prodigious abilities, was not acting entirely alone and the police, by suasion and force, struck at his friends and supply lines. The first to feel the law's pinch was his young boy, with whom he had escaped from the pine forest. Camped in the Porcupine Hills with his remaining two wives and the boy, Charcoal had descended the previous night to a Piegan camp on a horse-stealing expedition. His son followed on a pony. Before Charcoal left to steal the horses, he hid the boy in the bushes. A subsequent gunshot frightened the boy who thought his father might have been killed; he left his shelter and entered the camp where, instead of finding his father, he was apprehended by the police. "After a great deal of persuasion," according to Steele, "he agreed to lead the police to his father's camp which was discovered abandoned."

The young boy was removed to the prison guardhouse at MacLeod and kept as a hostage. Charcoal's other relatives who aided his flight, or were thought to do so, were similarly dealt with. When a half-brother called Long Main, who lived on the Blood's Reserve, walked about scantily clad, it was thought he had lent some clothes to Charcoal. He was arrested with his family and placed under preventive detention. Another brother, Red Horn, employed on the neighbouring Walronde ranch, one day quit his job after reportedly announcing he needed to spend more time helping Charcoal. "A close watch was therefore kept on this Indian," Steele reported. More drastic measures were taken against Charcoal's other brothers, Bear's Back Bone and Left Hand, when it was discovered that Charcoal had appeared during the night on the Blood reserve, stolen a horse and escaped south. Bear's Back Bone was immediately arrested for aiding and abetting the fugitive while Left Hand was pursued south to Lees Creek where, following the receipt of his treaty annuities, he had gone with his family to trade with the Mormons. There he and twenty-two other relatives, mostly women and children, were arrested, charged with assisting the fugitive, and transported to the guardhouse at MacLeod. They were cajoled and interrogated, threatened and offered "kindnesses" by police officers and Indian Agent Wilson. Several days later, Bear's Back Bone and Left Hand were released for several days, on condition they immediately report on Charcoal's whereabouts and aid in his capture. The women and children were detained and the husbands warned that, in the event of their failure to assist in Charcoal's capture, they and their families would be charged with aiding and abetting and would suffer dark consequences.

Charcoal, in the meanwhile, was giving the fatigued search parties a furious test. He was sighted at widely different points, often fifty miles apart the same day. Spent, stolen horses were scattered through the district. Police parties and Indian agents traced down numerous reports of his sighting. They rushed to the Piegan agency after an Indian named Commodore complained he had been fired at by a mysterious assailant who was trying to steal a horse tied to a hay-rack near his house. When Corporal Armer of the Cardston Detachment stepped out one evening for some fresh air, he was greeted by a rifle blast fired by someone hiding behind the water-trough in the yard. The bullet's calibre was the same as those fired at the late Medicine Pipe Stem. Mrs. Lamb of nearby Lees Lake reported that one night, after bedding down without her husband, she heard someone galloping furiously down the trail nearby. "She knew from the rate at which the person travelled," Superintendent Steele reported, "that it was not her husband and she was very much frightened." Mrs. Lamb then heard a strange noise in the storeroom behind the house which moved her to bury her head in the pillow. On entering the storeroom in the morning, she discovered a quantity of bread, butter and flour had been removed.

Chief Red Crow, no friend of the fugitive, shared some of Mrs. Lamb's fears. Charcoal galloped furiously about but he always returned to the vicinity of the Blood Reserve where he helped himself to fresh horses and provisions. The Chief trembled at these visitations and for the entire duration of Charcoal's freedom vacated his bed for the floor, for fear of being shot through the window. White Calf, another Blood warrior who had incurred Charcoal's enmity, took to sleeping in a hayloft and pulling the ladder up after him.

So the chase continued, for days and weeks: up the Porcupine Hills, down the valley of the Old Man's River, around the Cochrane ranch, near Olsen's Coulee and Bull Horn Coulee, at the head of the Belly River, and along the north fork of the Kootenay River. The Piegan reserve was scouted, spied and searched while thirty miles south the Blood's home, where Chief Red Crow was plagued by insomnia, was given a similar attention. More abandoned horses were recovered, hobbling and sweating, and occasionally the carcass of a dead steer stumbled upon. But no firm contact with the outlaw was made until November 10, when a party consisting of two Indian scouts and several constables, led by non-commissioned Sergeant Wilde of Pincher Creek, pursued the Indian through heavy snow south from Beaver Creek across the Old Man's River, in the direction of the Blood's Reserve. The party sighted Charcoal near Thibaudeau's ranch on the north fork of the Kootenay and received firm instructions from Sergeant Wilde not to approach closer than fifty yards. Charcoal rode his pony bareback and led a second horse, saddled and carrying provisions. He paid scant attention to the pursuers at first, but when they began to fiercely push their horses through the snow and close ground, he changed horses, turning the unsaddled pony loose. When the distance between was cut to 150 yards, Constable Halloway, accorded the first delicious opportunity in weeks to shoot the outlaw, hurriedly dismounted from his horse, cocked his rifle and misfired: the oil on the striker pin had been congealed by the cold. The officer finally did get off a shot but, by then, Charcoal had opened the distance to half a mile. At this point the entire party, except for Sergeant Wilde, had spent themselves and dismounted from their fatigued horses which had lugged thirty-five miles through the snow. But Wilde moved steadily ahead, closing the distance. He was soon abreast of Charcoal and, placing his carbine across his thighs, reached over to take hold of the Indian, who suddenly turned in his saddle and fired a bullet into Wilde's stomach. The officer fell wounded and lay bleeding in the snow while the Indian, who had moved ahead twenty yards, wheeled his horse around, rode up to his victim and fired a second shot into Wilde's abdomen, killing him. The outlaw then dismounted, turned his horse loose, requisitioned the dead man's carbine and his horse and rode off at an even canter.

The first of the sergeant's party to reach the scene of his death was an Indian tracker called "Tail-feathers-around-his-neck," who siezed Charcoal's abandoned horse and set out in pursuit. Wilde's body was removed by Constable Halloway and another Indian to a neighbouring ranch and, the following day, transported to Pincher Creek where an inquest was held and a verdict of murder returned against the Indian Charcoal. The dead sergeant, who had served seven years in the Royal Irish Dragoon Guards, three years in the Second Life Guards and fourteen years in the mounted corps, was buried the next day with full military honours. The funeral was attended by Chief Red Crow and a large body of Pincher Creek citizens who later erected a monument to his memory.

Similar honours were not accorded the outlaw who was trailed by Tail-feathers-around-his-neck to a refuge at the head of a branch of the north fork of the Kootenay River. Here the Indian tracker was joined by a party of Pincher Creek hunters, including a Mr. Herron who sighted Charcoal at the timber's edge and drove him with gunfire deeper into the woods. The search party then divided and conducted a close search until nightfall. The next morning Charcoal was nowhere to be found. Again, he had eluded his captors and commenced, in the brutal cold of a winter's night, a long and final visitation to the reserve he called home. The man who emerged from the timber was a ghost, exhausted by the chase, worn during weeks of hounding by frantic posses, starved with hunger and drugged with sleeplessness. But he was determined on a last journey, seventy miles long, a tortuous flight through massive drifts of snow, heavy timber, endless hills and ice-bound lakes.

Around three a.m. of the next morning, November 12, a weak knock was heard at the door of Bear's Back Bone and Left Hand who had bedded down for the night after a glum evening contemplating their own and their family's fate. The visitor was Charcoal who briefly stared at his roused kin, turned and staggered back to his horse tethered in the bushes nearby. Before he could mount, the brothers were upon him and he was dragged into the house. Charcoal was in a weakened state. With a moccasin awl he had punctured a series of holes in his arm in an attempt to bleed himself to death. The brothers stopped the flow with flour, bandaged the arm with pieces of flour sack and sent an Indian named White Top Knot to inform the police, camped nearby, of their prize.

Sick from loss of blood, the outlaw was removed from his brothers' care to a Roman Catholic mission and later conveyed to Stand-off where he was attended by a hospital steward. The next day Charcoal was transported to the guard room at MacLeod, interrogated and force-fed since he had refused food, preferring a voluntary death to the fate which awaited him. He was soon removed to the prison, chained to the wall and guarded by five policemen. As a precaution against a suicide attempt, he was not allowed to use either a knife or a fork. During his outings for exercise, he was chained and escorted by several guards.

Charcoal survived long enough to be tried, convicted and hanged; and life around Pincher Creek quickly returned to normal. The Indian scare abated; the *MacLeod Gazette* became less strident; hunters washed down accounts of the chase's hardships with swills of rum; Red Crow returned to his bed; and White Calf swung the ladder down and climbed from his loft. The dead man's wife and children grieved and remembered his defiance but the settlers, ranchers and police were mostly relieved it had all ended. Most pleased of all was Superintendent Steele who was so impressed with Charcoal's resistence that he was moved to describe him in his memoirs as "at least the equal if not the superior in character and prowess of the ideal Indian of Fenimore Cooper's novels."

Sam Steele had some anxious moments but, overall, he thought the pursuit operation economical and bracing of the moral fibre of the community. "His brothers Left Hand and Bear's Back Bone . . . were induced to act by promises I made them," he later reported to his superiors, "which have been fullfilled without costing the country anything . . . The careful management of the Indians for years past, kind and just treatment coupled with firmness, has caused success in gaining their confidence to a degree unknown in the past. I may conclude by saying . . . the circumstances have had a beneficial effect on the community, because the settlers have seen whites and Indians work together under police officers to carry out the most determined pursuit of a criminal that it has ever been their experience to know of."

The community of the hunters which warmed the superintendent's heart was not nearly as evident, in the autumn of 1896, further north and east around the fork of the Saskatchewan River where Almighty Voice continued to elude the search parties sent out to inflict upon him Charcoal's fate. By inducing a delicious 'Indian scare' in the border country south of the Saskatchewan,

Charcoal's mad defiance momentarily diluted the Cree fugitive's notoriety and diverted police energies and settler hysteria into the neighbouring ranching country. The Blood's death, however, revived speculation about the Voice's location and, during the winter months of 1897, a careful reconnoitering of the Cree's home territory was maintained. Rumours continued unabated. One report had him dead in Montana; another, alive and well in the north around Lesser Slave Lake. The Nut and Quill Lake Indians and the Fort a la Corne Reservation were investigated while white traders who did business with the Voice's home reserve were enlisted as spies who reported regularly to the police. Two well-provisioned search operations were maintained throughout the cold winter months, one centered around Crooked Lake, the other south-east of the Voice's reserve where the neighbouring farm of a Métis settler named Venne was used as a base camp.

The police were not pleased with the proverbial inscrutability of the destitute Indians who, defying the laws of political economy and rules of Jeremy Bentham, were not quick to surrender their man and collect the reward. The Métis around Batoche, whose crops were failing and who faced starvation during the winter months, were no better and most refused to join the search operation. But there were some exceptions, among them Mr. Napoleon Venne, farmer and tracker, who, one day late in the month of May 1897, reported to the mounted police detachment at Batoche the killing of a cow on his farm. For weeks preceding the animal's demise, it had been widely rumoured that the Voice had returned to his home reserve. These rumours were reinforced by the mysterious wanderings to and from Batoche of his father, no friend of the Vennes. Accordingly, when Corporal Bowridge, head of the Batoche police detachment, heard of the cow's killing and Venne's suspicion, he immediately joined the Métis in a search around the farm. The mountie and the Métis were barely on the trail when they suddenly came upon a pair of young Indians, one of whom retreated to the edge of a bluff of poplars. As Bowridge approached with Venne at his side, a shot from the poplars struck Venne's shoulder while a second shattered the butt of his rifle. The corporal and his guide did not stay for the fight.

They turned their horses and raced to Duck Lake where they informed Bowridge's superiors, headed by Inspector J. Wilson, of the shooting. A further message was dispatched by telegraph to Prince Albert where Inspector "Broncho Jack" Allan rounded up a group of rough-riding constables and interested citizens and departed the same evening for the Minichinas Hills. By early morning they joined with the Duck Lake bunch and began scouting operations from a cabin owned by a man named Couture, located on the crest of a hill overlooking the surrounding valleys, several miles distant from the scene of Venne's shooting.[1]

It was not long before the hunters sighted their quarry. From his bird's-nest location, Allan and a fellow scout McKay trained their field-glasses on several figures, resembling sandhill cranes, moving single file across the valley floor towards a bluff beyond. On closer examination they proved to be Indians wrapped in blankets. Nearby, an Indian was frantically chasing at racing speed a small group of cayuse ponies past a clump of willows. Allan recalled his scouts and flanking parties, mounted his horse and descended about a mile when a second report, from a Constable Ascott, confirmed the Indian's proximity. Ascott had seen several figures, loping on all fours through the wolf willow, which he first thought were deer. Shielded by a thicket of poplars, he spied them again and observed they were Indians, three in number and wrapped in blankets, who disappeared into the bluff nearby. He confirmed as well the recent proximity of the Indian boy, on a fast buckskin who urged on, with a frantically waving blanket, a pack of ponies. The Indians were evidently surprised and horseless and had retreated into a thickly wooded poplar bluff, rectangular and about five acres in extent, matted with bush and interspersed with clumps of willows, located on a hill among barren neighbours, known to the Cree as the Beautiful Bare Hills.

The police were soon at the bluff's edge. A party led by Sergeant Raven, who had come down from Prince Albert with

1 The locale was about ten miles due east of the spot where General Middleton's column branched from the main trail to enter Batoche in May 1885. The marks of the small drains dug around their tents, as well as other signs of General Middleton's camping places, were still evident.

Allan, dismounted and cautiously began scouring the woods. Several flankers, on horse and foot, controlled the wood's edge, while Broncho Jack circled the perimeter in anticipation of a run for freedom. The Raven party were the first to make contact when, after advancing fifty yards through the thickly matted underbrush, they were greeted by a fusillade of fire from a pair of Indians crouched in a clearing twenty yards away. Raven was hit in the thigh and dragged from the bush by his colleagues, who slowly retreated. Allan, in the meanwhile, was searching the bluff's west side when he suddenly spied three Indians crashing through the bush, one of whom fired a quick shot which brought the inspector's horse to its knees. After raising and calming the beast, Allan raced towards the southern extremity in an effort to close off a possible escape. Broncho Jack had guessed right and for his wisdom received a bullet which shattered the bone in his upper right arm and felled him from his horse. The shot had been fired by an Indian the inspector recognized as Almighty Voice. Short of ammunition, the Voice moved towards the fallen officer, covered him with his rifle and, with his left hand extended, beckoned for his pistol and ammunition belt. A quick round of firing from Allan's approaching colleagues, including the bleeding Raven, drove the Voice and his two companions back into the bushes.

Here, in a lone island of high poplars and gaunt, white willows, padded with underbrush thick and fierce enough to tear a man's skin, surrounded on all sides by wide spaces of short grass and beyond, by the bare beautiful hills, the Indians prepared themselves for a siege. The Voice was not alone in his misery. In recent days he had been joined by friends and family: by a tall and tough Indian called Dublin from Fort a la Corne and by a brave young cousin, fourteen years of age from Nut Lake, known as Little Saulteaux. With him as well, in heart, were the people from One Arrow's Reserve who slowly drifted onto the adjoining hills in full view of the besieged bluff. Among the sullen squatters were the trapped Indian's mother and wife who, with their friends and relatives, resisted the importunities from local officials to vacate. The mother alone chanted encouragement. The Voice's father, arrested the preceding day on a charge of aiding his outlaw son, was in jail.

The reserve Indians, gloomy and quiet, may have conveyed to the trapped men, by their mere presence, a moral support. But there was nothing material forthcoming. The people had come to witness as much a burial as a battle. The trapped men well knew that for them there were no supply lines, no routes of transport, no buckboards, railways, telegraphs, cannons or parties of outfitted and aroused friends on saving missions. The Voice had not arrived at the bluff to satisfy an "ambition to be great." He had been driven into a lair, horseless and unprepared. Contrary to early press reports, the outlaws had no cache in the woods, no food supplies and ammunition to sustain a lengthy stand. So they made do with the implements at hand: a pair of rifles, a pistol, a few rounds of ammunition, and a hunting knife which, lashed to a stick, served as a shovel. In the hours following the engagement with Broncho Jack's roughriders, they fired warning shots at the attacking party and, with the makeshift shovel, dug a pit five feet deep and eight feet wide in a dense thicket near the west side of the woods.

While the Indians spied and dug and fired an occasional shot, Broncho Jack's party withdrew and reassembled. The bushes were surrounded again and a message conveyed to the outlaws by a pair of Métis scouts, in Cree and Saulteaux, to surrender or be smoked out, an unlikely prospect since the trees and brush were still wet with the spring's waters. Requests for help were sent off to Batoche and from there conveyed by telephone and telegraph to Duck Lake and Prince Albert where the Volunteers, a local militia formed in the days of the Northwest Rebellion, assembled and dispatched an emergency relief party. With Broncho Jack removed to Duck Lake in a buckboard, and Raven incapacitated, the field command fell to Corporal C. H. S. Hockin, a son of Admiral Hockin of the British Navy, who had spent twelve years as a commissioned officer in the Imperial Service and several terms in India, before joining the Mounted Police, three years previous.

Hockin's scanty forces were reinforced by recruits from Batoche and Duck Lake and plans made to invade the bluff. As night approached, Hockin and his men grew impatient and fearful of a break for freedom by the desperate outlaws under the night's cover. So they decided to assemble a line of men and, arms in hand, slowly comb the woods in a series of sweeps commencing at the bluff's southern extremity. The men found the going tough and on two separate forays, failed to make contact with anything except a thousand twigs and burrs. On their third rendezvous, however, after making a short advance, they were met head on by a line of fire which felled three of the search party. The Indians, it seemed, had stationed themselves in the pit and withheld fire until their enemies were practically upon them. The strategy worked, resulting in the killing of a constable named Kerr and the Duck Lake postmaster, Ernest Grundy, a friend of the late Sergeant Colebrook who had ridden out that afternoon on a mission of revenge. The third casualty was Hockin, dragged badly wounded from the bush by his retreating colleagues. Hockin soon died and his body was removed to Prince Albert. Kerr and Grundy's bodies were abandoned to the outlaws.

The fatal pit fire suddenly escalated the fight from a desultory smoking out operation into a veritable battle. Huge fires were lit during the night as the search party's remnant kept up a lonely vigil. The killings had shaken the field troops' confidence and the men anxiously waited for reinforcements, which arrived the next day: from Batoche, where C. E. Boucher, M.L.A. led a group of Indian fighters; from Duck Lake, where Inspector Allen marshalled extra troops and volunteers; and from Prince Albert, where Superintendent Gagnon gathered an eager pack of Northwest Rebellion veterans and a seven pound brass cannon. The call for help reached as far as Regina where a farewell ball for the local North West Mounted Police contingent was interrupted and halted mid-way. On orders from Commissioner Herchmer, a force was assembled and dispatched under Assistant Commissioner McIllree consisting of an inspector, twenty-four non-commissioned officers and men, a nine pound gun, a gun team, several saddle horses and a war correspondent from the *Regina Standard,* who was later joined by a similar representative from the *Manitoba Free Press.* The men departed before a cheering throng at the C.P.R. station in the mid-morning of May 29, gained Duck Lake late the same afternoon and, after a pause for feeding and watering their horses, arrived at the battle scene at ten o'clock in the evening.

While the surrounding forces swelled until they counted over a hundred men, the trapped Indians desperately improvised and prepared for the inevitable. To warm themselves during the cold and wet spring night, Dublin and Little Saulteaux appropriated the scarlet tunic of Officer Kerr and Postmaster Grundy's shirt. The Indians sustained themselves with a thin fare of crow meat and quenched their thirst with the sap of poplar trees, whose bark was stripped bare with a knife. They fired an occasional shot from their dwindling supply of ammunition to remind the police that they were still alive and prepared to fight on.

By the late afternoon of Saturday, May 30, a new factor came into play: the war cannons. Superintendent Gagnon's seven pounder began its exercise at dusk and several shells were lobbed into the bluff in the direction of the outlaws' dugout. The evening firing was brief and brought a taunt of recognition from the Voice, who shouted that the superintendent's men were doing well, but would have to do better. By midnight, the cannonading had stopped, huge bonfires were lit, and a tight cordon thrown around the bluff's perimeter. A desultory rifle firing, back and forth from the woods, continued until the early morning hours when the cannons were placed in position at opposite ends of the bluff. As the cannons boomed, One Arrow's people, camped on a hill east of the bluff, watched in grim silence. The day was cloudless and their view unobstructed. "A bright and beautiful Sabbath in a fair and lovely country," a *Globe* correspondent reported, "was heralded by loud cannonading." The firing began at six a.m. and the gun teams sent forth, intermittently, during the next four hours, a steady shower of cannister, shrapnel and ball. The bushes crackled as the missiles exploded and wreaths of white smoke swirled above the timber. But throughout the entire exercise, which Assistant Commissioner McIllree later described as "most excellent practice," there was no response from the woods. Soon after the guns died, the civilians became impatient and urged the police officers, who were under orders not to risk an early invasion, to rush the bluff. The police, however, resisted and the Volunteers brooded until two p.m. when they gathered a force under James McKay, Q.C. and William Drain, a captor of Riel in 1885, on the brow of a neighbouring hill and threatened an immediate assault. A hurried consultation between the Volunteer's representative and McIllree resolved differences and, in the mid-afternoon of the siege's third day, an attack on the bushes was launched.

The invaders were more fortunate on this, their third try. They were not long in the undergrowth when the outlaws' bodies were discovered. The Voice and Little Saulteaux lay together, in their rifle pit, which served as a grave. The Voice had been killed by fragments of shrapnel, which had shattered the top of his skull, exposing his brain. The body of his young cousin, also a shrapnel victim, lay on top of him. Dublin died alone at the timber's edge, dressed in Kerr's tunic and with a bullet in his forehead. Outside of the bluff's edge, a Volunteer in search of mementos discovered a makeshift crutch, built of a poplar branch and a rag and, beside it, a single moccasin which fit the foot of Almighty Voice. During his final night, he had attempted a long crawl to freedom with the aid of the crutch. His left leg shattered by shrapnel and bound in a rough splint, he had crawled to a point almost a hundred yards from the bluff's edge. But here he abandoned the enterprise and returned to his pit, to die.

The Voice died silently and mostly alone. No large battles or skirmishes followed the extinction of an outlaw finally "numbered among the class of Indians marked good."[2] In the century's last years, the Saskatchewan Crees abjured the fiery path of the neighbouring Cheyennes in Montana just as those Bloods who marvelled at Charcoal's exploits and aided his escape, preferred for themselves the path of peaceful extinction. There circulated, to be sure, in the weeks following the deaths of the Voice and Charcoal, many rumours which invited a host of explanations and remedies. Reports of restless braves leaving their reserves, of cattle killing around Nut Lake, of a dead cow here and a butchered steer there circulated freely, feeding the vitriol of journals

2 "Controller White thinks that Almighty Voice, knowing that he would assuredly be killed, decided to make a greater record than Charcoal, the Indian who ran a month last year. He was certainly successful." The *Globe*, June 1, 1879.

like the *MacLeod Gazette* which warned about "false economies" and demanded a bigger and better police force. Some authorities, including police officers and the eastern press, discerned in the poverty and degradation of the Plains Indians both the causes of past events and the seeds of future rebellion. "The Indians in this district," NWMP Saskatchewan District Superintendent Cotton wrote, "are not as well off as they have been in the past . . . the treaty Indians find it hard, they say next to impossible, to earn money by working for, or making sales of wood, to white men; in other words, the Indians' power to earn something over and above what they receive in aid (in the shape of rations) from the Government has in the past been over-rated. A hungry Indian, like a hungry white, is not so docile or as contented as he is found to be under more favourable circumstances." The *Toronto Telegram* endorsed the superintendent's view: "Almighty Voice was the champion of the race that is 'up against it' in civilization. The wonder is not that an occasional brave cuts loose, but that all the braves do not prefer sudden death to the slow extinction of their people."

The authorities, however, did not seem terribly concerned, and in the months following the Voice's death, they occupied themselves with more positive matters, such as the logistics of settling carloads of Ruthenians on the bare plains in mid-winter, or the triumph of Sir Wilfred Laurier at the Diamond Jubilee Celebrations in London, where the NWMP paraded their scarlet uniforms and prancing horses. Among them was a horse once favoured by Sergeant Wilde, which Superintendent Steele thoughtfully included in the overseas contingent, for presentation to the dead man's regiment by the Prime Minister of Canada.

Notes

The best accounts of the Almighty Voice and Charcoal affairs can be found in the annual *Report of the Commissioner of the North West Mounted Police Force,* Ottawa, Queen's Printer, 1895, 1896, 1897. Almighty Voice is the subject of a useful pamphlet by Frank Anderson, *Almighty Voice,* Frontier Publishing Co., Calgary, 1971. Among the many articles written on the Cree outlaw are, W. B. Cameron, "Outlaw," *Scarlet and Gold,* Second Annual; Chief Buffalo-Child Long Lance, "The Last Stand of Almighty Voice," *Maclean's Magazine,* Feb. 1, 1929; A. Cooper, "The Brave They Fought with Cannons," *Maclean's Magazine,* July 1, 1951. *The Saskatchewan Herald* and *Manitoba Free Press* provided good coverage of Almighty Voice's last stand. Worthwhile material is contained in several North West Mounted Police histories and biographies including: S. B. Steele, *Forty Years in Canada,* Toronto, McClelland, Goodchild and Stewart Ltd., MCMXV; R. C. Fetherstonhaugh, *The Royal Canadian Mounted Police,* Carrick and Evans, New York, 1938; and T. M. Longstreth, *The Silent Force,* The Century Company, New York, 1927. A precis of the Charcoal affair is included in L. V. Kelly, *The Range Man,* Argonaut Press, New York, 1965.

Sable River

The Roman Line

Michael Carrol

Patrick Ryder

William Thompson

James Donnelly
Patrick Ryder

James Donnelly

John Whalen

John Cain

Patrick Whalen

Edward Ryan

John Carroll

Patrick Quigley

Martin Darcy

James Keefe

Patrick Ryder

Patrick Sullivan

William Casey

Thomas Ryder

Thomas Ryder

LUCAN

GRAND TRUNK RAILWAY

The Shape of a Dog

When he first settled in Upper Canada's Queen's Bush, James Donnelly was not terribly concerned about the legal title of the land he occupied. Donnelly was a curly-headed, handsome and dirt-poor Irishman from County Tipperary, in the southern province of Munster, happy enough to find a space to squat on. Like many of his compatriots, he had already suffered plenty from rack-rents, commons enclosures, absentee landlords, potato blights, famines, epidemics and a slow, punishing transport across the ocean to the new world.

James Donnelly's immigrant ship teemed with dispossessed Irish and diseases so infectious they consumed masses of human cargo before docking at a quarantine camp near the mouth of the St. Lawrence River. Grosse Isle, a desolate assemblage of rocks pelted by freezing rains, was a place of separation. The dead and dying were left to rot and fertilize the rocks. The living, which somehow counted James and Johannah (Judith) Donnelly and their two sons, James and Will, proceeded west to the gloomy immigrant sheds at Montreal, Kingston, Toronto and finally, the boom town of London.

Donnelly stayed briefly in London before moving north, into the adjoining township of Biddulph where, at lot 18 of concession 6 of a vast domain claimed by the Canada Company, he parked his family and began to scratch a living. The new Tipperary arrivals were not alone in the Biddulph bushes. A colony of run-away slaves, named after the British abolishionist Wilberforce, had been established by the Society of Friends around 1830, while a Protestant constable named James Hodgins sponsored a migration of Tipperary Protestants to neighbouring London township and Biddulph, where they lived in a row of settlements called the Protestant Line. The Tipperary Catholics, the Donnellys among them, came later, settling primarily in Biddulph, in a district known, understandably, as the Roman Line.

The Queen's Bush was a haven for the Donnellys who built a shanty and a few out-buildings on a spread of uncertain size known as Greenland. As the years passed, the old man cleared and improved the land and added to his family. The two oldest boys were joined by four brothers – Patrick, Mike, John and Tom.

The Donnellys became a close group, and the father, a respected Biddulph citizen who crowded his children into the tiny schoolhouse nearby, attended St. Patrick's church, drank gallons of ale at Andrew Keefe's tavern and quarrelled with his neighbours about politics, religion and other matters touching the human condition. The old man's quarrels were usually harmless and ended, at worst, with a bloodied nose or busted ribs. There was one dispute, however, with a neighbour named Patrick Farrell that took a decidedly fateful turn. It centered on Donnelly's land which he claimed by right of pre-emption. The Canada Company thought otherwise and sold the southern portion of the homestead, about 50 acres, to Farrell. Quarrels and lawsuits ensued, but Farrell clung to his portion until the evening of June 25, 1857, when the legal combatants attended a local barn-raising bee. Both drank heavily and soon entered into a fierce argument which ended when Donnelly seized "a certain wooden handspike of the value of one penny," and drove it into Farrell's head. Farrell died within three days and a coroner's inquest concluded that James Donnelly was the perpetrator of a "willful murder."

Donnelly did not wait around to be arrested. A poor Irishman with a deep distrust of judicial authority, he fled into the safety of the surrounding bush where he lurked, close to home, for almost two years. The fugitive often slept in the family barn, supped in the house and worked in the field, disguised as a woman, dressed in a long skirt and kerchief. His wife was busy during his absence. She staunchly cared for the brood which added two members: a daughter named Jenny, who arrived soon after the father's departure, and a young boy, William Farrell, the son of the victim, who was adopted as an act of charity and soon became a loyal family member. Judith Donnelly worked feverishly to prepare for her husband's return, which took place in the spring of 1859 when the fugitive surrendered himself to the local constable.

James Donnelly may have thought he would be lightly dealt with. After all, he had been an exemplary citizen before the Farrell affair, local opinion had cooled during his absence and it was common knowledge that Farrell's death had resulted from a rash act committed possibly in self-defence, in a heat of passion and under the influence of alcohol. But he was disabused of such calming notions at the trial held at the Huron Spring Assizes at the town of Goderich where the judge concluded that Donnelly had willfully and culpably murdered Farrell, and sentenced him to hang.

In the gloomy days following the trial, the Donnellys worked night and day, in homes, taverns and church to marshall support for a petition of commutation. A long list of local signatories, Catholic and Protestant, was gathered and submitted to the authorities who mercifully altered the sentence. Instead of hanging by the neck until dead, James Donnelly rotted in the penitentiary in Kingston where he remained for a full seven years.

The Donnellys were a patient people and dedicated themselves during the father's absence to preserving the family homestead.

When James departed the boys were young but they sustained the mother during her lengthy vigil. Judith Donnelly was a strong and independent woman who cultivated in her children a like pride and loyalty to the father and family. Instead of blushing and wilting during their father's imprisonment, the Donnelly boys developed a pugnacity and combativeness which earned them the respect and fear of their neighbours.

When James Donnelly returned from the Kingston Penitentiary in 1866, he found his family and homestead preserved and intact. The father's arrival was a boon and, in the following years, the farm was improved and expanded. Additional acreage was purchased, wheat and potatoes grown in abundance, pigs and poultry raised, and several fine Clydesdale horses installed in the barn. During the autumn of 1867, the shanty was torn down and replaced by a larger structure built of nicely dovetailed logs and consisting of a large kitchen, living room and three bedrooms on the main floor, with additional space upstairs. Beside the house was a small milk house, and behind, a pair of barns. The new home, one of the largest and most pretentious in the area, stood a short distance off the small road leading to the neighbouring village of Lucan, where the local farmers marketed their grain and purchased supplies.

Here, along the Roman Line, in the first years of his return from Kingston's tomb of the living, James Donnelly settled routinely into a society barely civil. The Lucan district, in the years preceding and following Confederation, was a place of crime and terror so endemic that Donnelly's cashiering of Farrell seemed an almost ordinary event. Petty thefts, assaults, burglary and highway robbery were common occurrences from the earliest days of settlement. Election days were the signals for fisticuffs and mêlées fought in the streets and taverns. Nor was murder an exceptional occurrence. The killing of Farrell was one of five committed in a space of four years, beginning with the robbery and slaying of a Protestant cattle drover named Richard Brimmacombe in 1857 and ending with the smiting of William Calahan, father of eight, by John Cain in 1859. Another local pastime was barn burning. In the year ending August 1865, seven district barns were consumed by fire, at least three of which were set by arsonists.

Biddulph's chronic criminality sprang from the usual infirmities of human nature set free to wreak their havoc in a frontier society where legal institutions had barely formed. But it had, as well, a special flavour, traceable to the place of origin of many of the criminal practitioners. Biddulph Township, after all, was New Tipperary, where the rough transplants from Munster province faithfully replicated their old quarrels, grudges and factions. Old Tipperary, since the Protestant invasion, had been a hotbed of terror, crime and violence. The grinding poverty of the Irish peasant, his victimization by absentee landlords of a different religion, his cynicism towards legal authority and penchant for violence were directed inward toward his own Irish kin as well as outward against the English.

Tipperary people were chronic fighters. They scuffled with the landlords and spawned a host of secret organizations – including The Whiteboys, The Rightboys and The Ribbon Society – which terrorized the countryside. And they fought wildly and bitterly among themselves. Whiteboy vengeance was directed as much against the Catholics, who were thought to collaborate with the enemy, as against the English and Protestants. Frustrated in their war against poverty and degradation and a powerful land-owning class, the poor fragmented into factions, wallowed in drunken stupors and beat each other's brains. "The lower classes in this country," Toqueville observed from a visit to Ireland's Waterford Assize Court in 1835, "are very prone to quarrels and fights, and . . . almost every village forms a kind of faction with a code name. Factions which started nobody knows when, and which continue nobody knows why, and which take on no political colour. When men of different factions meet, at a fair, a wedding or elsewhere, it is exceptional if they do not come to blows just for the love of fighting. These quarrels very often end in someone getting killed; generally speaking, human life seems of little value here."

Tipperary quarrels varied. Some were political, others nonpolitical. Some were directed, others apparently anarchic. They had, however, several common attributes, among them a fierce loyalty to faction or group and a hostility to the legal authorities who found the road to justice strewn with perjured witnesses, secret oaths and intimidation. Tipperary people, according to one account "look with indifference upon the most atrocious acts of violence, and by screening the criminal, abet and encourage the crime."

Matters were not very different in New Tipperary where, after a respite of several years following their father's return from Kingston, the Donnelly boys thickly entered the fray. James Donnelly had served his time and carefully avoided further skirmishes. His sons, however, showed no similar reticence and, by the early seventies, had already gained a host of enemies. The Donnellys quarreled with their neighbours over a range of matters from love to livelihood. And they fought many interests, among them the Conservative-Catholic political oligarchy and the local railroad and stagecoach companies.

When it came to affairs of the heart, the Donnellys displayed a curious exuberance which sometimes landed them in court. The case of Will Donnelly, the club-footed, second-oldest boy, gifted with a keen intelligence and biting tongue, was an excellent example. When Will found neighbour William Thompson sulking over his daughter Maggie's affair with a Donnelly, he raided his home with a group of family and friends and started a scuffle. Not content with this, he subsequently removed himself to Maggie's brother's house where, at a charivari welcoming young Thompson and his new bride, Will and friends broke every pane of glass, used the chimney for target practice, heaved sticks and stones, and tore down the rail fence whose components were used to build a bonfire, which almost burned down the house. The Thompson capers soon earned Will and several of his brothers court appearances, which resulted in acquittal.

Will's brother Jim's quarrel with a James Caswell, who lived at Biddulph's eleventh concession, was a more serious matter. Donnelly, according to Caswell, squatted on some fifty acres of land adjoining Caswell's before departing for an extended stay in the United States. During his absence, several of the brothers and the father worked the land which James claimed he owned. The Canada Company, however, claimed the legal title and advertised the sale of the parcel. Among the interested purchasers was Mr. Caswell who was warned by Bob Donnelly that the Canada

Company had no valid title to the land and no right to sell it. Caswell ignored him and purchased the acreage. Henceforth, he suffered a string of reverses. On Christmas eve, 1875, his stables and sheds burned to the ground. Not long after, his hay was consumed by a fire in the field and a pair of horses killed. When Caswell tried to buy new horses, he found his neighbours reticent to sell, for fear of retaliation by the Donnellys. Several years later, his crops were consumed by a fire and his reaping machine destroyed. "I was afraid for my life to prosecute any member of the Donnelly family," Caswell later complained, "who were continually trying to pick quarrels with me, and on one occasion a Lucan magistrate declined to grant me protection from them, saying that if they attacked me all Lucan could not save me." Caswell was convinced the Donnellys had authorized the wicked deeds which eventually cost him his farm. No court, however, had an opportunity to support his assertion.

More serious and protracted disputes followed from the Donnellys' entry into the stagecoach business in 1872, when Will took a job as driver with a company owned by Hugh MacPhee. Will proved a tough and ambitious driver and, in partnership with his brother Tom and Patrick Whelan, soon bought out the company which carried passengers and small freight between London and Exeter. Will did a good business initially, until the inauguration of the London, Huron and Bruce Railway which severely pinched the small coach companies. The railway had come to stay, but its early years were not free of dangers and depredations. Track inspectors in the township of Morris, between Lucan and Goderich, one day found a large hardwood tree slung across the track near a precipitous turn. Earlier, near Clandeboy, someone had sawed through the timber supports of a bridge. It was thought, among the family's legion enemies, that the Donnellys had done the carpentry.

The railways eventually killed the stage business which, in Biddulph Township, died painfully and with a good dose of violence. When the Donnellys entered the field, it was already, on account of the rail competition, constricting. The diminishing traffic inspired not mergers, but a bitter competition between rival companies resulting in threats, collisions, fist fights and the destruction of property. The major rivals were the Donnellys, who claimed brother Mike as one of their drivers, and the Hawkshaw Stage which fell into the hands of a tough Irishman named Flanagan. Neither side owned timid drivers and everywhere along the sixteen mile Proof Line Road connecting London City and Lucan Village, at stations, stables, and roadsides, the feuding drivers pursued their vendetta. "The boys who drove the stage were continually quarreling with the drivers of the opposition stage," an East London constable reported, "one party or the other getting a beating every other day."

In the Stage War the Donnellys held their own. They regularly threatened their rivals, showered them with abuses, engineered collisions and engaged in scuffles. In the autumn of 1876, Flanagan discovered his stables and barn burnt to the ground and several of his prize horses without tongues. One of his drivers was severely cudgelled one night in a barn. A Flanagan carriage was burnt and another drawn down a road and sawed into pieces of firewood size.

The drivers argued and collided in the streets and in the courts. When Will Donnelly's coach was bumped by Flanagan's, several of his passengers were injured and awarded court damages against Donnelly, who was charged with careless driving. Mike Donnelly charged Pete McKellar, a Flanagan driver, with threatening to kill, and John McLeod, an employee with the same rival firm, with "maliciously colliding with and damaging" the Donnelly stage. Mike, in turn, was charged with threatening to kill McKellar, the use of abusive language against an ex-constable named Henry Brien and perjury.

When the Donnelly enemies did get them into court, minor convictions involving fines sometimes resulted. But the Donnellys were not easily drawn to the law's bosom and their resistance to arrest landed them in further difficulties. When a powerful detective named James Berryhill became embroiled with them at a hotel near the Lucan station, he was attacked by Pat, Tom and James, and by a friend named James Keefe, beaten with clubs and stones, and, if we are to believe Berryhill, detached from part of his nose by Tom, who took a healthy bite. Another snooper, named James Currie, was similarly treated and dispossessed of some of his money. When Rhody Kennedy, a county constable, arrived one evening on the Lucan stage to arrest James Donnelly on a Berryhill assault charge, he was given a rude reception. Kennedy suffered from a minor disability: he had only one arm which Donnelly, being a perceptive sort, shrewdly noted. When Kennedy seized his prey, Donnelly drew a gun and before an audience of spectators asked Kennedy to desist. Lacking an arm, Kennedy could neither draw his own gun, or take Donnelly's, without releasing his quarry who, noting the constable's quandary, began to beat him about the head. Donnelly escaped arrest and Kennedy pressed charges.

Rhody Kennedy's complaints were soon registered and arrest warrants placed for execution into the hands of three London constables – John Reid, John Bawden and John Cowsey. Upon arrival in Lucan, the constables heard that the wanted Donnellys, James and John, were attending a wedding for a family friend at Fitzhenry's Hotel, known as the Catholic hotel, located on a small dark side street. The officers repaired there in the late evening and discovered, to their consternation, that the Donnellys were in no mood to leave the reception early. Reid was fired at twice and badly wounded by William Farrell, the late Patrick Farrell's boy. While the officers dressed their wounds, the Donnellys fled in a sleigh, decorated with jingling bells.

The hotel meeting did not end well for the Donnellys who faced a host of charges at the Spring Assizes in London in 1876. The stage dispute sharpened opinions against the family whose fierce pugnacity invited contrary sentiments of revenge and hatred. The Donnellys boasted of warm and loyal friends – the Keefes, the Donaghues, the Hogans and others – to whom they were kind and generous. But they counted as well an assortment of enemies whose numbers swelled as the battle thickened. The dark Tipperary legacy, the violence of the stage war, the chronic outrages throughout the district – often committed by persons unrelated to the Donnellys – the family's bluster, combativeness and readiness to use threats and force, their support for the Grit party against the Catholic-Conservative hierarchy, their friendship with the Protestant merchants in a community where remnants of Whiteboy sentiments survived, drove their enemies to pursue a policy of organized and violent retaliation.

A shadowy Vigilance Committee, on which the Donnelly family had no representation, appeared early in 1876, charged with keeping the peace and protecting upright citizens from the wicked deeds of evil persons. Private detectives scoured the district collecting evidence and witnesses in an attempt to build a legal case against the boys. Prominent among them was Hugh MacKinnon, a muscular Scotchman who later headed the police force in Belleville, Ontario. MacKinnon arrived early in 1876 and interviewed several local citizens who readily complained about the Donnellys but were curiously reticent to repeat their stories in court. MacKinnon did not himself always resort to gentlemanly tactics. When he and several cronies heard that a man named Atkinson was friendly with the Donnellys and might be persuaded to talk, they visited the gentleman at his house and removed him forcibly in a carriage for an airing in the country. When Atkinson proved uncommunicative, he was strung to a tree and gently raised and lowered several times, with little result. He was then returned to his home with an assurance he would be murdered if he recounted recent events. Atkinson later fled to Michigan and, on his return, was persuaded by the Donnellys to press charges of abduction against the MacKinnon gang. Proceedings were initiated, the abductors, including the Belleville future police chief, were arrested, and a trial date set. In the forenoon of the day fixed for trial, Atkinson sat in the courtroom. But when summoned to testify the next day, he could not be found. The charges were dropped.

MacKinnon had been employed for a purpose: to build a case against the Donnellys. The results of his labours were evidenced at the London Spring Assizes of March 1876, where five of the boys – Thomas, William, John, James and Patrick – together with several of their friends, including young Farrell, faced an array of charges including arson, assault, larceny and shooting with intent to kill. But the prosecution had trouble making some of their charges stick. When the Donnellys and their enemies committed their outrages, especially barn burning, they were not easily detected. Nor were they readily charged by persons fearful of intimidation. When charges were pressed, convictions rarely followed. The Donnellys were fierce courtroom fighters, retained good counsel – among them a London lawyer named David Glass – and were not usually troubled by long lines of hostile witnesses. So long as their strength and numbers remained intact, few persons rushed forward to lay informations or testify against them, for fear of retaliation.

The March 1876 Assizes in London represented the first concerted attempt to curb the family's power. But the Lucan Vigilantes enjoyed only a modest success. While many of the charges were dropped or dismissed, several stuck and three of the boys were sent off for short terms to the penitentiary. Will received nine months for his Fitzhenry Hotel performance while John earned three months on charges arising out of the same affair. James, charged with assault in the Berryhill fracas, was imprisoned for nine months.

The jail terms induced not a halt, but a pause, in a feud which assumed a ferocious intensity in the winter and spring of the following year. Both sides fought fire with fire and the Lucan streets and taverns filled with alarums about burning and dark reports of animal mutilations. The incendiaries did not discriminate. Barns, storage buildings, homes, hotels and post offices were reduced to ashes. When a fire watcher employed by Lucan village took a lively interest in his duties, he received a bullet in the groin. The Donnellys were naturally cited as perpetrators of the outrages which made Biddulph "the shame of the townships" but they, or their allies, were victims of nearly half of the dozen burnings during the fire feud of 1877. On two separate occasions their stables and barns, together with valuable horses, were consumed in blazes which invited bitter retaliation. Brother Mike, who commuted to the Lucan district while employed as a brakeman with the Canada Southern Railway Company, barely escaped a fire which destroyed his lodging place.

Mike was less fortunate in a scuffle he engaged in two years later at a hotel at Waterford Station, Norfolk County: one of several adversities which, in the months and years following the fire war, weakened the strength and numbers of the Donnelly faction. An inveterate brawler, who had more than held his own during the stage fights, Mike landed in a dispute over the treatment of a dog and was stabbed to death by a sometime Biddulph resident named William Lewis. The cause of the death of James, who quietly expired in the home of his parents in May 1877, was more mysterious. Word circulated that he died of gunshot wounds following an attempt to either vandalize a barber shop, rob a Grand Trunk grain elevator, or set fire to the Queen's Hotel. Whatever the distal events, it was locally presumed the immediate cause of his death was "lead poisoning," a disease which almost consumed Lucan constable Samuel Everett who, late one night outside the door of his home, was fired at by a shrouded figure from behind a woodpile. Everett thought the assailant was Bob Donnelly, a commuter from Glencoe. With the aid of a pair of informers planted in the cell of the accused, Bob was sent away in March 1878 to the Kingston Penitentiary for two years.

The jailing of a Donnelly was music to the ears of the Lucan Vigilantes who, in the closing years of the decade, pursued their vendetta with renewed intensity. The Vigilante Committee, at the outset, was a mysterious body of uncertain size, appearing intermittently in the penumbra of Lucan politics. In 1879, however, it revived in virulent form and assumed a clear shape and purpose. The committee was organized by hardened Donnelly enemies and counted anywhere from thirty to a hundred people who, for one reason or another, shunned and hated a family rapidly descending "from Popularity to Ishmaelitism." It met, irregularly, in the Cedar Swamp schoolhouse, swore members to secrecy and included an inner core of members who tightly controlled meetings, agendas and membership. The core consisted of respected Lucan citizens and Roman Line residents, including neighbours of the Donnellys such as Patrick Ryder and Martin McLaughlin, a substantial farmer and recent convert to the anti-Donnelly cause. It harboured men with old and festering grudges such as William Thompson, another neighbour, whose daughter had been courted by Will Donnelly, and John Kennedy, whose sister married Will. And it counted among its most fanatic workers a brawny bearded farm implement salesman names James Carroll, a recent immigrant to Lucan from the township of Stephen.

The Lucan Vigilantes, known to the Donnellys as the "Black Militia", were a secular body consisting exclusively of lay

Catholic Irish. But they did enjoy a certain religious sanctification volunteered by Father John Connally, an eager and meddling Irish priest sent to St. Patrick's parish by his superiors to straighten matters away. When the tall, grey-haired priest in his early fifties arrived in Lucan in February 1879, he had no intention of pursuing the timid policy of non-intervention in the Biddulph feud preferred by his German predecessor, Father Lotz. Connally's parishioners, after all, were his own kin, and immediately on arrival the father pursued a lively interest in their frenetic affairs. He soon took sides with the anti-Donnelly faction, a resolution inspired, in part, by an attack on his person, clad at the time in a wolf-skin coat, by a wicked dog owned by Will Donnelly whose home the priest was visiting. Thereafter the Donnelly enemies approvingly listened every Sunday while Father Connally hurled fire and brimstone at the beleaguered family, warning that the Lord would smite the devilish perpetrators of evil deeds. And he meddled in specific cases, in and outside of the courts: an intervention which moved the Donnellys to petition the priest's superiors, with little result. Father Connally's crowning achievement, however, was the collection of a stack of signatures appended to a page in a book he placed one day on a table near the front door of his church, in full view of his parishioners as they entered for their morning prayers. The signatures, which did not include the names of any of the Donnellys or their allies, were entered below a pledge, composed and drawn up by the priest, to assist the "spiritual director and parish priest, in the discovery and putting down of crime" in the parish.

Father Connally did not create the Vigilance Committee. As he later disclosed, the only organization he had ever formed was a temperance society. Nor did he define for any committee or group an offensive purpose. The priest merely wished his parishioners to unite to protect themselves from thieves and rogues. If property was stolen from someone, he later stated, then it was the job of the others to aid in its recovery.

Whatever the priest's real intent, the Cedar Swamp Vigilantes were hugely pleased with his intervention, and with his sponsorship of an anti-crime pledge, which they interpreted as an endorsement of their own organization. Like Father Connally, they protested that their sole concern was with self-protection through mutual aid. As they moved into action, however, in the latter part of 1879, it became apparent that the Lucan Vigilantes had a larger, offensive purpose: to rid the township of the Donnellys, root and branch. Although formally nameless the Committee might properly have registered itself, under a Companies Act, as a "Society for the Suppression of the Donnellys."

Among the vigilantes' major peeves was the alleged reticence of police and court officials in arresting and convicting criminals like the Donnellys. They consequently began to press for the appointment to judicial and police positions of men from their own ranks. They enjoyed good success. A firm committee member named William Casey earned an appointment as justice of the peace, while a second partisan, Martin McLaughlin, was placed as a magistrate. But the tough work, in the streets, fell to the constables, and it was here that the vigilantes enjoyed their greatest success. Following a petition to Judge Elliott, the vigilantes heard the glad news that their fearless nominee for the police, James Carroll, had been appointed a county constable.[1]

Flashing his credentials, Carroll doggedly pursued the Donnellys. An old robbery charge, in which a Ned Ryan accused Tom Donnelly of stealing from his person, was revived. Although Donnelly had already been tried and acquitted in one court, Carroll pressed the case in another court and district. When Donnelly heard of Carroll's intention, he fled the scene on horseback and was pursued by a posse of vigilantes. He was again tried, and acquitted. Carroll accused Tom's brother John of supplying a horse in aid of the escape and pressed charges. He also escaped conviction.

The Donnellys did not take kindly to Ned Ryan's accusations and their retaliation further confounded the vigilantes. When Ryan needed his grain threshed and approached a man named Curtin who owned a machine, he found Curtin reticent following a warning from Tom Donnelly not to work for Ryan. Curtin then

---

1 In April 1879, Carroll had been arrested and subsequently acquitted on a charge of threatening to shoot Mrs. Donnelly. Later, he confessed to Edward Sutherby, a Whalens Corner blacksmith, "I will have them out of Biddulph if it costs me my life." The *Globe,* October 17, 1880.

went to Father Connally who agreed to stand security for the machine in the event of its damage. Curtin went ahead and threshed and found pieces of iron in the damaged works. The entire machine was wrecked during a later threshing job, prompting excited Cedar Swamp meetings where compensation was discussed. According to one account, no rewards were made since it was alleged Curtin had ruined the machine himself to collect damages.

The case of William Thompson's cow led to further vigilante frustrations. Finding a heifer gone, Thompson brought the matter before his Cedar Swamp colleagues who concluded the Donnellys were the likely thieves. When the vigilantes were denied a request for a search warrant by Reeve Stanley, they decided to go ahead and look without one. Early in the morning, before the Donnellys had risen, the search party of forty members armed with clubs and guns descended on their residence and searched it roughly. An altercation followed in which James Carroll asked, in reply to a taunt from the old man, whether Donnelly wanted his ribs kicked in. The vigilantes then withdrew to the neighbouring village of Whalens Corners where Will Donnelly had moved with his wife. While the vigilantes glowered and searched, Donnelly played them "Bony Crossing the Alps" on his violin, and inquired of one of the party whether he was searching for his mother, who could be found in a poor-house in Ireland. The Thompson cow was eventually found in a neighbouring pasture, but the court proceedings dragged on. John Donnelly pressed the charge of trespass against several vigilantes who, benefitting from their colleagues' testimony, were acquitted. The vigilantes in turn initiated perjury proceedings against John, which never came to trial.

For the beleaguered Donnellys, Thompson's cow proved less fateful than Patrick Ryder's barn. In the evening of January 15, 1880, while four of the Donnelly boys attended a wedding, Ryder looked out his back window and noticed a conflagration. Somebody had set fire to his barn and granary which quickly burnt to the ground. Ryder was a Committee man and his sad loss was mulled over at the Cedar Swamp schoolhouse where it was concluded that Ryder's long-time neighbours were the likely perpetrators. Informations were laid against four of the Donnelly boys whose obvious wedding alibi dissuaded William Casey from issuing warrants for their arrests. Since, however, it was known to all that the boys' parents had not attended a wedding that evening, additional informations were laid against them before Casey, who issued warrants for their arrest. Carroll executed the warrants and the elder Donnellys were brought before a Lucan magistrate and freed on bail. Henceforth the vigilantes made slow progress. On Carroll's own admission, the crown's case, after four adjournments, was ready to "fall to the ground".[2] A final hearing date was set for Wednesday, February 4.

The case was never heard. In the early evening of February 3, old James Donnelly and his youngest son Tom visited the home of Michael Connor in East Lucan and returned home with his boy Johnny who agreed to tend to the farm during the absence of the Donnelly elders at the Grantown court the next day. Young Johnny, a bright and precocious eleven-year-old, spent an easy and pleasant evening at the Donnelly home. He munched apples, helped with the feeding of the pigs and horses, ate a full supper and, while Judith conversed in the kitchen with son Tom and niece Bridget – who boarded with the family – he went to sleep. In a room adjoining the kitchen Johnny shared his bed with the old man who, after saying his prayers, retired early with his young visitor. Johnny Connor did not sleep long. Around two o'clock in the morning he was awakened by a noise and light. Standing in the doorway was a squarely built bearded man dressed in a soft black felt hat, a black coat and grey flannel pants, who announced to James Donnelly that he had come to arrest him and his son John. When Donnelly answered that John was not there, the man repeated his intention and held a candle while the old man dressed. James asked his visitor what he had against him and the man replied he had another charge. Donnelly searched briefly for his coat then walked into the kitchen

2 Carroll was initially so pessimistic about the prospects of acquittal that he contemplated reviving a two-year-old arson charge against Bob that would return him "to Kingston for a long term of years." The Donnellys let it be known that they were prepared to press a case for malicious prosecution.

and asked his son Tom, who slept there, whether he had been handcuffed. Tom replied in the affirmative and requested the night visitor to read his warrant. The man in the black hat replied there was plenty of time for that. Mrs. Donnelly, in the meanwhile, had awakened in the adjoining bedroom and asked Bridget – who shared her room – to light the fire.

But Bridget ran for the stairway as a group of men, about twenty in number, stormed into the house. Several of the night visitors wore blackened faces, while others were dressed in women's clothes. There were three, however, who wore no disguises and were recognized by young Connor: James Carroll, the man with the candle; Thomas Ryder, the bearded son of Patrick Ryder; and James Purtell, an orphaned and drifting farm labourer who performed odd jobs around the Lucan district. The night raiders made short shrift of their quarry whom they beat with sticks and clubs. When Tom broke free and escaped from the house, he was pursued, dragged into the kitchen and beaten over the head with a spade. Young Bridget's flight upstairs did not save her. Her leaving was noted and she was pursued into the attic and attacked. The visitors closed their assault in true Lucan style. Coal oil from the lamps was poured on the beds which were ignited just before the visitors departed into the night.

While the flames roared through the wood-frame home of James Donnelly, wildly licking and dancing around the battered bodies of its residents, the vigilantes sped through the winter snows to Whalens Corners where Will Donnelly slept quietly after a warm evening spent with his brother John and a visitor, Martin Hogan. John and Hogan stayed for the night, sharing a bed in a room adjoining Will's. The vigilantes rushed to the front door and shouted to Will about a fire. Since John was closer to the door, he answered the alarm and was met, upon opening the door, with a pair of volleys which tore a hole in his chest. "Will, I'm shot," he shouted, "may the Lord have mercy on my soul." Nearly dead, John was dragged into the bedroom where a blessed candle was placed in his hands; he held it, with the aid of Hogan, until his expiration. Nobody moved from Will Donnelly's house for fear of interception the entire night; a lonely and trembling vigil was maintained until the slow dawn of the morning sun.

The coroner's examination and wake were held at the home of Michael Connor, where James Donnelly's charred body together with the remains of his relatives were delivered in a sleigh by a pair of London constables, Brown and Clark. The house was filled with mourners drawn from the far corners of the township, including Mrs. James Currie of St. Thomas, the Donnellys' only sister; son Patrick, a Thorold carriage maker; and Bob, a resident of St. Thomas since returning from the Kingston Penitentiary. Bob Donnelly collapsed with grief over John's coffin and was led away to a neighbour's residence.

In all, several hundred people arrived in an assortment of sleighs on the morning of Thursday, February 6 and joined the funeral procession headed by the hearse carrying John's body and a sleigh filled with the remains of his fellow victims. The procession moved slowly, through a bitter frost, to the Roman Catholic Church at Ryan's Corner, two miles from Lucan, where it was met at the door by Father Connally. He preceded the coffins up the aisle to the front of the church where they rested during a remarkable ceremony.

Events had plainly shaken the priest who broke down and sobbed several times during an occasion he pronounced as "the most solemn ever brought before the gaze of humanity." "To come to Biddulph," he complained, "I left a quiet place, and a Christian place, where the laws of God and the laws of man were observed. I came to a district where neither the laws of God, nor the laws of man were obeyed." Father Connally spoke of the rumoured depredations of the Donnellys, confessed he "did not think that anyone could bring such disgrace upon his religion" and protested his friendly inclinations, towards the mother in particular, who confessed frequently and tried "to get her boys to come to confession . . . but they did not come and here is the consequence. O, God of Heaven, forgive them!"

During his brief address, which ended with a spasm of tears, the priest spoke neither of the vigilantes nor, specifically, of the Donnelly depredations: an omission which moved Patrick to rise at the close of the address and ask Connally to give a "detailed account." The priest was astonished at the request, but recovered quickly enough to speak in some detail of his differences with the family, protest that he would "willingly have laid down" his life "to save them," and defend the Vigilance Committee, composed of men "incapable of committing such a terrible murder as this one." The father concluded with the resigned wisdom that all that remained to be done was to pray for the departed: "Let us try in our hearts to pray for them, for no matter how we die, whether by the hand of God or the hand of wicked men, we have to stand before the Great Jehovah and account for all our earthly actions. How will those guilty people appear before their God with a cry for vengeance coming up from earth? Ah! it will be a terrible day for them."

Being avid churchmen, the Lucan Vigilantes doubtless contemplated the heavenly reckoning, rating it at a discount in light of their convictions about the demonic qualities of their victims. The earthly reckoning, however, was another matter, and in the days following the Donnelly burial a score of police and detectives from London, led by Chief of Police Williams, descended on Lucan and conducted an investigation so earnest that it shook the foundations of the Cedar Swamp schoolhouse. The vigilantes would have rested easier had they known there were no eye-witnesses to their final solution. But they were apprised of what soon became common knowledge in the township: that two persons had seen several of them in the flesh during the commission of their crimes and were prepared to tell their story to the police and courts.

The first was Will Donnelly, the real target of the Whalens Corner raid. Donnelly did not hide under the bed, or covers, during the shocking moment of his brother's death. Instead, in the moments following the shooting, he drew the curtains of a small window overlooking the house's front yard and peered into the yard, where he recognized several old friends. "I heard John open the door," Donnelly later testified, "and immediately after that I heard the shots; before the outside door was opened I heard McLaughlin's voice and that of young Ryder; I did not make any motions to get up because I was afraid; I heard the next shots fired at the south-east corner of the house; I turned the edge of the curtain back and saw Kennedy standing within three feet of me; I saw one part of his face and his head; he had dark clothes;

he had something in his right hand . . . Carroll and James Ryder stood beside him; I knew Carroll before he spoke."

For his brother's murderers, Will Donnelly's nocturnal perceptions were not a cause for great concern. The Donnellys, after all, were tainted people who, like other Lucanites, were said to practise perjury as a daily art. The other likely crown witness, however, had no such darkened reputation. Johnny Connor was a nice, honest and beardless boy, who, through a quirk of fate had witnessed as an impartial spectator the commission of awful deeds. And, remarkably enough, Johnny Connor lived to tell what he had seen.

When the raiders entered the Donnelly home, Johnny had been in bed with the old man whose folded coat served as his pillow. When the beatings began, and young Bridget raced for the attic stairway, Johnny followed her but, finding the door closed, returned to the bedroom and hid under the bed, behind the clothes-basket, where he witnessed the brutal conclusion of the night's work. He was able to recall events of the brutal killing, from the time of the raiders' entry until their hurried departure following the dousing of the beds with coal oil. And he remembered persons. "I was waked up about two o'clock," he later stated "I know the time, because it was that time when I got to Whalens; the old man got up; I saw James Carroll holding a light for him to dress himself . . . I saw Thomas Ryder and John Purtell; I knew them before; I knew them well; I also knew Carroll well; they were all standing around when I saw Ryder; I saw one in woman's clothes; two or three had their faces blackened; and the three I've named had not their faces blackened at all . . ."

The vigilantes did a thorough job, except for their failure, through a strange and momentary assertion of conscience, or sheer neglect, to finish the trembling boy. When they left the burning home, Johnny Connor crawled from under his bed, put on his britches, tried to extinguish the flaming bed with a jacket, stumbled through the kitchen over the prone bodies of Judith and Tom Donnelly and raced out of the house, across the road to the home of Patrick and Ann Whalen who lived fifty yards away.

Although he was barefoot and freezing, Johnny Connor was given a cool reception. "I ran up to the door," he recounted, "and

Mrs. Whalen asked who was there; I said 'Connor's boy' and then I went in and whispered to her that Donnelly's house was on fire; Mr. Whalen got up and told me I was dreaming; I told him a lot of men came in and hunted them out of the house, and I thought the old woman and Tom were killed; I told her to call up the boys Joe and Will; she said 'No, if they go over there they'll be killed.' "

The Whalens invited Johnny Connor in and suggested he warm himself near their fire. But when he began naming people, they told him to keep quiet about what he had seen. It was a full ten or fifteen minutes before Patrick Whalen, the Donnellys' near neighbour, took it upon himself to investigate the scene of the murder.

Johnny Connor stayed the night at the Whalens' and, in the morning, after visiting the burnt wreck of the neighbouring home and noting the four bodies amidst the blackened ruin, returned home to his family in Lucan and recounted his story. He told his parents what happened; and he told an *Advertiser* reporter who printed an account, without names, on the front page. Johnny gave his story to police investigators who kept him under close guard before and during the series of ensuing trials. And he repeated it, with little significant variation, at a coroner's inquest, a preliminary hearing in magistrate's court and two subsequent trials in London before eminent judges.

Johnny's and Will Donnelly's stories brought results. In a full sweep through the Lucan district, the police collected thirteen persons who were brought for a preliminary trial before a police court in London in late February. The accused were exclusively Biddulph people and known Vigilante Committee members, or friends of vigilantes. They included Patrick Ryder; his brother and two sons; the substantial farmer and justice of the peace, Martin McLaughlin; John Kennedy, who bore a spite against his brother-in-law Will Donnelly, favoured by the elder Kennedy; William Carroll, the dull younger brother of the Lucan constable; James Maher and his beardless son who, relatives of James Carroll, farmed on the sixth concession, a mile or so from the Donnelly farm; and John Purtell, the estranged farm labourer who wandered the district. But the prime suspect, apprehended by negro constable Charles Pope as he walked one day along the Roman Line, was James Carroll, who "appeared excited and shook a little and changed colour" when he first encountered the officer.

The men accused of the Donnelly murders were neither hired assassins nor the dregs of the countryside. They were, on the contrary, respectable Lucan citizens, pillars of the community: farmers, labourers, yeoman, landholders and officers of the law. When reporters, who quickly filled the front pages of the nation with lurid accounts of "The Biddulph Tragedy" and "Lucan Horror," began sampling local opinion in the weeks and months following the murders, they found a marked sympathy, not for the victims, but for the accused: a sympathy which increased as the trials progressed. Lucan, after all, was a lawless place, the seat of a vendetta pursued for a decade by bitter factions. The Donnellys' fierce tenacity, their chronic skirmishing, their remarkable ability to hold ground – in the streets, taverns and courts – their refusal to accept an Ishmaelite status, had so frustrated their opposition, and its sympathizers, that a "final solution" was looked upon more as a welcome relief than a terrible and punishable act. The Lucan citizenry had long ago taken a moral holiday. They supped nightly on a diet of hatred and revenge. The pre-meditated murder of five members of a Canadian family asleep in the dead of night was an outrage across the country. In Lucan, it was a blessing.

The reporters heard this when they interviewed the local people. "Wasn't that fine work last night," a gentleman commented to a friend. "It was," came the reply, "May a felon never grow on the finger that pulled the trigger." One Roman Liner observed that the Donnelly murderers "ought to have a first class seat in heaven," while another affirmed that "the jury that would hang them ought to be hung themselves." When he first heard of the arrests, a gentleman wondered "What are they making all this fuss about? Why don't they leave the two sides to themselves." Another citizen was prone to emit aphoristic bursts of folk wisdom: "As a man lives he dies"; "A workman earns his wages, and they got their just dues; they burned and cut and were cut and burned."

The Lucanites made no distinction between good or bad Donnellys or between the parents or children. "They were a bad family," a prominent resident concluded, "and the only difference between them and a dog was in the shape . . ." "There need be no sympathy for Mrs. Donnelly," a reporter was told, "she was kind-hearted and did lots of little acts of kindness, but she had a wicked mind. Why, it is said that she prayed on her knees that the souls of her sons might forever and ever burn in Hell if they ever forgave an enemy or failed to take revenge." Belleville Police Chief MacKinnon was moved to recall "that the old lady was a hard talker and may have said to some of the neighbours that she would never be satisfied till each of her boys had killed his man like the father."

Lucanites were equally indulgent to the Vigilance Committee and, in several published interviews, made no attempt to hide their views on the likely authors of the killings. And they were quick to predict the outcome of the trials. "There is no doubt that it was the members of the Vigilance Committee who killed the Donnellys," a leading village resident volunteered, "the Committee was organized for no other purpose than to wage war on the Donnellys." A local Catholic was convinced the Committee was "in on the secret but they will keep it." He added that "the people of the neighbourhood are under a debt of gratitude for their action to rid the place of the Donnellys, and no one will testify against the Committee . . . if the truth were known it will be found that the murderers are the most respectable people in the township, good farmers and honest men, but they had to do it – there was no other way. . . There will be any amount of money at their back. The best counsel will be procured, and nothing will be left undone. The murderers . . . are respectable men who would not harm a fly, but they had to kill the Donnellys, just as they would a mad dog. People cannot live in a state of terror forever." A local Protestant thought the prisoners "among the most decent and respectable men in the township" and predicted a certain acquittal. "It will be hard to get anyone to swear against the prisoners, except the Donnellys. I never knew an Irishman yet who would act as an informer. If even an enemy of the men saw them committing the murders they'll not tell."

There was ample opportunity to tell, and perjure, at the series of inquests, hearings and trials beginning with the coroner's inquest, where a Lucan jury found that James, Judith, Thomas and Bridget Donnelly "came to their death by being murdered and burned by parties unknown," and that John Donnelly was killed "by gunshot wounds . . . at the hands of a party or parties unknown to the jury." The London preliminary trial, which heard a mass of evidence, sorted out the primary suspects and resulted in the discharge of all of the accused except six – James Carroll, Martin McLaughlin, Thomas Ryder, James Ryder, John Kennedy and John Purtell – who were committed to stand trial at the London Spring Assizes in early April 1880.

The proposed London trial seat did not please the crown attorneys, led by Emilius Irving Q.C., who received the hearty endorsement of editorial opinion across the province of Ontario when he applied for a change of venue, alleging that a fair trial was impossible in Middlesex County.[3] Irving knew the culture, opinion and practices of Biddulph and conveyed his intelligence in the Court of Common Pleas and, again, in the Court of Queen's Bench. He argued that fear and intimidation were the rule in the area, that local feelings and opinion were inflamed and bitterly divided, that the accused knew persons throughout the county, that no jury could likely be found to hear the case without fear and prejudice. But Justices Hagarty, Armour and Cameron of the Court of Queen's Bench thought that since Biddulph was in the extreme north of Middlesex County, it was unlikely that a juror from a southern portion would be more exposed to fear than jurors of Wellington and Bruce called to trial in their own counties. Mr. Justice Armour remarked that if jurors "were to be afraid of their lives to bring in an honest verdict, what were they to say about the judge who tried these persons – was he to be massacred too?"

As it turned out, neither judge nor jury were done in during the London trial of James Carroll, charged with arson and the murder of Mrs. Judith Donnelly. The Crown built its case around

3 Irving was assisted through the various trials by Charles Hutchinson, The Middlesex Crown attorney, James McGee, representing the Ontario Government and Edmond Meredith.

the testimonies of Johnny Connor and Will Donnelly, supplemented by a host of corroborating witnesses. Connor, cross-examined for three hours and a quarter, repeated in substantial detail earlier versions he gave to the press, coroner's inquest and preliminary trial. Donnelly went through a gruelling examination and had his testimony substantiated by his wife and Martin Hogan, a resident at his home the night of his brother's killing. Crown Attorney Irving flushed out bits of information on the Vigilance Committee, alleged a conspiracy to kill the Donnellys, noted Carroll's intimate association with the Committee, cited his expressed malice towards the Donnellys and membership on the Committee and emphasized the good character, intelligence and reliability of his prime witness, Johnny Connor.

The defence's strategy was to weaken the Connor and Donnelly testimonies, build a case around Carroll's alibi – that he slept uninterruptedly at the neighbouring Thompson residence the entire night of the deaths – and vindicate the Vigilance Committee as a legal and proper civil-defence organization. Witnesses testified to Will Donnelly's family loyalty, prejudice and bad character, and to the respectability of the vigilantes who were properly and legitimately concerned with protecting themselves and the community from criminality. The Thompsons and Carroll's brother, who allegedly shared James' bed at the Thompson farm the night of February 3, testified to James' presence there without interruption. Similar testimony was advanced on behalf of Thomas Ryder and James Purtell, whose presence at home was attested to by the McGrath family. The defence's case and the prisoner's fate ultimately rested on the testimony of the boy who was submitted to a tough cross-examination. Only minor inconsistencies – relating to the position of Bridget Donnelly's body and other like matters – appeared in Connor's story. To defence counsel Meredith and McMahon[4], however, they were significant and they argued forcefully that the boy, a friend of the Donnelly family, was too young, unreliable, impressionable and excited to relate information accurate and truthful enough to justify conviction of a man for murder. The defence's case was good

4 Aiding McMahon and Meredith were George McNabb and J. J. Blake, both outstanding lawyers.

enough. Seven of the jurors favoured acquittal and James Carroll faced a second trial, again in London, Middlesex County in late January 1881.

Neither the Crown nor the defence substantially altered their strategy during Carroll's second ordeal. McMahon repeated his tactics and arguments. The Connor boy was roughly handled and minor contradictions in his testimony – relating to the valance of the bed, the placing of Bridget Donnelly's body, the position of the spade allegedly used to kill Tom Donnelly – were loudly exposed. The boy's parents, who received monetary support from the Crown during the proceedings, were accorded a similar treatment. McMahon argued that the Crown's case rested exclusively on Connor who was a confused and impressionable boy. He defended the alibis of Carroll, Ryder and Purtell, and luridly documented the bad history of the Donnellys – which he said explained the apathy of their neighbours following the killings – and also accounted for the creation of the Vigilance Committee, purely a self-defence organization innocent of any designs destructive of the Donnellys or of the processes of justice.

Crown Attorney Irving added little to his earlier case. He again argued the basic consistency and sense of Connor's description of events in the Donnelly home on February 4, emphasizing the remarkable memory and intelligence of a boy possibly "gifted for a great purpose, and by a far higher power than had yet been suggested." The Vigilance Committee was trotted out, together with Carroll's membership in it and persistant antipathy to and harassment of the Donnellys. The purpose of the Vigilance Committee, Irving alleged, was not merely to curb and destroy the Donnellys, but to protect, cover and defend persons, including the accused, who performed the Committee's work. Irving attacked the Carroll alibi claiming that the Thompsons and his own brother, who supported the alibi, were interested witnesses who gave contradictory testimony. Since the defence argued that the Connor boy was wrong in his impression of the presence at the scene of the crime of Ryder and Purtell – and therefore was likely wrong about Carroll's presence – Irving methodically attacked the Ryder and Purtell alibis, bringing forth a new witness named Robert Cutt to counter Ryder's support witnesses.

Emilius Irving's closing address, over two hours long, was spirited and forceful. But it failed to sway the jurors who possibly subscribed to the view that, under the circumstances, Johnny Connor "may have been in such a state of mind that it would be unsafe to rely on what he said." The death of the Donnellys went unavenged, James Carroll was acquitted of the charges of arson and murder and the Lucan Vigilantes were vindicated in their effort to restore law and order to their divided township. Bail was taken out for the remaining prisoners and their cases soon dropped since Carroll had been the candidate most likely to be convicted.

The London acquittal invited no provincial or national approval. On the contrary, there was wide recognition that the ends of justice had been confounded. Editorial writers spoke of grounds for national humiliation, dark stains on the cherished Canadian mosaic. But there was little humiliation in Lucan, except among the Donnellys' beaten friends and remnant family. When the prisoners returned home they were greeted by exuberant family and friends who boisterously drank, sang and danced at the several resorts favoured by the Biddulph people. At the Western Hotel, however, there was an unpleasant incident when Bob Donnelly approached a group of revellers and said: "Now I want all you murderers to come up and have something with me." There were no takers.

Notes

The Donnellys are the subject of a sensationalist and inaccurate treatment by Thomas Kelley in his *The Black Donnellys,* Winnipeg, Greywood, 1969. A more sensible and reliable account is Orlo Miller's *The Donnellys Must Die,* MacMillan, Toronto, 1967, which provides useful background material on early Biddulph crime and violence, and the Donnelly family's involvements. James Reaney has written an informative note on James Donnelly in the *Dictionary of Canadian Biography.* W. Stewart Wallace's *Murders and Mysteries,* MacMillan, Toronto, 1931 includes a well-written chapter on the Donnelly story. The *London Advertiser* and the *Globe* are filled with detailed accounts of all aspects of the Donnelly case.

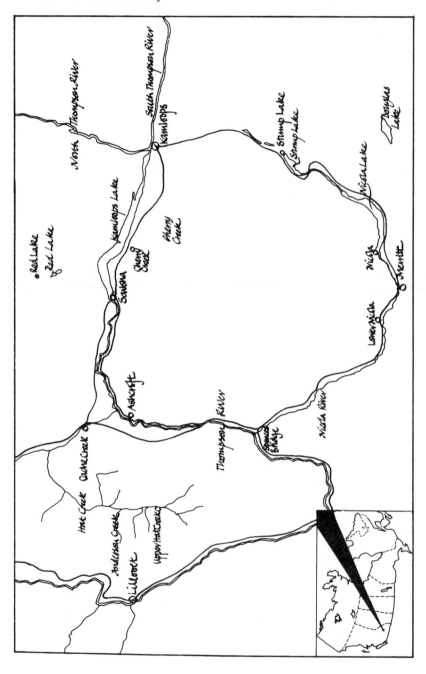

The Waifs

At the foot of Long Lake, a few miles below the town of Kamloops in the Canadian province of British Columbia, four young men camped on a bitter cold day in early December, 1879. The oldest, a tall and muscular youth with a black beard, called himself Allan McLean. With him were two younger brothers: Charlie, a swarthy seventeen-year-old with high cheek bones and a scant moustache, and Archie, the glum family baby at fifteen. The group's fourth member was shorter and squatter than the rest. He had a wide forehead, a long bent nose and wore a look of ineffable sadness. His name was Alex Hare, a recently inseparable companion of the McLean brothers. Like his friends, Hare was part Indian, the son of Cherry Creek rancher Nick Hare and a Siwash Indian woman.

The boys had barely started their fire when they were suddenly approached by a short bearded man astride a brown horse. William Palmer, a Stump Lake rancher, had lost a black stallion and thought he saw it in the possession of the boys. But as he neared their camp, he decided not to press the matter. Two cocked and ready shotguns, pointed by Archie and Allan, greeted his arrival, and the meeting which followed was brief. Palmer begged his hosts not to shoot and assured them of his friendly intentions. When Allan asked why he had approached so fast and warned that anyone trying to arrest them would be killed, Palmer replied weakly that he had merely wanted company. He then rode away towards Kamloops where he laid an information for horse stealing against the McLean boys and Hare before Justice of the Peace John Edwards.

William Palmer's supposition was entirely correct. The horse grazing near Charlie McLean, a large black stallion, had been stolen from his ranch on December 3. Nor was this all. Most of the possessions of the McLean-Hare group, including a brown horse taken from Palmer's neighbour McRae, had been acquired in the same way. The McLeans at their Long Lake camp were well-supplied with food, cooking utensils, guns, ammunition, saddles and bridles. When they needed something, they took it – from a variety of places and persons in the sparsely settled country between Cache Creek, Kamloops and the Upper Nicola Valley.

The McLean boys were poor and helped themselves to what they could get. Not all of their family were this way. Their mother Sophie lived quietly on a few acres at Hat Creek. Their half brothers and sisters from their father's first marriage were mostly respectable people scattered over the north-central interior in a variety of gainful occupations. One sister had married a member of the provincial parliament, Preston Bennett, who sat for the district of Yale.

The boys' troubles stemmed from their father who had so misarranged his life that his younger sons found themselves displaced and resentful persons. Donald McLean had found a place for himself in the Hudson's Bay Company which he joined as an apprentice clerk in 1833. A hard and bitter man from Tobermory City on Scotland's Isle of Mull, McLean rose over years of service in the Pacific Northwest to the position of chief trader. He served at a variety of posts and places: at Forts Hall, Boise and Colville below the 49th parallel; at the northern Forts Chilcotin and Alexandria where he won the post of chief trader in 1853; and finally, at Fort Kamloops, the growing Thompson River post in the Company's New Caledonia district.

Donald McLean was an arrogant and abrasive man whose life was an endless round of quarrels. Some of his arguments were domestic. He fought with his first wife, a Spanish Indian woman from the Kalispell country in the south, who accompanied him on the arduous trip north, more than a thousand miles, from Snake River to Fort Chilcotin. McLean's wife gave birth to six children before he abandoned her and, in 1854, took up with another woman Sophie Grant, also Indian, from Fort Colville, who brought five more McLeans into the world.

McLean's other quarrels had to do with company business. Though an able employee, whose services were appreciated and rewarded by his superiors, McLean's ambition and temper resulted in a constant round of disputes with subordinates and senior company officials. In 1860, when the company had passed its best days, McLean had a final quarrel with Mr. A. G. Dallas, who headed operations west of the Rockies following the resignation of Governor Douglas. The quarrel began with the management of the new forts of Dallas and Verens in the Lillooet district, whose construction was supervised by McLean, and ended with a recommendation from Sir George Simpson that McLean be transferred east of the Rocky Mountains. McLean balked and quit the Company's service. In the spring of 1861, he settled down as a rancher and roadhouse operator at Hat Creek near Fort Kamloops.

Donald McLean did not long enjoy his new vocation. Among his most violent enemies were the local Indians, whom he had always held in profound contempt. Like other company employees, McLean had often been brutal with the Indians whose labour power fueled the company profits. When, in 1849, a Métis employee of the company, Alexis Bélanger, had been killed by an unknown assassin, McLean concluded a Quesnel Indian, Tlhelh, had done the deed and organized a posse to right matters. When the posse arrived at Tlhelh's village, they found it deserted, except for several huts occupied by the fugitive's relatives. McLean did not ask many questions. When informed by Tlhelh's uncle that the suspect was gone, McLean replied, "Well then, for the day you shall be Tlhelh," and shot him dead. The Indian's son-in-law and his baby were similarly disposed of before McLean resumed the hunt for the fugitive.

McLean enlisted as an aid another of Tlhelh's uncles, Netzel, who was threatened with death if he failed to return with the nephew's scalp. Netzel eventually did kill Tlhelh and was so overcome with remorse that he attempted suicide. When Netzel reported the deed to McLean, he lost control of himself and in a fit of grief and anger furiously whipped his white tormentor's face with Tlhelh's scalp.

With this legacy, it is little wonder that McLean enthusiastically volunteered to head a force of men against the Chilcotins led by the chief Klatsassin when they rose in 1864. McLean awoke one morning in his retreat on the Bonaparte River and declared he wanted to kill a couple of Siwash before breakfast. Near Tatla Lake he got his chance. An Indian guide told him that several Chilcotins had been seen on a nearby hill. Accompanied by the guide, McLean went for a look and was shot in the back by a brave named Anukatlh. Had the assassin fired into his victim's chest, McLean would likely have survived – since he usually wore a heavy iron breastplate on Indian-hunting expeditions. It was said that Anukatlh, who was never punished, knew of Captain McLean's frontal armour and carefully ambushed him from the rear.

McLean's death was mourned, not by the Indians, but by many of the white settlers in the Kamloops-Nicola ranching district, including his own numerous progeny. But they soon dried their tears and began quarreling over the division of his estate. McLean was not a wealthy man, but neither was he poor. He had prepared for his retirement from the company and owned a nice piece of acreage in good ranching country, as well as some cattle and horses. But there was hardly enough to go around among the eleven children of both marriages, the two wives and, it appears, the deceased's sister Anna Brown McLean, the wife of a London wine merchant who claimed the whole of the property for herself. The quarrel over the estate dragged through the courts for years. Among the losers was Sophia, Donald McLean's second wife, who received a small Hudson's Bay Company pension, discontinued within five years, and little else.

Sophie's boys grew up strays and waifs. There were settlements everywhere. Donald McLean's estate was settled and they were left impecunious. The Nicola Indians settled onto inferior land reserved for them but not for the half-breeds, which counted the McLeans. The best range land was settled by a new class of whites who found no place for Donald McLean's disinherited younger sons. Nor was there any niche for the boys in the Upper Nicola caste system. Their mother was rejected by the whites, who deprived her of her husband's legacy. The father was despised by the Indians who deprived him of his life. The younger sons and their sister Annie fitted nowhere.

School was no place for the McLean boys. Young Archie, sent off briefly to an Indian boarding school, was the only one among them who could sign his name. Nor did the boys develop any fixed occupations. They worked as cowboys, shepherds and ranch hands, drifting from ranch to ranch in the Kamloops, Cache Creek and Upper Nicola Valley districts. The boys had some skills. They rode well, tended cattle and sheep and built fences, barns and houses. They were excellent hunters who knew how to track animals and finish them with a gun. But they had no capital, or land, or fixed position.

The young McLeans matured in the 1870's when the grasslands bounded by Ashcroft and Spences Bridge in the west and Kamloops and Douglas Lake in the east became the province's major stock-raising centre. For the Indians, the 70's were years of retreat and surrender onto reservations whose boundaries were niggardly drawn. For the whites of the district, who streamed in from the far corners of the continent, it was a decade of progress when ranching developed into a stable and profitable business. For the McLeans and other half-breed drifters these were long years of sulking, scavenging and freebooting.

Having settled into a drifting existence, the McLeans slowly entered into a collision course with the ranchers and townspeople around them. They drank heavily, quarreled with their neighbours and cursed the world in which they had no place. But their first real skirmish with the law did not occur until the spring of 1877 when Charlie picked a fight with a young Indian. Charlie knocked his opponent to the ground, pounced on him, and in a fit of pique, bit off the unfortunate's nose. There is no record of whether he chewed and swallowed it. For this act of violence Charlie McLean was hauled before Hudson's Bay Company Justice of the Peace John Tait and sent to jail for three months.

Charlie did not relish his stay in the Kamloops prison which hosted, as well, a young Italian named Antonio Lamprone. Charlie and Antonio soon hatched a plot, escaped during the night and took off around the countryside. Antonio disappeared, but Charlie was joined by his brother and by his old school chum, Alex Hare.

The boys roamed freely and committed numerous robberies from Ashcroft to Douglas Lake. They grabbed whatever they needed wherever they could find it. From G. Wilson, a teamster, they took provisions and a saddle. Four race horses and several saddles were removed from Johnny Wilson's large Savona ranch. A horse and a saddle disappeared from the Kamloops Indian reserve. A shepherd named Kelly was robbed of brandy and freshly-baked bread. J. Uren's storeroom at Savona's Ferry was broken into and a large body of provisions removed. The ranch of a man named Thadeus Harper, nine miles from Kamloops, was raided and a supply of blankets and armaments taken. James Cavanagh of Cache Creek lost several items of clothing while George Caughill and Tom Cavanagh were dispossessed of saddles. A Chinese merchant was stopped between Copper Creek and Savona, robbed of his money and severely beaten.

The McLeans did not discriminate. They took from everybody: from the rich and poor alike, from white, Indian and Chinese. But they bore special grudges against several pillars of the local community whom they threatened to kill on sight. One of their favourite enemies was the Hudson's Bay Company J. P. John Tait who, after jailing Charlie, trembled for his life. Another was John Andrew Mara, a wealthy Kamloops merchant, with interests in steamboats, saw mills and land. Mara sat as a member of the Legislature, and served as a justice of the peace. He had seduced Annie McLean, the boys' younger sister – loved by Alex Hare – and she, it was rumoured, bore Mara a child. The boys resented this and swore vengeance – against Mara personally and the entire town of Kamloops, jointly controlled by Mara and the Hudson's Bay Company. They threatened, in fact, to burn Kamloops to the ground.

The McLeans' threats and depredations continued throughout the year 1879 and peaked in the month of November when settlers from Kamloops and the Upper Nicola district retired indoors early and anxiously trained their guns out the window. "This is a fine state of things," a *Daily Colonist* correspondent wrote, "to be terrorized over by four brats, who have threatened to burn the jail in order to destroy the records of their deeds. If these vagabonds are not either arrested or driven to American territory, it may become pretty hot for us. This is a nice state of things for us, and a nice Government to allow it. At present nothing is being done and everybody scarcely likes to leave his house for fear of being robbed."

The problem, it appeared, rested not merely with the McLeans. It lay as well with a weak provincial government driven into a policy of retrenchment by the mid-seventies recession. Among the casualties were the county and mining districts of Cassiar, Yale and Lillooet whose police forces were either removed or pared down under a system of "cheap government."

The new system in Yale resulted in a raft of dead warrants against the McLeans. The warrants were issued by a variety of J.P.'s: by John Edwards and John Tait in Kamloops, Charles Semlin in Cache Creek and by Senator Clement Cornwall. Some were dated 1878 and others 1879. They listed a variety of charges, from assault to robbery. But they had one characteristic in common: they were never served. The problem was that the Yale district had only one regular constable, a frail thin man named Johnny Ussher. Son of a Montreal Episcopalian minister, Ussher joined the Caribou goldrush before settling into a ranching vocation on the North Thompson River. Ussher was a policeman only part of the time. Besides ranching and running a sawmill in partnership with J. A. Mara, Ussher exercised a number of official functions. He was government agent, tax-collector, jailer, assessor, mining reporter, clerk of the county court and registrar of the supreme court.

Being the only regular policeman around, Ussher was overworked and neglected his duties. Instead of chasing outlaws he tended to other businesses, including his own. When he did pursue, it was without ardour, stamina or adequate reinforcements. Ussher sometimes hired special constables like John Kennedy and Caughlin. But he thought twice about doing so, since the government habitually returned their expense vouchers unpaid. On several occasions, Ussher, together with some local ranchers and merchants, had to pay his deputies' expenses out of their own pockets.

When the McLeans were apprehended, they had little trouble breaking out of the Kamloops jail, a one-room affair whose door could be opened with the curled end of a rusty nail. Charlie easily escaped after the nose incident, just as his brothers quietly removed themselves following arrest on a robbery charge. The instrument of freedom, in this instance, was a rope dropped over a wall into the adjoining yard by Alex Hare. When Ussher requested $100 from the government to make the prison safer, following the presentation of a grand jury, he was refused.

Premier Walkem's "cheap government" and anaemic constabulary had a livening effect on the brash McLeans. It encouraged their anarchy and fueled their juvenile delusions which assumed heights of grandeur during the early days of December, 1879. After a month of uninterrupted depredations, the boys began to entertain the notion that they were immune from arrest, an attitude which William Palmer discovered when he found them in possession of his favourite black stallion at Long Lake.

Palmer's flight to Kamloops did have some effect. After hearing his complaints, Justice John Edwards issued a brand new warrant for their arrest, which was handed to Johnny Ussher for execution. Ussher was not lax on this occasion. The gang's roving had lately inspired official concern and a renewed effort was contemplated to effect their capture. The Hudson's Bay Company offered $250 as an inducement. The provincial government, following a spate of local complaints, raised the ante by $500. Johnny Ussher did not leave on his saving mission alone. He took with him the aggrieved Mr. Palmer, who knew the outlaws' likely location, and an emigré Mormon named Amni Shumway, who had freighted and ranched in the Upper Nicola region for three years. The trio first jailed Hector McLean, an older step-brother of the boys and, in the early afternoon of December 6, set out on the gang's trail near Anderson Creek, south of Kamloops. They stopped along the way at a ranch operated by an ex-Glasgow man named John McLeod, who had lost a horse to the gang, and recruited him to the mission. The posse slept overnight at a government camp used by a Canadian Pacific Railway survey party, where several government horses had been reported missing. The tracking resumed early next morning along the Brigade Trail, used in past days by Hudson's Bay Company porters to haul furs to and from the Upper Nicola Valley.

The trackers had been gone several hours when they came upon four saddled horses on a high ridge sixteen miles from Kamloops. Nearby in a clearing Archie McLean stood, rifle in hand, by a fire. His brothers were with him. When his men momentarily balked, Ussher took the lead and urged them forward with an assurance that the fugitives would "never fire a shot." Charlie proved him wrong. When the Ussher party approached within several feet of the fire, Charlie whistled and fired a ball which singed Palmer's beard and tore through McLeod's cheek. McLeod fell bleeding from his horse while Palmer exchanged fire with Charlie, Archie and Allan who hid behind several trees. McLeod was hit again, in the knee, and his horse wounded three times.

Ussher did not fire. Instead he calmed his frightened horse, urged the McLeans to surrender themselves and dismounted. As Ussher moved towards the McLeans, Alex Hare suddenly rushed out of cover with a Bowie knife in one hand and a pistol in the other. When Ussher reached for Hare's shoulder, Hare grabbed him and they wrestled momentarily. Hare began stabbing Ussher who fell to the ground. Hare jumped on him, held him down with his knees and left hand, and drove the knife continuously into his neck and face. When Ussher screamed "Boys, don't kill me," a voice from the bushes replied, "Kill the . . ." It was Allan, whose brother Archie ran out from behind a tree, held a pistol within eighteen inches of Ussher's head and fired. Palmer saw the gun flash and Ussher's feet kick. He knew he was dead.

The wild firing continued briefly until Palmer, Shumway and McLeod, who had succeeded in wounding Charlie, retreated to Kamloops where they announced the death of the local constable. A posse headed by J. A. Mara and John Edwards was rounded up and raced to the scene. The fire was still warm but the McLean boys and Alex Hare had disappeared. Ussher was still there, unmoved. His left cheek was badly gashed and there was a hole through the centre of his forehead. His face was covered with caked and frozen blood. His light brown overcoat and fine leather boots were gone. The body was frozen stiff.

The McLeans had graduated. During years of quarreling and robbing, they had never killed a man. They were, in the words of Cache Creek rancher Charles Semlin, "reckless, lawless" and "a hard lot," but they had stopped at robbery and assault. Now that the threshold had been crossed the boys ran for their lives towards the Indian reservation at Douglas Lake. But they stopped along the way to spread terror, boast of their deeds, search for their enemies, gather supplies and collect weapons – for their own use and for the Indians whom they hoped would join their cause.

Near a swamp the boys met shepherd James Kelly who was not a McLean favourite. They had previously taken his bread and brandy and Allan had quarreled with him recently in the mountains. Their meeting by a wagon road was brief. Archie was in the lead when they approached. When Hare spotted Kelly, he levelled his gun saying, "Don't say we passed you." Kelly replied, "What have I to do with you?" Hare then shot him in the chest and Charlie added a bullet in the stomach. Hare then jumped off his horse which Archie held and collected the shepherd's pistol and Waltham watch and chain. Kelly's body was dragged off the road where it was later discovered, face up, by a posse. The shepherd's two collie dogs stood guard over the body, licking the wounds. His chest and face were clammy with spittle.

The boys repaired to Kelly's cabin, relieved it of flour, salt and other provisions, and rode to the home of Thomas Trapp, a rancher who lived seven miles from the scene of Ussher's murder. Trapp heard the knock at one o'clock in the afternoon and was presented with a request for his rifle and pistol. When he refused, Charlie and Archie drew their guns and threatened to shoot him. Trapp changed his mind and the boys collected the weapons. They spoke excitedly of their achievements. When Allan flashed a pair of shackles, Hare told Trapp there was blood on them – "Ussher's blood, we have killed him." Charlie waved his knife and said he would kill anyone who came to arrest him. Archie said, "Do you think that they will ever get the drop on me? Not much." The boys collected other articles including cartridges and warned Trapp to tell no one of their visit. As they prepared to leave, the boys became generous. Hare offered Trapp a fifty cent piece, part of Ussher's pocket money. When Trapp refused, Hare insisted he take it. Trapp did and laid the money on the table where it was collected and repocketed by Hare. Upon leaving, the boys promised to return Trapp's weapons when they had finished with them. And they assured him they had no intention of killing him.

From Thomas Trapp's the McLean gang galloped to John Roberts' ranch at Stump Lake. Mr. Roberts was killing pigs when they arrived and had a large fire going. The boys dropped their guns from their shoulders and levelled them as they rode up. "Good evening," said Mr. Roberts, "It's a cold afternoon." Charlie replied that it was cold, "But there's a good many colder nights," to which Archie added, "And a darn sight hotter times." Hare, Archie and Allan dismounted, approached the fire, fondled their guns and inquired about several enemies, whom they threatened to kill. They were particularly interested in the location of an Indian named Canda known for his bravery in fighting three bears. "This will be the last night he will have to face three bears," Archie said, "He'll have to face four boys; I'm only fifteen, but you bet your life I'm brave." The conversation then turned to Johnny Ussher. When Allan boasted of his killing, Roberts was incredulous. "Upon my soul we killed him," Hare said, "Here's the knife that went through him, and here's the blood on it." Hare waved the weapon and pointed to the blood on his grey coat and on his face. Archie raised a foot and said, "Here's Ussher's boots." Hare added, "Here's his coat and gloves," and Allan remarked, "There's his horse, saddle and canteen."

Having made their point, the boys spoke briefly about having killed a sheepman, then returned to Mr. Ussher. "Here's the handcuffs Ussher brought out to put on me," Allan announced, "but he didn't get them on. I'll keep them for Palmer." Charlie added, "Yes, and we'll give him fifty lashes every day and fifty every night before he goes to bed; we'll keep them to torment him." This broke the boys up and they laughed heartily. But they quickly fell serious, inquired about Palmer and several others, and departed with an assurance they had no intention of hurting Mr. Roberts since he had a large family.

William Palmer was another matter. When they arrived at his house, the boys looked mean and ready. Palmer, fortunately, was not around. But his wife Jane was. "I recalled the 8th of December last," she recounted, "(They) came to our house; they had guns with them; I invited them in to warm themselves and asked the little fellow, Archie, to warm his feet by the stove. Allan said, 'This is a good gun, I want to take it.' It was my husband's gun. Allan continued, 'If you had not been good to me, I would have shot your husband today; your husband is bringing a crowd from Kamloops against us; I shot young McLeod but did not kill him; we shot a sheepman today coming here.' He said it was Kelly; Archie said, 'He (Kelly) would not growl anymore for a piece of bread.' Kennedy was after them; this was the last night he had to live; they would kill him at first sight . . ."

The boys spared Mrs. Palmer after availing themselves of some of her brandy and collecting a supply of guns, caps and spurs. They departed in mid-evening towards Nicola. Near the front gate, in the snow, they left behind John Kelly's silver watch.

The McLeans did not need the watch. What they wanted were more guns and ammunition which they gathered at intervals along the route to the Indian reservation. Several of their hosts along the way offered free advice. They suggested the boys ride south through the Okanagan country to Osoyoos and across the border into the United States. But the McLeans had no illusions about a warm greeting there. They had already visited the border country where they stole cattle and antagonized the Indians. They did, however, have other hopes, centered on their tenuous blood ties and imagined affinity with the Nicola Indians. Allan had recently married Chief Chillitnetza's daughter and he was intent on rousing the Chief and his men to their cause. Like the Indians who brooded over land rights on their scant reserves, the McLeans had been snubbed and abandoned by the white men. They shared a common misery and oppression. What the Indians lacked were weapons and will. The McLeans brought both. When Allan and his brothers entered the Chief's log house, loaded with guns and ammunition, they offered him a chance to rise and drive the white man away towards the western sea.

Chief Chillitnetza listened, but was not impressed. He was, after all, a sensible man, who knew the McLeans were a wild bunch. They spoke his language and flaunted their mother's heritage. But the chief remembered their father, a heartless man, who lost his life fighting Indians. The Nicola Chief was a practical man, a prudent Canadian who recognized a lost and futile cause when it presented itself. The Chief had no wish to be a hero or a martyr. Those days had long passed. He wished merely to survive.

The Chief realized this could best be assured if the fugitives removed themselves from his presence and village. The boys stayed the night but departed the next morning, with neither aid nor promises, for a sanctuary on the reserve's edge near a creek running into Douglas Lake. Charlie's wound, it appeared, had badly weakened him. He needed a rest. The small log cabin, surrounded by bushes, with an adjoining corral and stable, seemed a sensible place to rest up, nurse their wounds, store their supplies and brood over their rejection by the ungrateful Indians.

The gang's removal to the cabin was common knowledge among the local residents, one of whom embarked upon a profitable enterprise. He decided to disclose the boys' location, for a fee. The Indian contacted George Caughill, a special constable tracking the outlaws near the reserve, and suggested a deal. Caughill agreed. For a promise of $100, the special constable learned of the outlaws' hideout and conveyed the intelligence by messenger to Nicola J. P. John Clapperton who, in turn, sent notice of the discovery to Kamloops. Clapperton, in the meanwhile, gathered a group of settlers and marched to Douglas Lake twenty-four miles away. When he arrived, Caughill and several assistants were already there, nervously spying on the cabin where the outlaws lay. The posse quietly surrounded the lair and set up a makeshift headquarters at an old cabin a few hundred yards away. The siege had begun.

Word of the cornering spread wildly across the province and invited a wave of excitement and mustering all the way from Spences Bridge to Victoria. In Kamloops, John Edwards collected a force of armed men including a contingent of Kamloops Indians and raced south along the Brigade Trail. Tiny groups of ranchers and cowboys from the Nicola district rode to the scene. Supplies of blankets, provisions and food arrived from nearby ranches and villages. Chief Chillitnetza, seeing the writing on the wall, prudently joined the siege and volunteered himself and twenty of his men. Volunteers from Spences Bridge, Ashcroft, Clinton and Cache Creek began a march to Kamloops via Savona Ferry, under the generalship of Senator Clement C. Cornwall.

The message even reached Victoria where the Walkem government sadly contemplated the likely loss of $1000 offered as a reward for the capture of the murderers of Johnny Ussher. Word of the siege and warning of an Indian rising were telegraphed from Cache Creek to New Westminster, where Superintendent of Provincial Police Todd urged the Cache Creek posses to do their best; then he boarded a ship for Victoria where he consulted with the Premier and his colleagues. Todd then took a ferry to Port Angeles, in the state of Washington, sent a warning message to American border guards around the Okanagan and returned to Victoria. Roman Catholic Bishop D'Herbonna was warned of potential Indian troubles and invited to remind his priests in the Williams Lake - Kamloops regions to do their duty in persuading local chiefs to keep their people out of the fight, except in aid of the government. Having enrolled the church, Todd gathered a posse and supplies on the steamer *Maude* which slowly lumbered towards New Westminster. The boat carried 8400 rounds of ammunition, eighty Snider rifles, several dozen small revolvers, and a party of "lusty and fearless fellows" including Officer Richard Quain, a veteran of the Maori war, where he had won some distinction, and Henry Roycroft, a member of the Wolseley Red River Expedition and the French army during the Franco-Mexican War. At New Westminster, Government Agent J. C. Hughes collected a batch of Henry and Snider rifles and several thousand rounds of ammunition in preparation for the sailing of two other ships, *The Gem* and *Royal City* to Yale, where stage-coaches were readied to carry the ships' cargoes to Kamloops.

While the government mustered and blustered and prepared loads for the boats and listened to advice from the Island press which suggested the employment of Hale's war-rocket batteries used "in Abyssinia and Zululand with great success," the Edwards-Clapperton posses of local settlers held the outlaws at bay. The boys in the cabin were not starved for provisions. They had boxes of canned food, salt, flour, and a supply of weapons and ammunition including single and double-barreled shotguns, revolvers, repeating rifles, pistols, and enough bullets and powder for a week-long stand. The cabin was made of logs thick and close enough to withstand heavy shooting. It had chinks and holes to serve as outlets for their own guns. And nearby, in the stable, were five ready horses including Ussher's and Palmer's prize stallions.

The siege settled into a protracted affair. The posse surrounded the cabin on all sides and mounted a round-the-clock vigil. After two days, seventy-five armed men stood guard. Sporadic gunfire alternated with intervals of negotiation. Clapperton and Edwards sent the outlaws notes, urging surrender and offering safe custody. These were carried by Indian and Métis messengers, including Allan McLean's brother-in-law, who rode up to the cabin unarmed and alone waving white handkerchiefs. The messengers spoke with the outlaws and slipped notes from the posse heads through the front door. The outlaws returned the signals with waves of a white shirt and sent replies in the cramped hand of Alex Hare. When Clapperton threatened to burn the house down, Hare replied, "We will not surrender; burn away." Hare later wrote, "You can burn the house a thousand times over," and appended a query to Clapperton: "I wish to know what you all have against me. If you have anything, please let me know what it is."

The desultory notes and sporadic shooting continued for several days during which the outlaws made several proposals, including a request for horses and a five hundred yard headstart to Kamloops. But Clapperton and Edwards were prepared to starve them out. By the third day, the boys grew so desperate they threw open the doors and ran for the horses. A fusillade of fire from all sides drove them back and resulted in the loss of three of their horses. In their return fire, the boys made some hits of their own. Two Indians were wounded and an old enemy named Johnson Stevenson, who ranched at Douglas Lake, was felled as he chased a stray horse.

By Friday, December 13, the war of nerves had reached a breaking point. The men tried burning the place. They loaded a wagon with hay, doused it with coal oil and slowly pushed it towards the cabin. But the hay was wet and sent up smudge and smoke. A further assault was contemplated behind a portable battery of timber. It was not necessary. After five days in the cabin's gloom, wallowing in urine and excrement, short of ammunition and suffering from a fierce thirst which swelled their tongues, the boys knew the end was near. They waved a flag and offered to surrender in return for a promise to be removed on horseback, without shackles. Edwards agreed and sent ahead a special constable to search them as they came out. They emerged one at a time. Hare came first and Charlie second. The other boys followed. They threw down their weapons as they walked forward. The circle of men slowly converged on them and closed fiercely. No chances were taken. The boys kicked, punched and swore as the settlers wrestled them to the ground. While the government steamboats bulging with recruits and arsenals were readied in New Westminster – to fight an Indian war if need be – the McLean boys and Alex Hare were dragged to William Palmer's ranch, shackled in iron and removed to the town of Kamloops.

There were no tears in Mara's town, except at the funerals of Johnny Ussher and James Kelly, held on Sunday, January 15. At a preliminary hearing held in the Kamloops courthouse, Messrs.

Cornwall, Tait, Edwards and Mara heard several witnesses and committed the boys – including their older brother Hector, who was charged with aiding and abetting – to trial in New Westminster. They had a rough trip down. Shackled and poorly clothed, they nearly froze in below zero weather on the way to Cache Creek where J. P. Charles Semlin warned the attending constables of their sickly state and supplied the prisoners with warm clothing and blankets. The prisoners were then removed, face down in a stagecoach, to Yale where Provincial Secretary T. B. Humphrey arranged for a further conveyance in several canoes down the Fraser River.

The trip covered thirty miles until ice conditions became so bad that the entire party, constables and prisoners, were almost lost. At a place called Cheam a wagon was procured and the frozen and manacled prisoners were placed face down again on the floor. It took four days to reach Chilliwack and another three to get to New Westminster where, at three o'clock in the afternoon of Christmas Day, the wild McLeans and Alex Hare hobbled dejectedly across the river's ice. The telegraph had buzzed all week and a sizeable crowd – white, Indian and Chinese – awaited their arrival. Idle jokes and snickers passed as the boys boarded a stage sleigh which carried them up a gently rising ascent to the jail.

The provincial penitentiary was not a model prison. It consisted of two cell blocks divided by a narrow courtyard and bounded by a wooden fence, decorated at the top with broken bottles and sharpened spikes. The boys were committed to alternate cells on the same side of a single block. Their cells were modest places, about nine feet high, and nine by seven square, ventilated by a small barred window near the top of each cell. The walls were white-washed and the skirting boards covered with coal tar. Besides a small cot there was nothing for the prisoners to rest on.

The boys abhorred their stay and, from the day of entry, harrassed jailer Moresby and assistants who sometimes chained them to the walls of their cells. They spat and cursed, threw dishes at the walls, refused food and engaged in bouts of whistling, shouting and dancing to relieve their solitude. Though separated by intervening cells and bounded by walls nine inches thick, they regularly conversed with one another in Chinook jargon, to the consternation of the guards. Knives were hidden under mattresses and blades fashioned from tin cups. Little escape plots were hatched and exposed. Sometimes the boys threw metal pails at their guards, or they simply refused to move when asked to. "Allan, return to your cell," Mr. Morseby once said, waving a revolver. "I won't," was the reply, "Shoot! you son-of-a-gun, shoot! I'm not afraid of an ounce of lead." Allan did soon return to his cell where a search yielded a knife, hidden in a blanket.

Mr. Moresby and his prisoners had a hard time and dearly wished for speedy proceedings. Nothing, however, moved quickly or easily with the Walkem government, which spent several months gathering witnesses and quarreling with lawyers and judges over the trial's time and venue. It was not until mid-March that the trial began in New Westminster. Appearing for the Crown was Mr. J. F. McCreight, a former premier and senior Victoria lawyer, aided by the assistant Attorney-General Eli Harrison Jr. Alex Hare was defended by Theodore Davie, a young bearded native of Surrey, four years a member of the provincial bar and later a premier and chief justice of the province. The McLeans were represented by an emigré Irishman W. N. Bole, who had practiced in Quebec before moving, two years earlier, to British Columbia where he settled into a practice on the mainland. The case was heard by Mr. Justice Henry Pelling Crease and had a peculiar finale.

Justice Crease thought the trial vitally important and presented the jurors, in his opening statement, with a learned disquisition on the sociology of half-breeds and the dangers to civil society posed by weak government and the absence of parental authority. "Quick shots, unrivaled horsemen, hardy boatmen and hunters," the judge expounded, "they knew no other life than that of the forest. They learned next to nothing of agriculture. They never went to school or had the semblance of an education and when the wave of civilization, without hurry, without delay, but without rest, approached, it met a restless roving half-breed population, who, far from initiating, did not even understand the restless agency which was approaching them. So long as the white father lived, the children were held in some sort of subjection, but the moment he was gone, they gravitated towards their mother's friends and fell back into nature's ways. Is it any wonder then, that, remaining unchecked and uncared-for they should at last adopt the predatory Arab life which in a scattered territory is fraught with such danger to the state."

The Crown attorneys evinced little sympathy for Justice Crease's errant nomads. A parade of witnesses including Palmer, Shumway, Edwards and McLeod were trotted out to testify to the McLeans' brutality, chronic depredations, cruel killing of Ussher and determined resistance to arrest. To Mr. McCreight, their violence was contemplated, boundless, dangerous and systematic. "Every act of the prisoners," he remarked in his closing address, "showed that they had entered on a systematic opposition to authority."

The defenders put up a stout fight. They chose not to put their clients on the stand or summon any witnesses. Objections were made, in opening parries, to the venue of the trial. Arguments were advanced that the Crown's evidence relating to Kelly's killing was weak and circumstantial, that there was no clear proof Archie McLean or Hare had killed Ussher, that no murder was contemplated, that the Ussher posse started the quarrel and frightened the boys into an insane excitement. The defense pleaded mercy in light of the younger McLean's tender age and the government's lax enforcement of the law preceding the Ussher murder, a matter raised by Justice Crease in his opening statement when he said, "We must go below the surface and see if other causes do not combine to produce the ill results. Ask yourselves is it a magistrate the less or a constable the less at Kamloops that has caused or could have prevented these murders? Look deeper." The jury peered, and saw only the dark stain of the McLean-Hare gang's guilt. It took them only twenty minutes to decide. When the boys appeared the next day for sentencing, they made rambling and garbled statements before Justice Crease pronounced his sentence of death on each of them separately. Of the four, only Hare was moved to comment, "Thanks, a well-deserved sentence." But his contrition was withdrawn when, upon leaving the courtroom, he spied William Palmer nearby. Hare screamed violently at Palmer, and struck a blow before he and his excited colleagues were subdued by the police, one of whom was punched on the head by Archie.

It was the boys' last scuffle. The prisoners were returned to Moresby's charge and the Superintendent readied his men for a group hanging. But the ordeal was not yet over. Just as the government had earlier invited the McLeans' outlawry, so now it prolonged their misery in captivity. In the weeks following the trial's conclusion, the defence lawyers argued that the Westminster Special Assize Court, which heard their case, had been irregularly convened. The government had established the court by proclamation, but without a commission issued to any judge or person authorizing them to hold the court. The matter was fought before a panel of Supreme Court judges who, in late June, concluded in their wisdom that the defendants' contention was correct: that the Special Assize had been irregularly convened, that a Queen's Commission was required to set it in motion and that no such commission had been issued. Since no legal court had been convened, no legal trial had taken place. It would have to be done all over again.

And it was. In mid-November 1880, the McLean boys and Alex Hare were brought into court for a new trial, which lasted a full six days. The evidence, the arguments, the witnesses, the legal pyrotechnics were the same as in the earlier trial. The jury's verdict and the judge's sentence were also identical. The only variation was in the boys' attitude. They made no statements, rambling or otherwise, before or after the judge sentenced them to hang, and they listened to the concluding statements with "an air of indifference, bordering on stoicism." Nor did they bother cursing or punching anybody before they left the courtroom.

What remained, in the matter of the dispute between Regina and the McLeans and Alex Hare was the gibbeting, scheduled for the morning of Monday, January 31, 1881. The boys' final weeks were quiet and they spent many hours with Father Harris, the ministering priest "unremitting in his efforts to bring them to a proper state of mind as well as a proper sense of their position." They were told of the date of execution in the office of the jailer who on Thursday, January 20 interviewed them separately and offered to convey messages to family and friends. Charlie and Hare declined the offer. Allan, however, asked the sheriff to "write to Hector and tell him not to take any revenge on Palmer or anyone else for our death. It can't be helped now." On returning to his cell, he sent a message to his wife in the Upper Country imploring her to take good care of the children. Archie was bitter on the matter of messages: "No, I have nothing to say or send to any friends. They have done nothing for me and I wouldn't care if all my friends got hung."

Apprised of the final day, the boys sank into a gloomy silence. But on the day before the execution, they cheered momentarily and asked to see the scaffold. Allan, being the oldest, was given the first tour. He stood beneath the traps, inspected the work, said a prayer and praised the carpentry. "Mr. Moresby, that's a fair piece of work and well put together." After returning Allan to his cell, Moresby summoned Hare and Archie who also ducked under the scaffold and inspected the construction. Under the trap door canopy, the boys shook hands and Hare remarked to Archie, "Under here we'll meet again and bid a last good-bye to each other."

Charlie had no interest in the scaffold and stayed in his cell until five-thirty the following morning when Mr. Moresby arrived with a blacksmith who removed the prisoners' irons. The blacksmith was followed by the priest who led them in brief devotions before a light breakfast consisting of hot buttered toast and coffee. Devotions were resumed after breakfast until eight o'clock when the prisoners were moved to the yard where there had gathered an assortment of notables including city councillors, members of the press and the scaffold contractors Messrs. Fry and Colbeck. The executioner, a clumsy fellow named O'Brien, who earned $200 for the multiple hanging, pinioned their hands in front with stout leather straps. There followed a procession which included the executioner, the sheriff, the prison surgeon, the chief of police, the warden of the jail, Father Harris and a pair of assistants. The boys mounted the scaffold in the company of the priest and made brief statements offering and begging forgiveness. Allan apologized to Mr. Moresby for causing him so much trouble and joined Hare in shaking the hand of the hangman.

The ropes were then adjusted and Mr. O'Brien, on instructions from Sheriff Morrison, did his duty. An attending priest, Father Cheruse, cried out "Courage, mes enfants, courage!" as the McLean boys and Alex Hare dropped the appointed nine feet through the trap door below. They expired without a murmur. Everything went off well, the *Colonist* observed, not a hitch occurred.

Notes

The sole full-length treatment of the McLeans is Mel Rothenburger's *We've Killed Johnny Ussher,* Mitchell Press, Vancouver, 1973. F. W. Lindsay includes a short account of "The Wild McLeans" in his *Outlaws in British Columbia,* Regatta City Press Ltd., Kelowna, 1963. Background material on Donald McLean can be found in E. S. Hewlett, *The Chilcotin Uprising,* M. A. Thesis, Department of History, U.B.C., 1972; A. G. Morice, *The History of the Northern Interior of British Columbia,* Ye Galleon Press, Fairfield, Washington, 1971; and R. C. Lundin Brown, *Klatsassin and Other Reminiscences of Missionary Life in British Columbia,* Society for Promoting Christian Knowledge, 1973. A stream of articles on the McLean boys have appeared over the years, mainly in British Columbia. Several worth mentioning are: Cecil Clark, "The Fighting McLeans," *The Shoulder Strap,* Summer Edition, 1939; Louis Lebourdais, "Death at Murderer's Bow," *Vancouver Province,* May 28, 1933; and Walter Deccar, "The Last Stand of the McLeans," *Vancouver Sun,* November 16, 1933. *The Mainland Guardian* and *Daily Colonist,* 1879-80, are filled with accounts of the boys' outlawry, capture and trials.

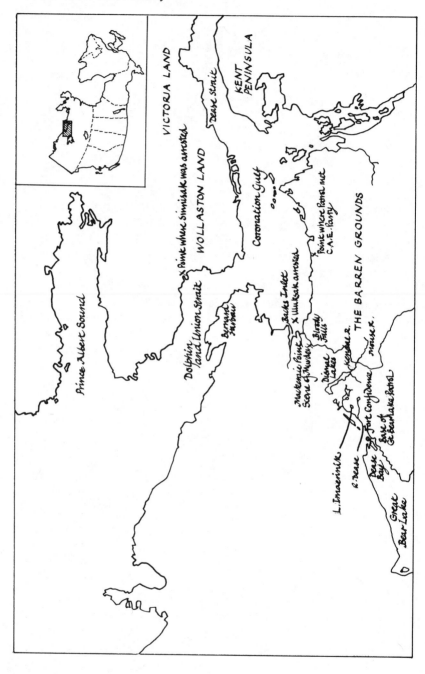

Igloo Badmen

In early July, 1911, there arrived at a small village in Canada's Northwest Territories a bearded missionary charged with the task of spreading Christ's message among the tundra heathen. The priest's name was Jean-Baptiste Rouvière and he was suited by inclination and training to endure the hardships facing the small brigade of white men who, in the century's early years, wandered into the frigid wastes of Canada's polar lands. Rouvière was a confirmed zealot who had enlisted himself in Christ's army and joined the Order of Oblates of Mary the Immaculate, soon after graduating from the University of Liège. A product of the town of Monde, in the southern French department of Lozère, the bearded Rouvière was a strong, resolute and practical man. He emigrated to Canada and briefly taught in Ottawa before dedicating himself to doing good work in the barren lands at the farthest northern edge of the Canadian Dominion.

Fort Norman, in the hour of Rouvière's arrival, was not much to look at. Sitting at the junction of the Bear and Mackenzie Rivers, over a thousand miles west and north of the city of Edmonton, it counted a few small and rough log buildings, the scattered shacks and tents of Indians, and little else. The village served as a way-station for the steamers of the Hudson's Bay Company and Northern Trading Company which plied the MacKenzie north and south of its meeting with the Bear River, and for the prospectors, traders and explorers who moved east in York boats and canoes to trade along the Bear River across Bear Lake, towards the edge of the Arctic Ocean at Coronation Gulf. The Hudson's Bay Company kept a log house at Fort Norman which they called a store. So did the Northern Trading Company who did a brisk business in furs and other goods with the neighbouring Indians. Two churches shared the competition for the red men's souls: the Anglicans, who worked with uncertain success out of a tiny shack church, and the Catholics, whose zeal to succeed had forced, by 1911, the closure of the rival mission.

The Roman church's foremost soldiers at Fort Norman, as elsewhere in the Territories, were the Oblates, and Father Rouvière's burden was shared by two colleagues of the Order of Mary the Immaculate. The first carried the unlikely name of Frapsance. The second was Reverend Father Ducot, the sixty-three-year-old founder of Fort Norman's Mission of Ste-Thérèse and the local superior, accountable to Father Gabriel Breynat of Great Slave Lake, Bishop of Adrumetum and Vicar Apostolic of Mackenzie and Yukon.

Bishop Breynat's northern empire counted a huge acreage, mostly tundra and muskeg, and a few people, mostly destitute Indians. In Father Rouvière's district around Fort Good Hope, where he was stationed since 1907, the objects of Oblate efforts were the Hare and Dog-rib Indians of the Athabascan family who hunted, fished and traded with the white men and Eskimos along the upper Mackenzie and east towards the Barren Lands. The father proved himself a zealous worker, selflessly dedicating himself to rescuing the Dog-ribs' souls. No armchair priest,

Rouvière pursued his subjects in the field. He learned rudiments of the Indian language, taught the heathen to make the sign of the cross, baptized their children, instructed them in the catechism, administered the sacraments and explained that Christ had died for them. The good father spoke reverently of a better world beyond and above, in the skies, and by inducements, tangible and otherwise, coaxed occasional stray Hares and Ribs into his mission where they sang, prayed and crossed themselves, and generally gave outer evidence of an inner commitment to Christ.

Having rescued any number of Dog-ribs from centuries of barbarism, Father Rouvière and his superiors began, in the year 1911, to cast urgent glances north and east of the Dog-rib domain in the direction of the shores of the Arctic Ocean where there wandered a strange and exotic people virtually unknown and untouched by either the church's or polite society's dominion. The father's superiors first heard of these polar wanderers from the local Indians and traders who moved inland east of Fort Norman during the summer months, and they soon harboured a fear that the Anglicans, already sniffing at the edge of the Arctic Ocean, might enroll these Stone age relics into the heretic church. To forestall this sad possibility, the bishop summoned Father Rouvière to Fort Norman, which he reached after a hundred-mile voyage upstream on the mission boat *Sainte-Marie*. Here Rouvière consulted with Fathers Ducot and Frapsance and laid plans for a saving mission into the dark forlorn lands stretching northeast to Coronation Gulf, on the shores of the Arctic. "No one knows how many they are, or what they are like," Bishop Breynat wrote, "but we should like to send a few specimens to paradise."

The object of the bishop's zeal was a group of Stone age hunters designated by the explorer Vilhjalmur Stefansson as the Copper Eskimos, on account of their use of that metal, found in abundance west of the Coppermine River, in their cooking and hunting implements. Concentrated around Coronation Gulf and the Dolphin and Union Straits, and spread as far as Kent Peninsula in the east, Cape Bexley in the west and Victoria Island in the north, the Copper Eskimos enjoyed, with only brief interruptions, a remarkable and splendid isolation.

By the century's turn, however, a score of traders, explorers and adventurers set their sights on the Coppermine, and what began as a trickle threatened, by the end of the decade, an invasion.[1] David T. Hanbury, a gentleman explorer, came first in 1902 and wrote a lively book about his travels. A Danish trader named Klengenberg followed in a small schooner which patrolled southwest of Victoria Island. Klengenberg was succeeded by an American whaler named William Mogg and by Captain Joseph B. Bernard whose schooner, the *Teddy Bear,* cruised for three years in the vicinity of the mouth of the Coppermine, Bernard Harbor and Victoria Island. Two British adventurers named John Hornby and Cosmo Melvill lived and traded inland around Great Bear Lake and were joined by a pair of Canadian brothers, George M. and Lionel D. Douglas, and a geologist, Dr. August Sandberg, drawn by the copper deposits north of the Dismal Lakes and by rumours of gold. The most notable guest, however, was the young scholar and explorer, Vilhjalmur Stefansson, who in 1910-11 sketched the social contours of the Coppermine and drew a remarkable portrait of a "lost tribe" of Eskimos on the brink of cultural invasion.

What the traders exploited, Stefansson observed, and Reverend Father Rouvière determined to save from the twin clutches of Anglicanism and barbarism, was a hardy and industrious ancient people numbering less than a thousand souls who had

1 There have been, to be sure, brief encounters with white emissaries going back as early as 1771 when Samuel Hearne reached the mouth of the Coppermine overland from Hudson's Bay in the company of a band of Chippewayan Indians. It was a bloody first meeting. At a peaceful encampment on the river's west bank near a waterfall later designated Bloody Falls, the Indians fell upon and massacred to the last child a party of Eskimos. Hearne soon withdrew, but a score of other explorers followed his trail including Captain John Franklin who, in 1821, approached the Coppermine overland from Lake Athabasca and the Great Slave lake and met a group of people known as the "Deerhorn" Esquimaux near the very spot where the Hearne massacre took place. Franklin returned for a second look several years later and was succeeded by Back who observed a group of Deer-Horns during his descent in 1833. Back was followed by Dease and Simpson in 1838, Richardson and Rae ten years later and finally, in 1851-52 by McClure and Collinson who observed several hundred of the Deer-Horns in their fishing and hunting grounds during the summer months.

nicely adapted to the rigours of polar life. The Copper Eskimos were a brave race of diligent hunters who fished and sealed on the ice in and around Coronation Gulf during the winter months before moving inland in spring to meet and hunt the caribou. In winter, they built snow houses and skin tents on the ice, huddled in villages, fished for seals through ice-holes and, in early spring, made caches of seal blubber which they stored with other implements on high rocks, until their return to the coast in the autumn. The sealskins served as clothing, and the seal fat as food, cooking-oil and fuel for fires which were made by rubbing together several pieces of iron pyrite and catching the spark on some prepared oil. The Eskimos killed the seals with spears and hunted the deer and caribou with bows and arrows. Copper, present in a natural state west of the Coppermine River, was used to fashion arrowheads, knives, ice picks, and as a supplementary material for cooking utensils, which were usually made of soapstone. Some iron, steel and brass, collected from early European shipwrecks, found their way into the villages. And with the arrival of traders in the century's early years, high-powered rifles, animal traps, fish nets, metal cooking pots, matches and needles slowly and ominously began to diffuse through the Eskimo society.

When spring arrived, the Copper Eskimos forsook their makeshift winter villages, dissolved into groups and wandered inland in search of wood, which they used to fashion large sleds. Trout and salmon were retrieved from the inland lakes and riverbeds. But the major prize was the caribou who retreated in vast herds during the winter south and west from the Arctic towards Hudson's Bay, only to return north in vaster numbers during the following spring. Here they fed on the grass and moss in the numerous valleys and beds along Bathurst Inlet and east to the Coppermine, where they were diligently pursued by the Eskimos who valued their skin and meat. The skin served as tent walls and wind-breaks and were fashioned by the women into elegant clothing which sufficed the year round. The meat was succulent and consumed in great quantities during the brief summer and early autumn, when the herds began their return south. The Eskimos retreated with the caribou, but in opposite directions. By August, the group of Eskimos who hunted up the Coppermine and east near Big Stick Island and the Dismal Lakes had returned to the mouth of the river and begun preparations for the winter.

The Coppermine wanderers were a practical and enduring people. Thriving on the hunt under brutal Arctic conditions they displayed qualities of patience, endurance and hardiness. "The Copper Eskimos think nothing of spending 24 hours on a hunt," the ethnologist Diamond Jenness wrote, "tramping continually over stony hills without a morsel of food, and with only a few short halts to rest their limbs and look around them. In spring I have seen them spend whole days fruitlessly digging one hole after another through the thick ice of the lake and jiggling their lines without ever getting a bite. In winter they sit for hours over their seal-holes even in howling blizzards with the temperature 30 degrees and more below Fahrenheit."

The hunt was the Eskimos' life and it shaped their minds, social organization and culture. The Eskimos filled their social hours with long accounts, in minutest detail, of the events of the chase and they developed a philosophical attitude of practical Epicureanism. "It is not strange . . . that the Copper Eskimo should be a true Epicurean," Jenness observed, "holding that life is a short and uncertain thing at the best, and that the wise man will grasp at what pleasures he can in his course without stopping to ponder over those things that do not directly affect his immediate welfare."

Among the most crucial things affecting the Eskimo's welfare were his kin, and the Coppermine society, shaped in response to a harsh environment, was egalitarian and co-operative. In 1910, the one thousand Copper Eskimos were divided among eight or nine groups each closely identified with a particular locality. The groups intermarried, spoke the same language and shared an attitude so tolerant that violence between or among them was a rare thing. The Eskimos had no military organization although they feared and mistrusted the neighbouring Indians. The co-operative principle pervaded relations within and between groups. There were no hereditary chiefs and no visible heirarchy, although shamans played important religious roles. Marriage took place at puberty, polygamy was uncommon, women were sometimes shared with friends though not, apparently, with strangers, and children, the aged and the infirm were loved and cared for. The Eskimos were not known to abandon their infirm or aged under ordinary conditions. The spoils of the hunt were shared and a brisk trade in equivalents pervaded the communities. Since most things were shared among people virtually devoid of privacy, thievery was uncommon and frowned upon. "The Copper Eskimos are, in fact, a race of ideal communalists," a NWMP officer observed, "for all food seems common property; the sick are looked after by the strong and they seldom quarrel among themselves." Stefansson thought them a kind and hospitable people possessed of substantial virtues designated in the European world as Christian: "For two days they had entertained us with warm hospitality and had already grounded firmly in my mind the impression which a year of further association with them was destined to do nothing to weaken – that they were the equals of the best of our own race in good breeding, kindness, and the substantial virtues. They were men and women of the Stone age truly, but they differed little from you or me or from the men and women who are our friends and families. The qualities which we call "Christian Virtues" (and which the Buddhists no doubt call "Buddhist Virtues") they had in all their essentials. They are not at all what a theorist might have supposed the people of the Stone age to be, but the people of the Stone age probably were what these their present-day representatives are: men with standards of honour, men with friends and families, men in love with their wives, gentle to their children, and considerate of the feelings and welfare of others. "If we can reason at all from the present to the past, we can feel sure that the hand of evolution had written the Golden Rule in the hearts of the contemporaries of the mammoth milleniums before the pyramids were built."

It was to bring these Christian Icemen – or Stone age communists – into the true church that inspired another Christian, a black-robed emissary from the Age of Iron, to undertake in midsummer of 1911 a punishing and dangerous mission into the lands forlorn stretching to the very rim of the Arctic Ocean. Father Rouvière would have fared easier had he decided to cruise north and convert Indians along the Mackenzie River, traversed by the steamers of the Hudson's Bay Company and Northern Transportation Company and by the gasoline launches of the church missions. The upper Mackenzie had trading posts and prospector's camps and even an occasional NWMP patrol to aid troubled adventurers. But he chose the harder task and more dangerous path towards the barren land of the Copper Eskimo: east from Fort Norman along Bear River to Great Bear Lake; across the lake's vast expanse to its northeastern extremity known as Dease Bay; further north up the Dease River to the bleak lands around the Dismal Lakes where the Eskimos camped and traded with the Indians during the summer months; and finally, the descent down the Kendall River and the Coppermine to its mouth at Coronation Gulf.

The first leg of Rouvière's journey was fiercely difficult and prepared him for the inclemencies ahead. The Bear River, winding ninety miles through muskeg country flecked with small patches of spruce and birch, was simple to descend and could be covered by a skilled boatman in a canoe in a single day. But the ascent was more difficult and it took the father, who enlisted a brigade of Indians as porters and guides, over a week. Rouvière travelled in a Peterboro canoe while his auxiliaries drew and tracked a scow filled with provisions. Although the party left early in July, huge piles of ice were thrown up on the shores throughout the river's entire length, obscuring the patches of small white pine beyond. The current was swift and the freezing water so clear that the river bottom was visible at a depth of forty feet. The channel was usually narrow and well-defined but at intervals it widened and the water, strewn with large boulders, grew shallow, forcing the party to take to the land on lengthy portages. The rain fell in torrents for several days and was replaced by blizzards of mosquitoes and flies.

But Rouvière persevered until his arrival, exhausted, at a small bay on the western end of Great Bear Lake. Here he rested several days, consorting briefly with the trader John Hornby, who had departed at the same time from Fort Norman with a party of Indians on a parallel trading voyage; and, by mid-July, he commenced the journey's second phase across the length of Great

Bear Lake. Approximately the size of Lake Huron and stretching 350 miles to its eastern extremity, Great Bear Lake remained ice-free for only six months during the year, until the beginning of October. To traverse this vast inland sea in an open boat was a punishing task. The cold, clear and very deep waters were bounded by high, spruced-covered hills which alternated with low, bare rocky expanses. Good harbours were rare and the bays often slammed by great rollers which swelled and roared across the lake's breadth. Dangerous storms rose quickly and the pre-vailing northeast winds often blew with the intensity of gales. The lake abounded in fish, mainly trout and whitefish, and the traveller who survived the wind's buffeting and high rollers, which cast more than a few boats on the rocky shores, ate well, providing he had a fishing net or other similar devices.

It took Rouvière almost two weeks to navigate the lake in the company of a brigade of Bear Lake Indians, who ferried the father across in their York boat and deposited him near the ruins of old Fort Confidence at Dease Bay, at the lake's northeast end. Several days later, Hornby arrived and joined the father in a fur-ther probe eastward. Using as a base a cabin Hornby had built at the Dease River's mouth, the men fought the rapids for miles until they approached the land of the Dismal Lakes, a wilderness of sandy plains and spruce patches interspersed with numerous ice blue lakes, fringed with green marshes and bounded in the north by a low range of purple mountains, the Copper Moun-tains. At the edge of a small lake known as Imaerinik in the southwest of the district, in a clump of spruce, Rouvière and Hornby built a small cabin – a combination trading post and wilderness mission, where the father briefly lived in the company of an Indian boy named Harry and his widowed mother.

Father Rouvière did not have to wait long to meet the Eski-mos, who first spied the wandering Oblate on a hill near the Dease River soon after he began the ascent with Hornby. The Eskimo party of hunters immediately rushed forward to meet him, the lead Eskimo raising his arms above his head and bend-ing his body forward in a greeting reciprocated by the priest. The Eskimos were short and stocky in build, had dark oriental fea-tures and were dressed in their summer skin, mainly caribou.

Their leader turned to the others and announced, "Kabluna" – It's a white man – took the priest's arm and presented him to his colleagues who were warm and effusive. Rouvière was delighted with the meeting and took the opportunity to shake the hand of everyone and present each of them with a medal which he hung around their necks. The Eskimos presented the priest with a meal at their camp where Rouvière tried to impress them with the idea that he had come to live among them. The Eskimos noticed the priest's soutane and oblate cross and were told that the man on the cross had died for them. The following day, the father returned for a second visit in the company of several Indians and was again greeted with commotion and enthusiasm. "Everything seems to be in common among them," he observed, "They give wholeheartedly and appear pleased when one shows interest in them."

The priest's interest continued throughout September and early October and was reciprocated by the Eskimos who arrived daily in families of two or three at his cabin at Lake Imaerinik. The exchanges were always pleasant but, from the father's viewpoint, not very productive, since he had difficulty picking up rudiments of their language. When the October snows fell, the parting was amiable. The Eskimos set their faces north to the sea, where the priest eventually hoped to join them, and the father went west by dog sled to the Dease River cabin where he prepared for the long winter. Throughout the winter months, Rouvière was not short of either food or company. Although he had failed to kill any caribou, he was supplied with plenty of dried meat by the Indians and fished for trout in the lakes through ice-holes. Barely six miles from the cabin he shared with Hornby, at a place called Hodgson's Point, the Douglas brothers wintered and entertained. The father joined them in games of auction bridge, whist and chess, played with pieces so cleverly fashioned that only Rouvière and Hornby, who carved the set, could distinguish between kings and queens, or pawns and bishops. The Douglases entertained at Christmas and presented the father with a lavish polar luncheon of Arctic hare, plum pudding with blueberry jam, toddy and chocolate. For supper, the father feasted on the north's great delicacy, smoked caribou tongues.

With the first glimpses of spring in late March 1912, Father Rouvière began preparations for a renewed assault on the Eskimos. To replenish his dwindling supplies and augment his forces he set out in the last days of March for Fort Norman where he rested at the Ste. Thérèse Mission and briefly fraternized with Guillaume Le Roux, assigned to assist in the second phase of the campaign to thwart the Anglicans. Le Roux was a native of the town of Quimper, Finistère department in the west of France, who graduated from Liège before emigrating to Canada. Since 1907 he had worked out of Fort Good Hope, among the Mackenzie Delta Eskimos. Twelve years younger than Rouvière, he was a good linguist and fiercely dedicated. But he did not own Rouvière's gentle manner, nor his patience and self-control. Le Roux was an aggressive, overbearing man with a short fuse who, when frustrated, was prone to fits of rage.

It was not before mid-July that the priests departed east in large canoes, in the company of Indian guides and porters, along the route previously taken by Rouvière. The trip, as usual, was slow, treacherous and hampered by swarms of mosquitoes, gales and squalls and, if we are to believe the priests, by the laziness of the Indian porters. A full six weeks passed before they reached the Douglas cabin at Hodgson's Point which served as a temporary headquarters.

With the summer all but gone, the priests set to work building a house and expanding storage facilities at Dease Bay and Lake Imaerinik, catching and storing supplies of fish at Bear Lake, and meeting with the Eskimos, about sixty of whom camped in the area of Lake Imaerinik. Rouvière did the bulk of the fishing and building while Le Roux met with the Eskimos on twenty or twenty-five separate occasions until their departure north in early November. The father was pleased to discover that several had learned to make the sign of the cross and he spent difficult hours trying to pick up snatches of their language. The Eskimos, as usual, displayed a fine hospitality and invited the priests to their tents where they shared with them their food and showed every mark of respect. The priests, in turn, instructed the Eskimos in the basics with the aid of Father Lacombe's illustrated catechisms. Pretty pictures of priests administering the sacraments and bishops ordaining priests were displayed in order to disabuse their pupils of the frequent and pernicious confusion between merchants and priests.

But the engagements were brief and lacking in the sustained intimacy of joint residence. The fathers, to be sure, hoped to convince an Eskimo family to come and live with them and return in their company during the winter to Fort Norman where they could be trained and enlisted as interpreters, guides and language instructors. But several attempts, fortified with promises of rifles and other goods, failed and in early November, Fathers Rouvière and Le Roux found themselves forsaken by their errant flock who set out alone on the return winter pilgrimage to the Coppermine's mouth.

By the winter of 1912-1913, the missionary fathers were abandoned, but not disheartened. Informed via Indian courier mail of Anglican plans to invade the Coppermine's mouth by the arctic route through Bernard Harbour, they prepared themselves for the next summer's work. Both travelled by dog sled to Fort Norman in early winter. When spring arrived, Father Le Roux returned to the mission while Rouvière remained at Dease Bay where he finished the construction of a new cabin. During Le Roux's absence, Rouvière met the Eskimos several times near Imaerinik and, on one occasion, travelled as far as the Coppermine River. Upon Le Roux's return in early August, the priests again pressed their acquaintance. Their bearded figures became familiar sights to the Eskimos who came to refer to Father Le Roux as Ilogoak and Father Rouvière as Kuleavik. The priests were invited to their tents where they were fed the choicest portions and rendered a homage so grand that Le Roux felt "like a guest of quality." The fathers reciprocated with renewed instructional attempts. The Eskimos were invited to holy mass and one day witnessed the sacraments of baptism conferred on an Indian child. Lacombe's illustrations were again produced and stories told of Christ's martyrdom and a beautiful world beyond. "These two men were telling us about the land above the skies," the Eskimo Hupo later reported, "They showed us coloured pictures of heaven, and they said that after we died we would go there. They used to sing just like the Eskimo when they make medicine. They held our hands and taught us to make the sign of the cross, and they put a little bread sometimes in my mouth."

All summer long in the year 1913 the priests insistently broad-cast the message of Christ. But they were still not certain of its reception. Their main problem was time. They had not yet lived with the Eskimos long or close enough to win their confidence. Circumstances had prevented the development of a relaxed inti-macy, easy communication and trust. Their knowledge of the Eskimo language was rudimentary and they were unable, in two winters, to convince the Eskimo to come and live with them for a sustained time either in the field or at Fort Norman. They depended heavily on John Hornby, a trader not always liked by the Eskimos, who fell ill the second summer and had to be closely tended. Their slow descent the second summer badly truncated the evangelizing season. The Eskimos were suspicious, moreover, of the priest's apparent intimacy with the Indians, their tradi-tional enemy.

The Oblates' mission was spiritual. They had arrived at the cold heart of the barren lands to bring Christ to a lonely and foresaken people. But their relationship with the Eskimos, as with the Indians, was peculiarly material. The priests were the church's servants and emissaries but the Eskimos had trouble dis-tinguishing them from traders. The priests had material needs which they could not themselves satisfy in a world strange and forsaken to them. They could not build sleds or snow houses in winter. They were poor hunters and had trouble finding caribou. Womanless, they could not prepare skins or sew their own clothes. The priests began their voyage with the aid of Indian auxiliaries, but the closer they moved to the Coppermine and the longer they remained in the barrens the greater they came to depend on their Eskimo hosts. An Eskimo named Kormik, for example, hunted for Father Le Roux while Uluksak's wife sewed the priests' clothes. To ensure the Eskimos' labour and co-opera-tion, the priests distributed things like nets, traps and needles while other commodities were merely promised – to Eskimos like Kormik, who expected a rifle for his work.[2]

The Oblates' spiritual advance and gain in trust among their polar flock was still tenuous in the late autumn of 1913 when the fathers were faced with an excruciating decision dictated by external circumstances. The source of their dilemma was a man called Fry, an Anglican missionary who, according to the fathers' informants, projected a winter rendezvous with the Copper Eskimos upon their return to the Coppermine's mouth. The fathers were uncertain of their spiritual hold on the Eskimos and were not yet convinced they were welcome to live and travel with them. But they had already invested two years of hard labour in their enterprise and were loathe to see an Anglican interloper steal their subjects. "I have learnt that Fry, the minister, is advancing towards Coronation Gulf," Father Le Roux wrote his superior, "He will reach Cape Parry . . . and his objective will be a big island which lies in the strait at the west of Coronation Gulf; there will be 400 to 500 Eskimos there. If he reaches there he will probably see several of those we see here. Time presses, and he must be anticipated. Shall one or other of us go to pass the winter with them? I do not know."[3]

The decision had already been made, by Fry, and in late Octo-

2 The Eskimos had their needs and wants inflated by the intrusion of the trading economy which introduced goods and implements they had never before contemplated. The anthropologist Diamond Jenness wrote, "The Eskimos were particularly struck by the fact that many articles of inestimable value to themselves, such as tin cans, scrap iron and steel needles, were very little prized by the white men, who set more store on fox skins and other objects of little use to the natives themselves and therefore of small value in their eyes. The white men again were inferior in hunting, except for the advantage the rifles gave them and less hardy at enduring. They were ignorant of the art of harpooning seals and in building snow huts, so that they could not move from their houses in winter without their tents. Further, they often bought meat from the natives, and employed them to hunt for them, and the women to sew their clothes. The journey of the two French missionaries to the mouth of the Coppermine River in 1913 must have opened the eyes of the Eskimos to the difficulties under which the majority of white men labour when they try to cope with arctic conditions of life and travel. For many different reasons, therefore, the natives conceived a certain amount of contempt for white men, a contempt that was only qualified by a desire to gain some of their most valued possessions, their knives and axes and particularly their rifles and their ammunition."

3 Father Duchessois, an Oblate attached to Bishop Breynat, later stated, "It was a race between the two churches as to which should first occupy and hold that field of missionary effort." *Calgary Herald,* August 4, 1917. According to Father Rouvière, Fry was coming "to sow tares" in their field.

ber the fathers laid in supplies at their cabins and joined the Eskimos on their winter trek north. The Eskimos departed in stages, in separate family or tent groups, each of which travelled with a sled drawn by dogs. The fathers travelled with an Eskimo called Kormik in a group of seven or eight sleds which included Kormik's brother Hupo and a pair of young hunters named Sinnisak, who came from the vicinity of Victoria Land, and Uluksak, a sometime resident around Bathurst Inlet. The Eskimos headed due north across the Barren Lands to a point west and north of Bloody Falls where they descended to the Coppermine River, a few miles from the mouth. Here, on the frozen ice of their ancient preserve, the Eskimos unpacked their sleds, fed their starved dogs, set up their tents and began their winter fishing.

The fathers, however, found the descent difficult and fell out with their hosts soon after their arrival. Several Eskimos, it appeared, had become disenchanted with the priests, among them Kormik in whose tent the fathers still lodged after settling on the ice. Kormik thought the priests owed him a rifle and some traps for his labours and with his wife's aid removed and hid one of the several guns owned by the priests, along with a supply of food. The fathers demanded its return and when Kormik refused, Le Roux loaded a rifle and threatened his host who by then contemplated killing both of his guests. Le Roux's intimidation brought quick results and the rifle was returned by Kormik's mother upon the advice of several villagers who feared being killed. The rifle incident snapped the final feeble tie between the priests and their hosts and Rouvière and Le Roux took the only sensible course. "We cannot say what we will do," Rouvière had written on the eve of his departure north, "If we get along well with the Husky band, we will stay the whole year with them; but if we cannot live with them we will come back before Christmas."[4] It was the latter course the priests chose, earlier than contemplated. Within several days of their arrival at the winter quarters of the Copper Eskimos, Ilogoak and Kuleavik turned their backs on their flock and with dogs and sled moved south

4 Husky was a slang term for Eskimo used by traders, police and, apparently, missionaries.

along the river's east bank towards the sanctuary of the woods, which faced them some twenty-five miles ahead.

The priests made little progress under the harsh conditions. Winter had set in and the temperature dropped sharply. They could not hope for a fire until reaching the woods, and their advance was slowed by weak dogs, a heavy load and high drifts of blowing snow. They suffered terribly the first night, but grimly continued their slow march the next day when, camped near a lake, they noticed a pair of Eskimos without a sled or arms accompanied by a single dog. The visitors were Sinnisak and Uluksak who had earlier descended the Coppermine with the priests and, after settling in and fishing for several days, were returning upstream along the same trail to assist in the descent of the remaining Eskimo migrants, among whom was Uluksak's uncle.

For the desperate priests, the Eskimos' arrival was a God-send. Le Roux called them over and promised traps in return for their aid in hauling the sled. The Eskimos consented, joined the dogs in harness and pulled for hours until nightfall when, still distant from the woods, they built a snow house for the night's shelter. The next morning the Eskimos decided to retreat since they had already passed the junction of the trail used by their expected kin and feared being lost. This displeased the fathers who grew angry and remonstrated with them. But the Eskimos stubbornly departed and had gone only a short distance when they lost their way in a storm. Alerted by the dog's whimperings, Uluksak discovered a cache in the snow, made earlier by the priests, and invited Sinnisak to come over for a joint inspection. Sinnisak had advanced only a few feet when the priests appeared, led by Father Le Roux carrying a rifle. The priest was angry and when Sinnisak asked whether he intended to kill him, Le Roux replied in the affirmative. The priests ordered the Eskimos back into harness and pushed Sinnisak towards the sled. The Eskimos relented, donned the harness and began pulling the sled ahead of the dogs, through the raging blizzard. It was punishing work, but they had no choice. Whenever they relaxed or the sled stuck Le Roux pushed them or waved the rifle. When either began to talk, Le Roux, who remained behind the sled with Rouvière, stumbled forward and placed his hand over their mouth. "Ilogoak was very mad, and was pushing me," Sinnisak later explained, "I was thinking hard and crying and very scared, and the frost was in my boots and I was cold. I wanted to go back, I was afraid. Ilogoak would not let us. Every time the sled stuck Ilogoak would pull out the rifle . . . I was thinking I will not see my people anymore." Uluksak shared his companion's distress. "I wanted to speak and Ilogoak put his hand over my mouth," he stated, "I wanted to talk of my wife sewing clothes for Ilogoak in the fall. Kuleavik gave Ilogoak a rifle and a knife and Ilogoak pointed the gun at us. I was afraid and I was crying. Every time I wanted to talk Ilogoak came and put his hand over my mouth."

The Eskimos did eventually speak to each other and Uluksak soon heard that his desperate companion intended to kill the white men before they killed him. As they approached a small hill, Sinnisak sprang from his harness and rushed to the side of the sled. Le Roux pursued and began pushing him back when Sinnisak complained bitterly that he had to relieve himself and began to undo his belt. Le Roux momentarily relented, watched Sinnisak move behind the sled and turned his back. Sinnisak immediately stabbed him with a hunting knife. The bleeding priest rushed towards the sled where the rifle rested while Rouvière was held at bay by Sinnisak waving the blood-soaked knife. By now Uluksak had removed himself from the harness and grappled with Le Roux for the rifle. Le Roux beat him with a stick and was finally stabbed several times, slumping dead into the snow. Rouvière, in the meanwhile, had fled about 100 yards when Sinnisak seized the rifle and fired. The first shot missed but the second struck home and the priest sat wounded in the snow. The Eskimos raced towards their fallen target with knives and an axe. Rouvière was breathing heavily and stood up when Uluksak arrived with his knife readied. Uluksak struck twice before felling Rouvière on his back, and Sinnisak finished him with an axe blow across the head and several across the legs, one of which was severed near its extremity. "Uluksak struck first with the knife and did not strike him," Sinnisak later confessed, "The second time he got him. The priest lay down and was breathing a little and I struck him with an axe I was carrying across the face. I cut his legs with the axe. I killed him dead." But the Eskimos feared that the white men, or their spirits, might rise to haunt them and revenge their death. So they performed an ancient and necessary operation. "After they were dead," Sinnisak continued, "I said to Uluksak, 'Before when white men were killed, they used to cut off some and eat some.'" Uluksak cut open Rouvière's belly and removed portions of his liver which he shared with Sinnisak. Bits of Le Roux's liver were similarly eaten before the Eskimos covered the bodies with snow, removed several cartridge boxes and a pair of rifles from the sled, and left for the Coppermine's mouth. They camped during the night and returned to their village the next day when they disclosed the killings to their companions. Uluksak turned over his rifle and cartridges to the villagers while a group consisting of Kormik and several other villagers left the next morning to retrieve the priests' goods. "They started in the morning," Sinnisak disclosed, "and came back the same night. Kormik had two church shirts and some clothing. I can't remember the other things. Kormik sold the two church shirts to A. Nautallik. I do not know what he got for them."

In a tiny village of Stone age seal hunters, resting somewhere on the ice in Coronation Gulf, the commodities of a pair of dead Oblate priests began circulating, and, with them, rumours and suppositions of the disposition of their former owners. The late fathers had made it a habit of reporting to their superiors by letters carried by Indians at irregular intervals to Fort Norman. Several months before departing on their fatal voyage, they had posted several letters declaring their intention to winter at Coronation Gulf. Thereafter, nothing of a direct nature was heard from them all winter. Their Fort Norman superiors, Fathers Ducot and Frapsance, knew that this, in itself, was no cause of worry since the frontier priests had left their Indian postmen behind. But they began to worry during the spring and summer of 1914 when vague rumours began to trickle in, from certain Dog-rib Indians who travelled east to the edge of the Barrens to trade and hunt, that the priests may have met an unlucky fate.

Their fears were heightened by the report of a Mr. Darcy Arden, a former employee of the Department of the Interior, who traded and prospected with the Northern Trading Company out of its Fort Norman base. Mr. Arden ventured inland across Bear Lake in the company of a Métis named Hibbert Hodgson during the summer of 1914. He had barely made thirty-five miles up the Bear River when he met several returning Indians who told him that some "Huskies" had killed the priests. Arden later camped at Dease Bay, near the priests' house at the mouth of the Dease River, and came upon a camp of forty Eskimos and several Indians. When Arden approached, the Indians rushed forward and excitedly told him that the Eskimos had killed the priests and had some of their goods. The Eskimos seemed friendly enough, laid down their bows and arrows when their guests arrived, and welcomed them with raised hands and with a greeting which apparently translated as "White man, thank you very much."

Arden spent several days with the Eskimos, two of whom, it seems, were dressed in priests' cassocks. When Arden asked where they got them, the Eskimos replied from "white men, in the west." The Eskimos were equally uncommunicative about their possessions which included prism binoculars, several rifles and tools for remoulding bullets. Unlike their trader guest, the Eskimos found the chance meeting beneficial. Arden and Hodgson subsequently found that a supply of files, knives, axes, scissors and shirts had been stolen along with their underclothes and 400 rounds of ammunition. "It is impossible to keep anything from them," he later complained, "They steal right in front of your face and must hide the stuff in their clothes."

When Arden later visited the priests' house at Dease Bay, he found the lock broken and the interior in shambles. The flour, rice and sugar, covered with green mould, were untouched, but little remained of the cache of powder, bullets, axes, blankets and vestments, a theft subsequently confirmed by the Indian boy Harry, in whose care the fathers had left the house.

Arden's story did not make pleasant listening for the Reverend Fathers Ducot and Frapsance, who made urgent representations in the autumn of 1914 to Bishop Breynat at Great Slave Lake. The bishop, in turn, pressed the federal authorities. By the spring of 1915, the pleas for aid brought results and an expedition was organized, unique in the fabled annals of the North West

Mounted Police, to probe the northlands for the missing priests.

For the mounted police, it was a welcome opportunity. By the arrival of the first world war, the police glitter had dulled somewhat. The western frontier had closed, thanks to their solid intervention, and the sturdy peasants in sheepskin coats, plowshares in hand, proved more tractable than the sullen Indians and Métis who formerly hunted the open plains. With the evolution of democratic `self-government in the western provinces and establishment of several provincial police forces, the mounted police threatened to recede entirely from the Canadian Mind, by now fascinated with the widely-acclaimed heroics of the Canadian Forces in the European war theatre. By the war's beginning, the mounted police's lone and last frontier was the polar territories north of the new western provinces where a string of police outposts had been gradually extended as far as Herschel Island near the Mackenzie's mouth. But the barren far north proved, during the first years of entry, singularly pacific, a state confirmed by Inspector Pelletier who, after leading the historic Great Slave Lake-Hudson's Bay Patrol in 1908, concluded no vigorous police presence was necessary since law and order naturally inhered in a land unoccupied, except by Eskimos, who were a harmless and peaceful lot.

The disturbing report of the priests' disappearance rekindled the Force's adventurous spirit and, in the mid-spring of 1915, a young officer based in Regina was ordered by Commissioner Perry to undertake an arduous patrol north in search of the missing men.[5] [6] Charles Deering La Nauze was twenty-seven years old and a ten-year veteran, whose father had served with the Force in the Territories. The young Irish officer had been stationed for several years at northern posts and was familiar with arctic condi-

---

5 "On the word of Indians who had heard the news after it had travelled down a thousand miles uninhabited by white men," the *Calgary Herald* later announced, "on a message that for years travelled by moccasin telegraph, British justice in the form of the North West Mounted Police went out to the lips of the frozen sea to teach the people of a million dark nights that 'thou shalt not kill'." August 11, 1917.

6 There was, about this time, a second patrol organized to apprehend the murderers of two traders, H.V. Radford and T. Street at Bathurst Inlet.

tions. La Nauze departed from Regina in early May with two colleagues – Constables D. Withers and J. E. F. Wight – for
Edmonton, where they gathered three years of supplies, and continued to Peace River Crossing. Here, in mid-June, the officers
boarded a steamer, the *S. S. Northland Call,* bound for Vermilion
Chutes where, after a short wait, they transferred to another ship,
the *McMurray,* which ferried them across Lake Athabasca to Fort
Smith. The officers then boarded the *S. S. Mackenzie* which carried them down the North's great highway to Fort Norman.

La Nauze gathered enough intelligence at Fort Norman to
confirm the need for an expedition inland. Several Indians, the
fathers Ducot and Frapsance and Mr. Darcy Arden were interrogated and an Eskimo interpreter and guide recruited named Ilavinik, who had earlier spent four years with Stefansson. La Nauze's
party, consisting of the two constables, Arden, Ilavinik, his wife
Mamayuk and daughter Nagosak, departed July 23 down the
Bear River. They travelled in a York boat heavily-laden with personal baggage, freight and two canoes. The bulk of the supplies
was sent along earlier in a scow tracked by nine Indians as far as
Great Bear Lake. The transportation down the river was, as
usual, difficult and it was not until August 4, after grim days of
tracking through icy shoal water, rapids and mud-slides, that the
party reached the river's mouth.

Here they remained for over a week and engaged, at a price of
three cents a pound, a pair of trappers named Sloan and Harrison
to transport in their small homemade schooner, the *Wild Duck,*
the bulk of their freight across Great Bear Lake. On August 12,
propelled by a slight southwest wind, La Nauze's party began
their trip across the lake, feeding themselves and their dogs along
the way with trout and whitefish – some as large as twenty-eight
pounds – which came easily into their nets. But the passage was
slowed by gales and prevailing northeasterlies and huge white-
topped breakers rolling in 200-mile sweeps from McTavish Bay.
The party were forced to lay in for days in several of the lake's
few serviceable harbours.

It was not until September 8 that La Nauze arrived at the
mouth of the Dease River in the vicinity of the priests' house
which Arden had visited the previous autumn. The house was

deserted and the officer employed it as a base camp from which he foraged inland towards the Dismal Lakes. With autumn almost gone, La Nauze hatched no grand plans for a further expedition, preferring instead to explore the land around and prepare for a serious thrust towards the arctic in the following spring. He hunted for deer, moose and caribou, which supplied ready meat during the ensuing weeks, and for clues of the priests' whereabouts. Less than two weeks after arrival, a brief patrol was outfitted in the direction of the priests' cabin at Lake Imaerinik. Since winter had already set in, pack dogs were used in a run seventy miles northeast across the snow and ice to the edge of the Barren Lands which were observed to be "not unlike the Saskatchewan prairies." La Nauze visited an island of small spruce overlooking the northeast branch of the Dease River, where Vilhjalmur Stefansson had camped in 1910-11 and built a house, later discovered by Constable Wight. La Nauze observed, from the crest of a high hill, the valley of Big Stick Island, known to the Eskimos as the Sled Making Place. "A veritable oasis of tall dark spruce about two miles long," the inspector later wrote, "nestled at the foot of a high rocky hill and, to the north, turquoise-blue lakes lay tucked away among the frowning hills. To the east bald grass plains stretched as far as the eye could see and small herds of caribou were everywhere."

Inspector La Nauze, at long last, had entered the land of the Copper Eskimos which somewhere, among its ice-blue lakes, granite hills and mountains of copper, held the secret of the priests' location. From a neighbouring mountain, the inspector spied Lake Imaerinik which he soon reached through a small valley filled with recent Eskimo caches and trails. Kopjes, or stone piles used to trap deer, were visible everywhere near the small lake, which had frozen over. The patrol crossed the ice on September 29 to the far northeast corner, where the priests had located their tiny wilderness mission in a clump of dry spruce. The cabin was empty, in total disarray inside and without a clue as to where its residents had gone. The wind blew harshly, throwing up clouds of snow, as the officer turned back to Big Stick Island, reached in a days march. Several days later, on October 4, the patrol gained, in a heavy snow storm, the base camp near Old

Fort Confidence at Dease Lake where they settled in for the winter's duration.

While La Nauze recuperated and awaited supplies for the spring's projected descent of the Coppermine, a second patrol was organized, in the person of Corporal H. V. Bruce of the Herschel Island police detachment, who boarded the Canadian Arctic Expedition's *Alaska* in late August and sailed east along the Arctic to Bernard Harbour in Coronation Gulf. Upon arrival, the corporal enlisted the aid of members of the Canadian Arctic Expedition, including the ethnologist Diamond Jenness and biologist Dr. R. Anderson, who used the Harbour as the base of their scientific assault on the Arctic culture.

Corporal Bruce spent a useful and informative several months exploring the Eskimo villages of the Dolphin and Union Straits during the autumn and winter months of 1915-1916. Without exception, the Copper villages were warm, friendly and hospitable. When he entered their encampments they raised their hands in peace, rushed to greet him, grabbed his sled, fed his dogs, mended his boots and pitched his tent. They invited him into their homes to share repasts of raw fish, deer and seal meat and, on occasion, a delicious soup of deer blood served in a musk-ox horn. The corporal sometimes slept in the villages, in his own tent or in a snow house, and joined his hosts in their social activities including wrestling matches and dances held in the large snow house where the Eskimos, dressed in long parkas and deer skin pants, sang and cavorted to the accompaniment of a large skin drum ten feet in circumference. And he attended seances conducted by shamans in trances who, with contorted faces, summoned spirits in voices strange and haunting.

The officer, in all, came away with a positive view of his smiling hosts who seemed simple, egalitarian, brave, industrious and friendly to white men. But he strongly suspected that the Eskimos knew about the priests. His first inkling came from a cache he stumbled upon, soon after his arrival, in the company of one of the expedition's naturalists, Mr. F. Johanson. Among the hides, pots, tins, rip-saws and powder-horns, he discovered a Roman Catholic Bible lesson book with coloured prints, a small brass communion plaque and a priest's cassock marked on the inside of the collar in indelible ink "R. Père Rouvière." Several meetings with Eskimos in their snow houses further kindled the officer's suspicions. A chap named Kormik was very friendly and showed the officer some of his finest possessions which included a "Psalterium Breviarii Romani," several old notebooks with entries in French, two coloured prints of Jesus Christ and the Virgin Mary and several initialled linen handkerchiefs. Bruce met with Kormik a second time and obtained from him several objects of note, including a Latin prayer book, a small crucifix, two tassels, a linen communion cloth, a carmine and gold mass vestment and a cut and blood-stained altar cloth. When questioned about his possessions, Kormik mentioned he had obtained his initialled handkerchiefs from the trader Hornby and his pictures and books from "another white man." The Eskimo spoke briefly and confusedly about Ilogoak and Kuleavik whom he said he had met several summers previous, but he volunteered very little information.

Corporal Bruce had a similar experience with a shaman named Uluksak Mayuk, who invited the officer to sit beside him on the sleeping platform in his deerskin tent. The officer was barely comfortable when the Eskimo rose and hammered several nails into the wooden supports above the seal-oil lamp, on which he hung a few cups. A further nail was then driven into the supports immediately above the sleeping platform on which was hung a crucifix with a long black silken cord and two rosaries attached to the arms, one of ebony and the other alabaster. The shaman warmly admired his possessions and was pleased to display them before the officer who soon heard that "a white man near a big lake had given it to him, as a gift."

Uluksak owned other intriguing items and when he arrived at the Canadian Arctic Expedition's camp in mid-November, he traded several to the ethnologist Diamond Jenness who, in return for two boxes of 40/40 cartridges, obtained the crucifix and rosaries, a French Roman Catholic Bible lesson book with coloured prints entitled "La Religion en Tableaux" and a Latin breviary with the inscription, on the fly leaf, "G. Le Roux, Oblat de Marie Immaculée." Nor was this the first contact of the Expedition with the Eskimos' new found religiosity. "I returned . . . to Bernard

Harbour about April the first," Dr. R. M. Anderson, commander of the Expedition's southern party reported, "and sometime during this month I saw an Eskimo, one Uluksak, wearing a priest's cassock; all the members of the expedition saw him, and a few days before this they also saw him wearing a crucifix as well; I myself did not see him wearing the crucifix, but I saw one in his possession. Mr. Wilkins, the photographer, took a photo of him wearing both the cassock and the crucifix: these photos have been sent by Mr. Wilkins to the "Chronicle" in London, England."

In featuring, amidst grim accounts of the battles of war, a photograph of a short, smiling Copper Eskimo, resembling a Japanese, on the ice in the Canadian Arctic, dressed in an Oblate's cassock and wearing a crucifix, the *London Chronicle* doubtless scooped its competitors. A similar triumph, however, could not be claimed by Corporal Bruce in his friendly competition with inspector La Nauze to solve the riddle of the missing priests. During the autumn and winter months of 1915-1916, Bruce visited villages, camped with and interviewed the local Eskimos, collected and noted their circulating religious commodities and diligently probed for hard clues of the priests' condition and whereabouts. By the break of spring of 1916, however, the officer was altogether frustrated and anxiously awaited the arrival of La Nauze, whom he had vainly-tried to reach in the company of Dr. Anderson in the dead of winter along the Coppermine.

The corporal was not long waiting. La Nauze departed east from Dease Bay on March 29 in the company of Constable Wight, Ilavinik, Darcy Arden, several Indians – who soon returned to Fort Norman – and eight dogs who shared the task of hauling a pair of toboggans, one of which was weighted with a large canoe. The land abounded in deer and the patrol obtained a good supply of fresh meat which they sometimes smoked Indian-style. But the passage through the Dismal Lakes district east to the Kendall Valley over firmly-packed snow was slow and marred by several fierce storms which forced the party to seek prolonged shelter. Because the patrol was overloaded with freight, double-tripping was necessary and it was not until April 16, after a swift run through the Kendall River Valley, that the Coppermine was reached. "It was great pleasure to see a good sized river again," La Nauze later reported, "flowing as it does through the heart of the Barren Lands, between its high spruce-covered banks." Upon arrival at the Coppermine, the patrol was greeted by budding willows, soaring hawks and other signs of the arrival of spring in the river valley. And they discovered a blaze on a tree carved by Dr. Anderson, announcing the presence on the coast of the Canadian Arctic Expedition. After double-tripping and building caches, hunting for meat and refitting the sleds with iron runners, which delayed departure a further two weeks, the La Nauze patrol commenced on April 29 a final run across the hard packed snow along the river's high clay banks.

The passage was smooth and uninterrupted and the following day, from a hill near the river's west bank, a blue haze, announcing the Arctic Ocean beyond, was clearly visible. The sight quickened the patrol which soon reached the river's mouth where fresh sled tracks were observed on the ice, leading to an island nearby. The tracks were followed to a freshly broken camp where cans of pemmican were cached and, a mile beyond, to an Eskimo village obscured by a sharp cliff. Here the officer was greeted with the usual spontaneous effusions, raised arms and rejoicing, and proffers of deer meat cooked in large stone pots suspended over seal-oil lamps. The Eskimos, about fifteen in number, were dressed in deerskin and lived in large skin tents fitted with snow sleeping benches and snow passage ways. They owned rifles, tin pots and other civilized adornments and informed the officer, Ilavinik providing the translation, that several white men were camped in the bay nearby while, four days distant, there rested on the waters a great ship. La Nauze left Ilavinik to pry his hosts and had barely departed on his search for the white men when he was greeted by a lone figure on the ice who turned out to be Mr. Chipman, topographer of the Canadian Arctic Expedition. Chipman led La Nauze to Corporal Bruce, whose sled was nearby, and here, in a bay on an island off the Coppermine's mouth, the inspector first heard of the corporal's mission from Herschel Island and the curious results of his investigation.

Corporal Bruce joined La Nauze's patrol and they left on a tour of the Eskimo camps on the Coronation Gulf. With summer beckoning and the Eskimo migration inland imminent, the officers knew there was no better time for a careful search. They began with the village where Ilavinik had remained and spent a full day in futile interviews. The next afternoon, the officers struck another village of forty people near Point Lochyer, where they were warmly welcomed and informed, among other things, that Vilhjalmur Stefansson was the first white man they had ever seen. But the officers heard nothing about the priests and left the same evening for another large village located on the ice beneath Cape Lambert in the Dolphin and Union Straits. The inspector, with Ilavinik's invaluable aid, acquainted himself with several of the villagers, including a man called Ekkeshvina and his brother Nachin, who had nursed Stefansson's man Natkusiak at the Dismal Lakes after he had badly burned his face with powder. Nachim and Ekkeshvina knew of Ilavinik, who had also served Stefansson, and invited him and Inspector La Nauze to their snow house in the village's center, where they related an interesting story. "I sat back and let Ilavinik do the talking," La Nauze reported, "I heard him question them and I could see him trembling. I saw that something was happening, but I never moved, and in about five minutes he turned to me and said: 'I got him, the priests were killed by Husky, alright; these men very, very sorry.' And indeed they appeared to be; they both had covered their faces with their hands, and there was a dead silence in the igloo."

Inspector La Nauze soon retrieved Corporal Bruce who joined the confession in the snow house where Ilavinik asked them to write down the names of Uluksak and Sinnisak, the crime's apparent perpetrators. A lively discussion ensued, joined by several of the villagers who, one after another, entered the igloo and began contributing to the conversation. Among the new arrivals was an elderly man, Koeha, who acted as spokesman and recounted the entire train of events surrounding the deaths of the white men: from the priests' joint descent with the Eskimos of the Coppermine from Lake Imaerinik, the layover with Kormik's family, the quarrel over the rifle, the sudden departure of the white men, the later removal of Sinnisak and Uluksak, and their subsequent return and confession. The people in the snow house expressed their sorrow about what had happened and when asked why they had not spoken of the white men's death before, replied they were afraid. They admitted to carrying the knowledge in their heads for a long time but could not tell it to people like Arden who did not speak their language, or to the men of the Igloopuk (headquarters of the Canadian Arctic Expedition) who were too numerous. The trader Hornby, known to them as Hornbyeena had, moreover, said that if they killed white men, the white men would kill them.

The Eskimos spoke simply and La Nauze knew he had the answer. He departed for a pair of nearby villages where he observed the Eskimos preparing their seal catches, attended a dance and interviewed Kormik and Hupo who, apparently, corroborated the story of the priests' death. The approximate location of the wanted men was soon ascertained. Sinnisak, the prime culprit, was reported on the ice off Victoria Land while Uluksak was said to be located somewhere east of the Coppermine's mouth.

La Nauze's party first pursued Sinnisak. As they approached his village on the ice off Victoria Land, no peace signs or effusions of hospitality greeted the officers. But the residents gradually warmed with their guests' arrival, except for a lone Eskimo who sat on his haunches in a canvas tent near the village centre, busily constructing a bow. The man's name was Sinnisak, and he froze with fear when the search party entered. "What do you men want?" he asked, from his sitting position. "The white men here want you to go with them," the reply came. "If the white men kill me," answered Sinnisak, "I will make medicine and the ship will go down in the ice and all will be drowned." But the officers had come to arrest, rather than kill; the outlaw was pacified and told he could bring along his wife and effects.[7] Sinnisak came quietly to Bernard Harbour where he was placed under guard, given a preliminary hearing, whose legal import he scarcely appreciated, and committed on two charges of murder. After due warnings about self-incrimination, Sinnisak gave a full statement, duly recorded, outlining events surrounding the priests' killing. The

7 Sinnisak's wife was later returned to Coronation Gulf well fortified with several small gifts.

Eskimo at first refused to lie down and sleep and finally dropped from sheer weariness. According to Dr. Jenness, who met the prisoner at Bernard Harbour, Sinnisak feared being stabbed while asleep.[8]

The search now shifted south and east towards the Coppermine's mouth where Uluksak was reportedly headed, to join the large assembly of his kinsmen preceding their summer migration southward. Leaving Corporal Bruce in charge of the prisoner, La Nauze and Constable Wight commandeered Dr. Jenness' boy Patsy and his sled and in five days time reached the river's mouth, which they found deserted. Patsy proved a useful guide and from the top of an island spied with his field glasses six sleds moving across the ice towards them. The sleds soon disappeared behind an island, but the officers repaired in their direction and had travelled several hours when they came upon a village of skin tents. The raised arms of peace greeted the officers as they approached and the villagers rushed out to meet them. But one man, recognized by Patsy as Uluksak, hung back. When the two officers neared him, Uluksak ran forward with hands raised and shouting, "Goana, Goana (Thank you. I'm glad)."

8 An interesting account of the perilous task confronting La Nauze in apprehending the Eskimos was later given in the *Calgary Herald*, August 11, 1917. "It was a strange situation confronting the little patrol and its leader. They knew that in a few days' search they must find the two suspected men – then what? For forty years members of the force had gone single-handed into the out of the way places in Canada and brought back law-breakers; the work had been done without the use of fire arms. The white man outlaw had been confronted with the authority of the British law in the person of the 'mounty' and submitted without protest in most cases. The Indian of the Plains and the half breed could see when told to come the results of resistance and meekly submitted. They all knew if they killed one member of the force, two would come back – and if they killed two, four would come back. But here on the rim of the world were a people who knew not the law or the law bringers – by the slightest error the patrol would bring upon itself the fury of a thousand warriors – warriors who could send with their mighty arms the copper tip birch arrow through the body of the Caribou at a hundred paces. Warriors who knew no fear in battle. These men knew that between them and an avenging party who might follow in search of the few white men composing their patrol, stood a barrier of nature that must take the coming and going of a season to cross – they knew the Barren lands with their winds and they knew how to fight."

La Nauze was pleased as well and asked the outlaw if he knew why they had come. Uluksak replied that he well knew and asked whether they were going to kill him. "The other two white men hit me over the head," he recounted, "will you do this?" The officers did nothing of the sort. They merely explained to the outlaw that he was under arrest and had to come along. Uluksak agreed to go anywhere with them but asked whether they would first wait until his wife finished making his boots. But the boots waited, as did his distraught pregnant wife, who was pacified with gifts of a miniature silk tent, a cup and a box of matches which, according to Inspector La Nauze, "cheered her up greatly".

Inspector La Nauze was delighted with Uluksak's apprehension and made final arrangements for the disposition of the case. Constable Wight and Ilavinik were ordered to remain at the Coppermine's mouth until the gathering of the Eskimos and then proceed south to the murder scene to collect evidence. From there, they were to continue south and return to the Dismal Lakes and Great Bear Lake to Fort Norman. La Nauze and Patsy and their prisoner went the opposite way, to Bernard Harbour where Uluksak was held in a guard room and given his preliminary hearing. The Inspector conducted the hearing, heard evidence for the prosecution submitted by Corporal Bruce and committed Uluksak for trial on two charges of murder. The accused was forewarned, in the usual manner, before he confessed his guilt in a statement duly recorded, in a literal translation of the vernacular, virtually identical to Sinnisak's earlier confession. "I have not deceived the murderers in any way," La Nauze later wrote, "I have had it carefully explained to them that it is not for me to judge them, but that the Big White Chief must decide what he will do with them. But it is hard for them to grasp the meaning of this; in their life they have no chief, everyone is equal, and their word 'Ishumatak' for chief, literally translated means 'the thinker,' the man who does the deciding or thinking for the party."

For Inspector La Nauze and his captives the arrival at Bernard Harbour was not merely the end of a hard journey. It was also the beginning of a new and longer one towards Herschel Island, a bleak promontory 700 miles west along the Arctic coast. The party, consisting of the two officers La Nauze and Bruce and the two prisoners, left on July 13, 1916, on the *Alaska,* whose ultimate destination was Nome, Alaska – 2,000 miles away. The voyage had several reverses. Three days after departure the *Alaska* sailed into a fog from which it emerged the following day heading in the direction of Coronation Gulf. After several trying encounters with storms and massive ice fields, the ship finally dropped anchor at its remote destination, an alluvial, treeless land body, stretching sixteen miles long and four miles wide and located about six miles west of the mouth of the Mackenzie River. The most northerly portion of the great Yukon territory, Herschel Island formerly served as the wintering place of the American whaling fleet and remained as a port of entry for American trading ships descending the coast from Alaska. The island was deserted, except for an Anglican mission, a small Eskimo settlement, a Hudson's Bay Company post and the local quarters of the NWMP. It was here, on a bleak stretch of land remote from the familiar shores of Coronation Gulf, that the unhappy Copper Eskimos were lodged, guarded and employed in odd jobs throughout the long winter of 1916-17 in anticipation of their fateful removal to a world they had never heard of.

The message, from the federal Minister of Justice, via the police at Dawson City, arrived at Herschel Island in the early winter of the new year. Officer La Nauze was directed to bring his charges south to the city of Edmonton, Alberta,[9] the chosen venue of the trial. On May 9, after the ice along the MacKenzie had broken, the officer and his prisoners boarded the Hudson's Bay Company steamer the *McMurray* heading south to the Chutes near the Peace River Crossing. The party was augmented along the way. At Fort MacPherson the interpreter Ilavinik boarded, along with the ethnologist William Thompson, who observed the Eskimos to be growing fat from a ravenous consumption of white man's food including soup, potatoes, beans and bread, taken without salt and pepper, which the prisoners abhorred.[10] Patsy

---

9 Although the alleged crimes had been committed in the Northwest Territories, the courts of Alberta had jurisdiction to try the cases.

Klengenberg and the Eskimo Koeha joined the entourage as prospective translators and witnesses at Fort Norman. After portaging to the Peace River, the swelling party was greeted by another steamer, the *D. A. Thomas*, and by a host of curious villagers from the Peace River duly forewarned about the ship's exotic cargo. "About five o'clock the police party arrived at the *Thomas*," the *Edmonton Evening Bulletin* observed, "with the Eskimos fat, smiling and as happy as children on a holiday. The only disagreeable feature was the mud and mosquitos. The prisoners were dressed in brown overalls, grey shirts and common caps and not in their picturesque fur costumes of the north. In fact the only evidence that they had come from a cold climate was the fact that they had their mittens on. It is at once pathetic and yet a high tribute to the police in charge, splendid, reserved, sun-burnt men who have been in the north for the past two or three years. The absolute confidence the Eskimos have in them is clearly shown. They follow them about like faithful dogs and would no more leave them than a child would leave its parents or protectors. They seem to be the last familiar link that connects them with their home in the far North."

The final leg of the epic journey was effected by passenger train, later described by the Eskimo Koeha as a sort of self-propelled sled, which arrived in the trial's chosen venue of Edmonton in a great summer heat on August 10. The Eskimos, prisoners and witnesses, were lodged at the mounted police barracks, supplied with light summer clothing and a cooling fan, and fed good portions of "white man's food," which they consumed so deftly that the *Calgary Herald* thought the new converts used "a knife and fork with more grace than many 'bohunks'." While Sinnisak and Uluksak lolled, drooped and wilted – as captive Eskimos are supposed to do – the witnesses and translators toured

10 Thompson surmised that the Eskimos would never again "be content . . . with the food they existed on before." He noted further that the Eskimos worked well and performed their menial chores "without grumbling." Mr. Thompson reserved special praise for the policemen: "Had they sent three American detectives after these men there would have been three graves up north. On the other hand the Eskimos will do anything for the Police. They combine undoubted courage with tact. There is only one other force that approaches them in efficiency, the Guard Civil of Spain."

the town. Patsy Klengenberg, Ilavinik and Koeha gawked and marvelled at the tall buildings, attended movies and visited sporting goods stores where they admired the wide variety and plentiful supply of guns and ammunition. Ilavinik, an Anglican convert of sorts, was even escorted to the Pantages Theatre for a vaudeville show and delighted in the performance, until the women appeared. "He evinced a lively pleasure in the performance until the ballet came on," the *Herald* observed, "upon which he modestly put his head down on his arms, the sight of the naked limbs of the charming damsels offending his ideas of what a Christian Eskimo ought to look upon. Whether he did the Peeping Tom act or not can only be conjectured." The two prisoners, unfortunately, were not afforded similar pleasures while they awaited their historic trial, which began a few days after arrival. The trial was a celebrated event, widely attended: by interested citizens, who crowded the aisles and window ledges of the courtrooms; by several Oblates eager to see justice done; by local attorneys curious about the trial's unique procedural aspects; and by several distinguished visitors including a noted criminologist from the University of Pennsylvania.

The spectators witnessed an odd show. The jurors, Edmonton peers of the Coppermine Eskimos, sat serious and upright in cloth of varying shades of grey. The court officials wore white stockings and frowned and fidgeted in flowing black silken robes. The policemen stood rigidly erect, as if frozen by the heat, in their scarlet, royal blue and yellow uniforms. Sinnisak, brown-skinned, with almond eyes and black closely-cropped hair, first appeared in his brown caribou robes belted with deer, decorated with ptarmigan feathers and trimmed at the neck with white rabbit fur. A pair of ice-filled tubs of water cooled his feet, but the rest of him was so suffocated that the Eskimo, on trial for his life, dozed occasionally and had to be roused with gentle nudges. He soon discarded his native garb for a pair of light cotton trousers and a blue sweater which some observers thought made him appear Japanese, or like a Russian of the Mongolian type.

There were other curious and trying aspects to the proceedings. The heat, which suffocated the accused, forced the adoption of two-hour sessions. The translators Ilavinik and Klengenberg gave tortured and confused renderings of legal phraseology including the charge itself, crudely and ambiguously communicated to the confused accused. The Eskimo witnesses swore not to tell the whole truth, but to speak straight, with one tongue instead of two. The accused constantly heard about the Big White Chief, which sometimes meant the Crown and King, at other times the presiding judge and on other occasions the Minister of Justice of Canada. Delays as long as ten or fifteen minutes ensued while the translators sweated to phrase lawyer's questions in a sensible way. The witness Koeha, an elderly man who wore his straight black hair down to his shoulders and incessantly smiled, seemed a constant source of amusement and was himself amused when asked his age, which he did not know, or the age of the accused, which equally escaped him. Koeha thought horses were somewhere between dogs and caribou, and trains were sleds. During his lengthy tenure with the police officers, Koeha seemed to have picked up some of their mannerisms. He stood very erect in the witness box and kept a pressed and neatly folded white handkerchief in his sleeve, which he ceremoniously removed on several occasions to wipe his sweating brow.

The trial lasted several days and was heard by Chief Justice Horace Harvey and a panel of six jurors, none of whom were Roman Catholic. Assigned by the Justice Minister to defend the accused was an able local attorney, J. E. Wallbridge, K. C., who accepted the appointment after the government's first nominee, Mr. H. Landry declined. The Crown's case was handled by Charles Coursolles McCaul, K. C., a prominent Edmonton criminal lawyer, who decided, in the first instance, to press the charge against Sinnisak for the murder of Father Rouvière.

In his lengthy opening address and closing argument McCaul emphasized the trial's critical importance and uniqueness "since for the first time in history the Eskimos were brought face to face with the white man's justice." To Mr. McCaul, the trial had a higher civilizing purpose. "The Plain Indians, the Blackfeet, the Crees, the Chippeweyans and Stonies had been educated to the meaning of 'justice' and had come to know that justice does not mean mere retribution . . . the Eskimo had to be taught not only the first principle of the civilized administration of justice, but they had also to be taught that they had to recognize the authority of the British Crown and of the Dominion of Canada, whose jurisdiction extends to the furthermost limits of the frozen North." To Mr. McCaul, the prosecution of Sinnisak in conformity with the principles of British justice would help to bring civility to the Eskimos and ensure safety for the white man. "Just as it is possible today for a white man to travel through the country of the Blackfeet or the Crees under the protection of the aegis of justice, so must it be made possible for white men to have the same protection and safety for person and property among the far tribes of the North."

The Crown's case rested primarily on the statement of Sinnisak, recorded by La Nauze with Ilavinik's aid, outlining the events of the priests' killings. McCaul directed his examination of witnesses and argument to proving that Sinnisak was in league with the disgruntled Kormik and had trailed the priests, after leaving the Coppermine's mouth, for the express purpose of harming or killing them. He stressed the dire plight of the priests, their desperation, their need for help which justified their use of suasion in recruiting the Eskimo to pull the sled and holding him to it. Mr. Wallbridge was equally forceful in a different argument. He questioned the admissibility of the Eskimo's sworn statement and the sense of the entire proceeding to men of a Stone age mentality. He argued that the Eskimos had left their camp to help some of their party back from the Dismal Lakes and had no intention to harm the priests, who used force and threats of force to enlist their aid in hauling the sled. Wallbridge's position was that the Eskimo had acted in self-defence in killing the priests and his homicide was justifiable. Forced, at gunpoint, under inclement conditions, to drag the sled away from his appointed and familiar route, Sinnisak reasonably feared that he might not survive and return to his people.

Mr. Wallbridge and Sinnisak, who testified intelligibly on his own behalf and confirmed the facts cited in the written "confession," proved persuasive and the jury, after deliberating for an hour, acquitted the accused, following a peculiar charge from Mr. Justice Harvey which included an assurance that should the Eskimo be convicted, he would be lightly sentenced. Mr. McCaul was incensed at the decision and, rather than prosecute the case against Uluksak, due to be heard in several days, applied for a change of venue. He alleged that Edmonton opinion had become inflamed in favour of the Eskimos and against the priests, who had been the subject of dark rumours relating to sexual matters, and that a fair trial under the circumstances would be impossible.[11] The Chief Justice agreed and the entire contingent of lawyers, prisoners, witnesses and translators was shifted to Calgary, Alberta where, several days later, a new trial began of Sinnisak and Uluksak jointly charged with the murder of Father Le Roux.

In Calgary, the show was repeated. But the Calgary jurists knew their duty and returned a guilty verdict, softened with the strongest possible recommendation of mercy. The Chief Justice set October 15 as the date of execution but assured the accused through Patsy that he "would ask Big Chief far away" not to be too hard on them. "I have asked him by the way we have here (telegraph)," Justice Harvey continued, "and he says because they didn't know our way he won't have them put to death for killing those men this time. They must understand, now they know our law, that if they ever kill again they must suffer." Upon receipt of this assurance, in its translated form, the prisoners bobbed their heads violently and uttered something recorded as "Yeah, yeah."

The commutation, to life imprisonment at the NWMP Herschel Island post, came several days later and the prisoners returned to Edmonton to prepare for their long voyage to their polar prison. When their party boarded the train north, several familiar faces were missing, including Officer Bruce, who obtained a two-month leave of absence to marry a young Calgary lady, and Inspector La Nauze, who departed for Regina and Ireland where he visited with his family. But the prisoners did enjoy

11 McCaul felt that religious rivalries and propaganda stressing the childish innocence of the Eskimos influenced the jurors as well as ill-founded rumours spread by disreputable people that the priests had "immoral relations" with Eskimo women. The sexual issue was not raised at the trial. Bishop Breynat later maintained that, if anything, the abstinence of the priests may have upset their hosts who made it a practice of offering their wives to guests. Diamond Jenness, however, found no direct evidence of this "custom" among the Copper Eskimos.

the company of their Anglican friend Ilavinik, who was later rewarded for his service, on the recommendation of the Commissioner of the NWMP, with a gold watch and chain.

Notes

A full account of the search and capture of Sinnisak and Uluksak can be found in Dominion of Canada, *Sessional Papers*, Volume LII, 1917, No. 28. Report of the Royal North West Mounted Police, Appendix 0, 1916, which contains a series of reports by Inspector C. D. La Nauze, Corporal H. V. Bruce, Constable J. E. F. Wight and Constable D. Withers. Included in La Nauze's reports are sworn statements from the Eskimos Hupo, Uluksak Mayuk, Koeha, Sinnisak and Uluksak. In "A Police Patrol in the Northwest Territories of Canada," *The Geographical Journal*, Volume LI, No. 5, May, 1918, La Nauze describes the highlights of his trip north. Descriptions of the life and history of the Copper Eskimos are contained in Vilhjalmur Stefansson, *My Life With the Eskimo*, MacMillan, New York, 1951 and Diamond Jenness, "The Life of the Copper Eskimos," *Report of the Canadian Arctic Expedition 1913-18*, volume XII, Ottawa Kings Printer, 1922. Fathers Rouvière and Le Roux's lives and activities among the Eskimos are discussed in George Whalley, *The Legend of John Hornby*, MacMillan, Toronto, 1962; "Coppermine Martyrdom," an article by the same author in *Queen's Quarterly*, vol. LXVI, Winter, 1960, No. 4; and G. M. Douglas, *Lands Forlorn*, S. P. Putnam, New York, 1914. Accounts of the Calgary and Edmonton trials, in August 1917, can be found in the *Calgary Herald,* and *Edmonton Evening Bulletin.*

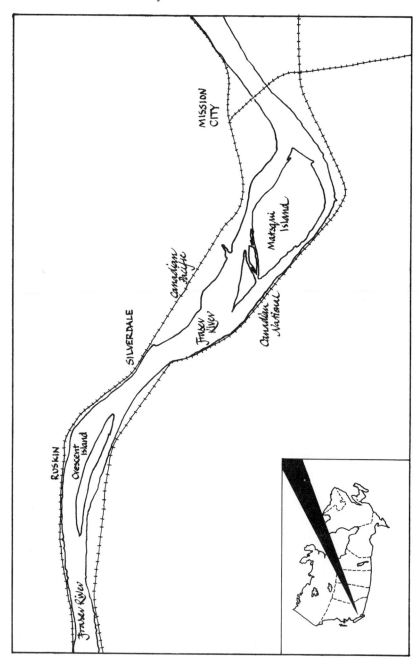

The Trainman

He was born in Bowling Green, near the Bluegrass country and buried in Georgia, under a magnolia tree. During half a century he marauded throughout the Southwest and Rocky Mountain States, robbed scores of stagecoaches and trains, and moulded in prisons from San Quentin to New Westminster. Among his nicest prey was Canada's national dream, the Canadian Pacific Railway Company, whose transcontinental train was halted and robbed in 1904 by a gang of hooded bandits as polite as they were efficient.

Bill Miner did not stay long in Bowling Green. Born around 1847, the son of a ranching father and schoolteacher mother, Miner left home at the age of sixteen and wandered west, working as a cowpuncher, bushwacker and, finally, as a mule driver in the Colorado mines. In 1863 Miner forsook these activities for the more dangerous vocation of express rider. When Brigadier-General George Wright, stationed in San Diego, offered a reward of $100 to anyone willing to deliver a message across hostile Apache country to a Colonel Corner, whose detachment was isolated in a fort on the Gila River, Miner volunteered. He rode all night, swam his horse across the Colorado River, ducked the Indians, dropped in at a ranch for a meal, delivered the note, mounted a fresh horse and returned home the next morning. Reward in hand, Miner went into business. He contracted to operate a pony express mail service and, at rates varying from $5 to $25 a letter, delivered mail throughout the region.

Miner soon found a more satisfying and lucrative vocation. The payoff as a postman was low, but among the fringe benefits was a ready familiarity with the routes and schedules of gold-laden stage coaches. So Miner turned his knowledge, and daring, to good account and abandoned express-riding for express-robbing. He did well enough in his new trade until April 1866 when he was sentenced to three years for a robbery committed in San Joaquim County.

Miner's San Quentin prison experience was edifying. He was dressed in a grey striped suit, shorn of half his hair, and employed, under convict overseers, in a jute mill. Prison conditions were an abomination. The convicts were crowded to the brink of suffocation, and sanitary and hospital facilities were non-existent. A variety of bestial methods – from thumb-stretching to bludgeoning with rubber truncheons, to forced standing for hours in a nine-inch circle painted on the floor, to the application of water through high pressure hoses to the prisoner's mouth and nose until the point of suffocation – were used to keep the convicts in line. But Miner was soon given a respite. Barely two months after incarceration, he was removed to Auburn, California where he was tried and convicted on a second count of grand larceny and his sentence increased to five years. He was then returned to his Spanish cell block in San Quentin, again shorn of his hair, refurbished in stripes, employed in jute and subjected to the old indignities. Only his number had changed. Whereas in April 1866 he entered the prison as number 3248, three months later he returned as number 3313.

Miner was back this time to stay, for four years and three months, until July 12, 1870 when he returned to his honoured vocation of highwayman. In the ensuing months he roamed Calaveros County, California, robbing and spending big, until his capture in June 1871 when he was sentenced to ten years for a robbery in San Andreas. The old process of committal and further trial was repeated. Admitted to San Quentin as number 4902 in June, he was hauled from the jail in February 1872, returned to San Andreas, tried and convicted for another robbery, rewarded with a twelve-year sentence, then returned to his customary resting place, where he was known as number 5206.

San Quentin had not changed during his absence and Miner did not find the place congenial. Two years after committal, he escaped, was recaptured several hours later, flogged publicly in the prison yard and committed to a dark cell in a dungeon, without light or ventilation, fitted with a windowless iron door and devoid of all furniture and amenities, except for a wooden bucket, which served as a toilet facility. Here Miner slept on a bare floor, fed on sour bread and tepid water, and occasionally choked at the lime fumes which the guards periodically employed to pacify the men. Released from the dungeon, Miner was hobbled with an Oregon boot, a heavy iron shackle attached to his right ankle to prevent escape. The shackle and other fortress devices sufficed and it was not until July 14, 1880, more than nine years after his committal, that the highwayman returned to the highways.

San Quentin, it appeared, had instilled, or reinforced, in Bill Miner an incapacity to perform routine labour in the usual, acceptable way. The dark prospects of further shackles, dungeons, and lime fumes, all issued under the majesty of the law by polite civil servants, did not deter him from returning to what he knew best. He took up his old vocation, under a new name, and in a new place. Calling himself William A. Morgan, he arrived in Denver, Colorado in November 1880 and formed a partnership with a Rocky Mountain adventurer named Billy Leroy – alias Arthur Pond – who, having robbed a stage in the San Luis Valley of $15,000, was tracked and arrested in Kansas City, then transported by train to Denver. Along the way, Leroy begged permission to relieve himself, visited the washroom, relieved his watch of the main spring, which he used to pick his handcuffs, and leaped from the moving train. Arriving in Denver, unattended and unshackled, he put his head together with Miner, known to the thieving fraternity as California Billy, and they soon departed on a prospecting tour to the southwestern part of Colorado.

Here the prospects were lucrative, especially along the line of the Del Norte stage which traced a treacherous route northward and up through the Rockies, from Del Norte, Colorado through Springcreek and Slum Gullion Passes to Salt Lake City. Miner and Leroy stationed themselves under cover along the way and robbed the coach of $3,600 in gold coin and dust, after due apology to the passengers for the short delay and a friendly warning to the driver to handle the difficult terrain with caution. But their own return proved more treacherous. A tough sheriff named Lou Armstrong, from Rio Grande County, assembled a gang of ferocious riders and pursued them so hotly that the pair went separate ways, Miner with the money in his saddlebag and Leroy with the posse in close chase. Dispossessed of both money and a riding companion, Leroy later recruited his brother, preyed again on the Del Norte stage, was chased, seized and jailed by Armstrong, and lynched by the good citizens of Del Norte whose rustic affirmation of the principles of law and order was preserved for posterity in two photographs, one showing the unfortunate Leroy hanging from a cottonwood tree, the other of the bandit sprawled dead against the prison wall.

Miner, in the meanwhile, decided to vacate Colorado for Chicago where he purchased a bale of fine clothes which were shipped in a pair of Saratoga trunks to Onandaga, Michigan, where the stage robber soon appeared in the guise of a Californian man of means. It was not hard for Bill Miner to pose as a gentleman. By the usual standards, he was a nice highwayman. He was of medium height and had a slender and trim figure. His face was warm and pleasant. He had warm and kindly blue eyes, a thin but large nose, and wore a nicely trimmed brown moustache and beard. Miner's manner was polite and he was loathe to use harsh methods when he went about his business. While he brandished guns, he rarely used them. His dislikes were directed more at companies than people.

Being a gentleman, William A. Morgan was well received by the residents of Onandaga. His attractive dress, easy manner, conspicuous spending and charming stories about elegant homes in Sacramento and San Francisco, rich gold mines in the Southwest, and an inherited personal fortune, were well received by the local burghers, especially the women, who entertained him in their salons. One local girl was so impressed she engaged to marry him. But Miner, his funds dwindling and feet aching, soon tired of the scene and began to talk of family obligations towards his mother who, in bad health, needed the resuscitation of an ocean voyage in the company of her son. So Bill Miner – alias William A. Morgan – bid the town of Onandaga and his betrothed a tearful goodbye and received return salutations of equal feeling at a large farewell banquet attended by the local dignitaries and presided over by the mayor, who spoke warmly of their distinguished visitor. From Onandaga, Miner returned to Denver where he adopted a new alias – William Anderson – traded in his finery for firearms, and joined fortunes with a troublemaker named Stanton T. Jones who robbed stages to and from his birthplace in Chillicothe, Ohio. Miner, Jones and a third man, James East, all in dire financial straits, headed for Del Norte where, at dusk, they held up a stage, bid the passengers a quiet "good night," and escaped with a few hundred dollars. The chase was conducted, with his usual determination, by Miner's old friend Sheriff Lou Armstrong of Rio Grande County, Colorado, who organized a posse and pursued the outlaws through Soguache, Marshall's Pass and finally Vila Grove, where they were captured after a pitched battle. But Miner was not yet prepared to face San Quentin. His prisoners tied together with heavy bailing wire and heaped in a buckboard wagon, Sheriff Brenagh, exhausted by the chase, camped overnight at Wagon Wheel Gap, twenty-five miles from Del Norte. While the sheriff slept and a guard dozed, Miner freed himself and Stanton, cashiered a pistol and, in one of his rare violent moments, succeeded in wounding the sheriff and both of his deputies in their arms, before escaping into the night.

Only East was recaptured. Miner and Stanton sped south to

Durango and Arizona, robbed awhile, then returned to California where they visited several mining camps in the company of a notorious horse thief named Jim Connor. Miner fell seriously ill with fever and chills at a place called Chinese Camp, but recovered quickly enough to attend a country ball on November 6, 1881 at Angel's Camp, a place made famous by Bret Harte in his "The Spelling School at Angel's." As usual, Miner danced until the late hours and charmed the women. He closed the evening with a fateful promise to a young girl to send along some sheet music from San Francisco, which he shortly intended to visit.

Anderson and friends did not head straight for San Francisco. They joined up with a former prison-mate of Miner's named James Crum, parked near Angel's Camp and when the Sonora stage approached on November 7, dispossessed it of $3,200 in gold coins and a sack of gold dust worth $500. Like Miner's earlier ventures, the robbery was brief, efficient and politely executed. It lasted a mere fifteen minutes and was concluded with the usual expression of regret at the unfortunate inconvenience.

Their resources replenished, the robbers sped five hectic days to San Francisco where Miner purchased a suit of clothes for $85, an overcoat for $50, a gold watch and chain, and some sheet music for his lady friend which he dispatched by mail. The arrival of the music was revealed to detective Aull of the Wells Fargo Express Company, who headed for San Francisco in pursuit of Miner. The chase continued to the ranch of Bill Miller at Woodland, a known resort for road agents, where Crum was apprehended and Miner and Miller pursued to the banks of the Sacramento River. After a bitter chase, Bill Miner was arrested without violence. On December 15, 1881 he was convicted of robbery and, six days later, began serving a twenty-five year sentence at San Quentin. His colleague Crum, who turned state's evidence, was given twelve years and released in three, after a pardon by Governor G. W. Irwin.

Miner was neither pardoned nor forgiven. Again, he endured the long strain of residency in a dank cell, the insolence of overseers, the rotting food, the absence of light and clean air, the drudgery of useless labour. An escape attempt in the early years failed and he lost four years and three months credit for good behaviour. Near the end of the sentence, he almost lost his life when attacked and knifed by convict Bill Hicks. But Miner was sustained by an iron determination and a sturdy body and, almost twenty years after his conviction for the Angel's Camp holdup, on June 17, 1901, at the age of fifty-four years, he walked through the gates of San Quentin free, and determined, it seems, to return forthwith to his old ways.

The world, in the meanwhile, had changed and the stage coach, whose ways Miner knew like the back of his wrinkled hand, had given way completely to the railroad train which, since its first runs through the golden empire of the west in the 1870's, was plundered by a fraternity of notables: by the James Boys, by Butch Cassidy, Kid Curry and The Wild Bunch, by the Daltons who struck the Santa Fe, and by Chris Evans and John Sontag, railroad haters, who preyed on the Southern Pacific. It was a war of robbers against bandits. The railways, by purchasing legislators, fixing rates, controlling land sales, gouging ranchers and sweating labourers, robbed the people, while the outlaws, through sheer malice, love of gain, pursuit of adventure, or by a habitual incapacity to do anything else, plundered the trains. To fight the trains, the bandits had to re-tool, upgrade their skills. Robbing trains was a tougher business than halting coaches; the Southern Pacific was a tougher foe than Wells Fargo. But the robbers adapted nicely and evolved standardized means of relieving their giant adversaries of their valuable cargo. They studied routes, stops, terrain, engaged informants, and when the final hour arrived, completed the task with a brief and chilling execution. The trains' bulk did not cow the bandits. The valuables sought – the gold taken from the mines, the payroll coin shipped to camps and towns, the bullion consigned to banks, the fine jewellery destined for the milk-white bosoms of fine ladies – were always in the express and mail cars located behind the engine and its tender, which carried the fuel. The train was boarded at remote stops and the engine reached by climbing over the tender into the cab where the engineers were persuaded at gun-point to disengage the express and mail cars and run them up the tracks, a safe distance from the passenger cars. The express cars were then entered through the application of dynamite or threat of it, and the guards inside, reluctant to risk their lives in a shoot-out, enlisted in a search for the valuables, or as aids in entering the safes, which were usually blasted open.

However brave and ingenious their labours, the bandits fought a rear-guard battle. The hazards and risks facing them multiplied as the railways buttressed their defences. Pinkertons were enlisted, guards doubled and baggage cars equipped with ramps, stalls and fast horses. Locomotives were readied on sidings at strategic places to transport posses. The photograph, telegraph and other new communications equipment aided in the pursuit. The railways consolidated, the economy surged, the telegraphs bleeped their frantic message and, one by one, gang by gang, the outlaws fell by the wayside. By the century's turn, when William Miner, alone and foot-sore, shuffled back into civil society, the bulk of the train-fighting folk heroes – The Jameses, The Daltons, Evans and Sontag, Bill Doolin and Black Barte – had been banished forever.

Their demise, however, was no deterrent to Miner who, having preyed on modest stages in the old days, prepared himself to take on the hulking engine. But he first took a sedentary respite and wandered north to Washington where he worked as a superintendent of an oyster bed planted in Samish Bay at the foot of Chukanut Mountain at Puget Sound. "From visitors who went up there to look at this development when the tide was out," a station agent at the Bow whistle stop reminisced, "we heard comments of his courteous manners, especially to the ladies when on hot summer days he would hand them an umbrella for shade. His name was Bill Miner. Occasionally, he walked down the tracks to Bow, returning on the evening train . . ." Miner, it appeared, did not devote his full attention to ladies and oysters. In his spare moments, he reconnoitered the Great Northern Railroad whose new line, along the waterfront from Bellingham to Burlington, passed his oyster bed. What he saw impressed him, and he soon recruited a willing gang of drifters and adventurers including Jimmy James, a distant cousin of Jessie; a mill worker, Harshman; and a seventeen-year-old orphan, Charles Hoehn, who had arrived at the age of twelve in Whatcom, Washington, where he lived with friends in a commune called the Equality Colony.

The operation was conducted at Troutdale, a few miles east of Portland, Oregon on September 23, 1903 when Miner and a spare, short colleague named Williams boarded train No. 6 of the Great Northern Railroad, climbed from the blind-baggage car over the tender and into the engine, where they presented themselves, revolvers in hand, to engineer Ollie L. Barrett and his fireman H. F. Stevenson. It was Miner's first train venture and the several blunders which followed indicated that the aging robber, who rusted in prison while his colleagues perfected the tricks of the trade, did not find the transition from Wells Fargo to the Great Northern terribly easy. Miner began by politely assuring the engineer that no harm would befall him if he kept still and obeyed orders. He then ordered Barrett to run the train down the track to Twenty-one Mile Post, where two other masked men, including seventeen-year-old Charles Hoehn, appeared from out of the bushes on the train's right side carrying two long willow poles at the ends of which were sticks of dynamite. The poles were handed to the engineer and firemen who were told to go back to the express car, order the messenger to open the door and, in the event of his refusal, to blow it open with the dynamite. While the bandits randomly fired a volley of shots by the train windows, as a warning to the passengers to keep their heads inside, the engineer moved past the express car to the baggage car – which was of little use to the bandits – and asked that it be opened. There being no response, the bandits seized the dynamite poles, lit the fuses, placed the sticks against the door and repaired with the engineer and fireman to the engine, where all watched as the car door blew open. Miner then ordered the engineer to lead the party back to the car. But Barrett ignored the order and fell in behind the bandit Williams who was twenty feet from the express car when a guard's bullet rang out from the dark, mortally wounding Williams and lodging in the left shoulder of Barrett. Miner momentarily examined the body of his dead colleague before sending Barrett and Stevenson back to the engine, and disappearing into the bushes with Hoehn.

It was a sloppy operation, badly executed, tainted with violence, which Miner abhorred, and consummated by a fierce police chase, ending sadly for Charles Hoehn who was caught and jailed for ten years, and Guy Harshman, apprehended at a Whatcom lumber mill and imprisoned for twelve. The rest escaped. James and a man called Underwood fled safely to Mexico, while the main object of the police search, a slender man with sad blue eyes who called himself William Morgan, drifted east to Bay City, Michigan, then south to Texas and Mexico, and finally, north again across the Washington border, to British Columbia and Canada.

Miner's arrival at the fount of law and order sometime in the year 1904, was unheralded and unknown. He was, after all, a tired and wanted robber and the Nicola Valley around Princeton was a quiet place where ranchers, miners, and retired outlaws could subsist unobtrusively. Assuming the name George Edwards, he prospected a bit, raised a few cattle, which he once drove through the mountains to Chilliwack, and generally endeared himself to the local people. He was known for his fondness of children, kindness to widows, generosity to orphans and occasional religiosity. When local churchgoers found themselves short a preacher one Sunday morning, old George Edwards volunteered and performed admirably. Children were bounced on his knee, showered with gifts and fed wonderful stories about adventures in distant lands. His worn old pistol and sad roan horse were local favourites. The women, it seems, adored his slender figure and easy manner and, Oregon boot notwithstanding, he danced long and well at local dances where, for some reason, he sometimes stationed himself near the door, as if in readiness to leave early. It is said that Edwards supplied widows in need with income supplements and when one was threatened with foreclosure for non-payment of a mortgage, he delivered to her in person the needed sum, which he subsequently forceably repossessed outside the widow's cottage from the unhappy collector.

Edward's exemplary behaviour fitted. Canada, our historians tell us, has always been a well-ordered state where good men found rest and security in a polite society built on the principle of mutual tolerance. Bad men were bred mainly in the lawless south where they waylaid stages, devoured trains and suffered ignominious deaths by lynching. The differences were maybe racial, or perhaps climatic. The humid air of the enervating south bred anarchy. In the frozen north ozone abounded, nurturing the flames of liberty and justice. There were, in addition, several bracing institutions which formed potent guarantors of order: the British parliamentary system, built on an inherent British respect for law and order; and the North West Mounted Police Force who, in addition to defending life, secured property. The trains in Canada, a well-ordered state, ran on time, especially the Canadian Pacific Railway Company, which, in addition to possessing an empire, enjoyed a substantial freedom from both government regulation and robber depredation.

Until September 13, 1904, that is. In the mid-evening of that day, during a brief watering stop at Mission, British Columbia, the blind-baggage car of the westbound C.P.R. Transcontinental No. 1 was quietly boarded in a thick, heavy fog by three masked men. One was slightly built, about thirty years old, with round shoulders and black hair. He wore blue overalls with spring buttons, brandished a 30/30 rifle, and carried himself nervously. The second man was younger, with square shoulders and a round face. He was clean-shaven, had a fair complexion, nervously sported a rifle and, like the first, was dressed in old blue overalls. The third man, who cooly directed the operation, moving with precision and confidence was older, perhaps fifty years of age. He had blue eyes and grey hair, was slenderly built and stood about five feet nine inches high. His hands were burnt a deep red and heavily calloused and wrinkled. The middle knuckle of his left hand was noticeably enlarged. The older man spoke deliberately in a quiet, almost effeminate voice and carried himself with the weary certitude of an experienced trainman.

The blind-baggage car was not the destination of the night intruders. As the train lurched into a start and lumbered towards Mission, they crawled over the baggage, mail and express cars where the older man, who did all the talking, stuck a revolver into the ribs of engineer Nat Scott, asked him to stop the train and warned him to obey at the risk of death. Annoyed at the silly intrusion, Scott muttered, "Get out," briefly considered pulling the coarse black mask from the robber's face and, finally, gleaning that his guests meant business, asked them whether he was "joking." The reply was a simple "No, I'm not joking," and its effect was underlined by the sight of the intruder's weapon, as well as the glistening gun barrels of the two younger men, who nervously held fireman Freeman under arrest.

Henceforth, the operation moved briskly. At the old man's direction, Scott moved the train a mile or two further to Silverdale where it was halted over a small bridge. The engineer was then held at gunpoint while the old man, his young assistant and the fireman quit the cab and walked along the track past the express, mail, baggage and two blind-baggage cars to the point at the end of the bridge, where the line of passenger cars began. An inquisitive conductor, who wandered into their company, was, with the utterance of a threat and wave of a rifle, ordered back into his car. At the juncture of the passenger and baggage car, the fireman was ordered to uncouple the train and the engineer, still under cab arrest, was ordered by signal to move the engine ahead twenty-five yards, to prevent an accidental recoupling.

The first stage cleanly executed, the two bandits and firemen returned to the cab. Relieving his younger colleague of guard duty, the old man ordered the engineer to drive on for another mile to Ruskin Siding, where the shortened train was halted again. This time the entire crew, robbers and trainmen, stepped down and walked back to the express car where the engineer, following the old man's instructions, tapped at the door and demanded entry. After a brief pause, the guard slid open the door, jumped from the car, surrendered his gun and returned to his car in the company of the old man. Waving a bag of dynamite, Miner asked the messenger to open a pair of safes. The messenger complained he did not know how to open the big one but he did open the small box which yielded $4,000 in gold dust, en route from Ashcroft to the Seattle assay office, and a further $2,000 in gold dust consigned to the Bank of British North America in Victoria. A valise containing $1,000 in bills was also taken. After questioning the messenger about a Victoria package, Miner leaped from the car and joined his colleagues below on a further visit to the mail car. Here the mail clerks threw open their doors and delivered up several bags of registered mail to the bandits. Miner then shooed the mail clerks back to their cars, suggested they go to bed, laughed gently when the engineer – whose oil torch was dying for lack of fuel – urged him to hurry up the operation, and directed the group's return to the engine. The fireman was ordered to uncouple the engine and his shovel disposed of in the bushes, in order to impede refueling. The cab was re-entered and the engineeer ordered to proceed, at full speed, about two miles to a creek a mile east of Whonnock and halt the train in front of the church. The robbers disembarked in the full glare of the engine's electric light. The old man said good night as he scrambled out of the cab. "Good night," answered the engineer, "I hope you have a pleasant journey." "We hope so," answered Miner, who by now had reached the edge of the siding. "You fellows have your nerve with you," the engineer ventured. From the rocks and trees below the siding, in the dark of the night, came the parting reply: "Yes, and we have something else."

Booty in hand, the robbers made for the river, commandeered a boat, crossed the Fraser and proceeded south by foot through a field of rocks, puddles and mud-holes for eight miles, until their trail was lost. When the news of the hold-up reached Mission and was relayed to Vancouver, a huge pursuit was organized. The provincial police around Mission, Abbotsford and Langley were alerted and organized into search parties. The C.P.R. search operation was directed by the National Superintendent of the corporation's special police division, Mr. George Burns, who was rudely interrupted, chopsticks in hand, in the middle of a Chinese banquet. The city police, headed by Chief of Police Sam North, who fested with Burns at the same luncheon, joined the search. And below the border, at Bellingham, Ferndale and Sumas, the Pinkertons, who knew the habits and haunts of William Miner, the very creases on the back of his red hands, the shape of the dancing girl tattooed on his left arm, the size of the heart pierced by an arrow on his right, the engraving in india ink at the base of his thumb, joined the chase.

The press beat the editorial drums and the authorities waved rewards. "The facts have created a genuine sensation," the *Colonist* declared. "It seems hardly possible that the men, with a large booty secured will be able to get clear away . . . It is not likely that the incident will be repeated on the Canadian side of the line. It is a fortunate circumstance that such incidents are and always have been, rare in this country, and when crimes of the kind are committed neither time nor money is spared to bring the offenders to justice. The fear of the law effectively administered has throughout these long years accounted for the immunity we usually enjoy from such outrages."

The C.P.R. initially offered $1,000 to anyone supplying information leading to arrest and conviction. A further $6,000 was advertised jointly by the C.P.R. and Dominion Express Company, with a proportionate amount for the jailing of the gang's individual members. Finally the British Columbia Provincial Government offered a reward of $1,500 for the lot.

Parties of provincial constables, supplemented by local volunteers, slogged day and night through the mud and rocks along the roads and trails in the vicinity of Whonnock. The men endured incessant rain, and sleepless nights in the cold under a tarpaulin ordinarily used to cover shingles in a local mill. On the American side, the Pinkertons scoured the country around Ferndale and Lynden checking abandoned cabins, logging camps and numerous side trails. Rumours of capture, of imminent arrest, of the identity and venue of the culprits appeared daily in the press. But as the days drifted by, the posse's energies and numbers diminished, and the press news thinned to a trickle. Within a week, the authorities were prepared to admit that the man with the red hands and quiet voice, and his two companions, had cleanly escaped.

The search was directed south but Miner, in the guise of Edwards, headed east to Chilliwack where he briefly lingered in a small deserted cabin. From Chilliwack he moved to Vancouver, then to Spokane, Washington and, finally, back across the border to the town of Hedley, which subsisted on the diggings of the nickle-plate mines. In the company of a young man and woman, he dressed elegantly and spent lavishly, though not as much as his friend, who was said to have dropped at games of black jack in the hotels, $250 a night during four consecutive sittings. The group soon split up and Miner lived briefly at a large ranch outside of Princeton owned by a short, red-haired American named Jack Budd. Here he leisurely smoked his worn old pipe, filled with something called "Black Strap" tobacco, swallowed opium pills, which he liked to call "poppy root" and otherwise continued his exemplary civic and social life. He dabbled in cattle, which he drove around some property known as Aspen Grove, hinted of a mine in Argentina and talked mining with mining men and cattle with cattlemen. He was even prone, on occasion, to discourse on socialist political economy. "I wish I had control of the air," he once complained, "I would dole it out to the rich and make them pay heavily for it too; but I'd let the poor have as much as they wanted." As usual, he was a great friend and favourite of the children. On one occasion, he spent two full days clearing and flooding a spot in a field for use as a skating rink.

He appeared at dances in Princeton, Hedley, Keremeos and Olalla, lavishly dressed in cut-away tails and adorned with diamond cuff links and a fine tiepin. When he danced with the local ladies, he invariably grasped a handkerchief to avoid touching his partner's dress. Sometimes he departed on mysterious prospecting tours. During a brief absence in November 1905, his Similkameen neighbours read in their paper of the hold-up of a Great Northern train outside Seattle, which yielded three masked men a sum of $30,000.

If Miner had taken this sum – a view held, though never proved, by P. K. Ahern, head of Pinkerton's Seattle office – then he plainly felt that his share of the booty was not enough to sustain him over the harsh Canadian winter. Six months later, in early May 1906, he departed north on another prospecting tour with several bay pack horses, his own roan and two straggling companions. The first, known as "Shorty" Thomas Dunn, was a snub-nosed, volatile part-Indian from Montana who, after several brushes with the law, sought refuge in the north where he trapped, mined and ranched around the Nicola Valley. He met Miner while a sawmill employee around Armstrong. Miner's second companion was a quieter sort. The youngest son of a substantial Ontario farmer, Lewis Colquon was a good student who finished high school, developed an accounting competence, drifted west, taught school briefly, lounged in jail at Walla Walla for two years on some charge unknown, and settled in Phoenix, British Columbia. A weak, irresolute man, with small, watery eyes, a lean nose and red moustache, Colquon quickly fell under Miner's persuasive influence and joined a prospecting expedition designed to lead either to an easeful world of glittering wealth or the gloomy torpor of prison.

The trio wandered north to the vicinity of Kamloops where they loaded their horses with supplies, including milk for the old man's ulcerated stomach and a stock of catarrh pills. They pitched camp in a secluded grove at a point five miles from where Campbell Creek emptied into the South Thompson River. To the local storekeepers, it appeared they were preparing for a lengthy prospecting expedition – which began on a warm, starlit evening at 11:30 p.m. when the coal-bearing tender behind the engine of the westbound C.P.R. Transcontinental Express No. 97 was quietly boarded by three masked men during a brief stop at Ducks Station, about eighteen miles east of Kamloops. The train had barely gone five miles, to the midway point between the Ducks and Furrer Stations, when engineer Callen's vision was suddenly obscured by the sight of a snub-nosed revolver. The man carrying the weapon was over fifty years of age, with blue eyes, high cheek bones, and a heavy greying moustache. Half of his tanned, weatherbeaten face was hidden by a black handkerchief and his slim body was wrapped in a heavy dark overcoat. He wore a pair of automobile goggles. The engineer, like his Silverdale predecessor, at first sensed a prank and asked, "What the mischief are you doing there?" The reply was straightforward: "This is no joke; we are going to rob this train." The operation proceeded smoothly. The train was halted and the robbers disembarked together with the engine crew who uncoupled the engine, tender and mail-express car from the rest of the train. When conductor Sam Elliott stuck his head out of the window of one of the passenger cars and shouted, "What's the matter? Has a hose burst out there?" he was informed of the true state of affairs: "This is not a hose-bust , but a hold-up. Get your head in or I will blow it off." None of the passengers, including several clergyman delegates to a Methodist Conference in Victoria, showed a similar curious inclination. "I was sound asleep," said Rev. J. S. Woodsworth of Winnipeg, Superintendent of Methodist Missions, "so I couldn't know very much about it, could I?"

While the passengers dozed, the men in front reboarded the engine and moved the few cars ahead a further mile and a half. Again the engine crew stepped down and the engineer was instructed to order the mail and express car attendants, Willis and McQuarrie, to open the door. They complied and Willis was ordered down while Miner joined McQuarrie in the car where he interrogated the clerk about San Francisco-bound mails and the contents of several red-striped pouches which usually carried American Express mail. Five large sacks were emptied and searched, and several letters, bound for Victoria, were picked out. McQuarrie was then ordered from the car and Willis brought in for a similar interrogation. But the results were no better. A large, red-striped bag at the car's end yielded only a pile of old mail bags. When Miner asked about the express safe, he was informed of its location in the second express car, attached to the passenger and baggage train down the line. Realizing his blunder, the old robber cursed, stood irresolute for a moment, then grew cheerful and resigned. With his paltry few letters in hand, carrying a total sum of $15 in cash, he jumped from the car, leaving untouched a case bristling with mail and carrying hard cash to the value of $35,000. In the express car behind was a cache of bullion worth an equal amount.

Only the escape mattered now. The engine was uncoupled and the robbers joined the crew for another short excursion down the track, to a dark tree-lined junction where the engine, as if exasperated, wheezed and puffed to a halt. Outside, a few yards down an embankment, waiting horses whinnied and stomped as the train approached. The robbers dropped from the car and made for the horses. The old man's final words on departure were friendly, as usual. "Well, so long, young fellow," he told the engineer, "take care of yourself."

Engineer Callen had no problem taking care. He made straight for the mail car, recoupled, backed up further to the stranded passenger cars, engaged again, then sped to Kamloops where the authorities were alerted and transported, by the same engineer, to the crime's scene. What followed was a pitiless, unremitting pursuit which gave the old man the run of his life. Rewards were immediately posted. The C.P.R. offered $5,000 for the capture of the men, dead or alive, or $1,500 per person. The Dominion government matched the C.P.R. while the province threw in an added $1,500. Company police and provincial constables from Kamloops and the lower mainland descended on the scene in droves and began beating the bushes. A C.P.R. light locomotive was lent full-time to transport posses and supplies. Ranchers and cowboys in the area between Kamloops and Douglas Lake in the Nicola Valley were sworn in as special constables. For trackers, the authorities relied on the usual staples: Indians and bloodhounds. Local Siwash trackers who knew every trail in the Kamloops district were enlisted. Bloodhounds in the care of provincial constables were shipped in from Calgary via Nelson while from Spokane, a crack team of dogs who had just finished pursuing the Salem, Oregon prison-escapee Frank Smith to his death – in a hail of gunfire at New Era – were shipped in at the peak of the hunt. A C.P.R. train from Calgary disgorged a contingent of seventeen NWMP constables who mounted local horses and headed for Chapperon Lake. And from Seattle, there arrived several Thiell detectives who carried with them carefully drawn files on the wayward activities and identification of a wizened robber known as William Miner.

The pursuit was treacherous, across swamps, abandoned Indian trails, and myriad thickets, ranges and dense woods. It followed south, from the locale of the robbery, through Campbell Meadows past sprawling ranches to the Douglas Lake area, where the scent grew hot. The trackers and dogs rarely lost sight of the marks of the hobnailed mining boots of Dunn and Colquon, or of the lighter, smooth imprint left by the old man whose feet, sore from decades of chase and prison toil, required a soft underlay. Along the way, the trackers came upon abandoned camps, strewn with old pots and pans, picks and shovels, and emptied bottles of catarrh cure. They found obscure cabins where the robbers rested and hid from the rain and stray horses abandoned near a thickly timbered cul-de-sac from which escape seemed impossible. Among the most dogged of the pursuers was provincial constable W. L. Fernie, a former rancher in the North Thompson area who had joined the provincial police force after serving with the Strathcona Regiment in the Boer War. After weeks of tracking in the company of Indians, Fernie had just called in at a local ranch two miles from Douglas Lake, when he suddenly came upon three men trudging slowly through an open range. The eldest of the trio, heavily moustached, hailed him and asked the way to Quilchena. Fernie replied and asked, as a return favour, the road to Chapperon Lake, which was easily volunteered. He then inquired further where they had come from. "Oh, we're prospectors," replied the old man, "We've been to Grand Prairie." The genial interchange continued for awhile until Fernie departed, in good humour. He checked the men's boot marks to confirm they corresponded with those he had been following on the trail, cashiered a horse, and rode madly towards Chapperon Lake where the mounted police squadron had just arrived from Kamloops.

The mounties wasted no time. They sped with Fernie to the designated spot, and located the tracks, which were soon lost. The mounties, it seems, never get their man, except with the aid of an Indian tracker. So one was brought in, and the hobnailed boot marks were located and followed. While Fernie rode to Douglas Lake, in search of bloodhounds, a mounted police party followed the tracks along a wagon road. They soon came upon a party of three men, huddled around a fire giving off a thin curl of smoke, and enjoying a snack of tea and boiled rice. "Well, boys, what are you doing here?" Corporal Stewart asked. "We're doing some prospecting," the old man replied. When the corporal inquired after the place of their prospecting, the old man answered, with a smile, "Oh, over there." The sergeant grew serious: "Well, we are looking for the fellows who held up the C.P.R. and you had better give an account of yourselves." This seemed to hurt the feelings of the old man who scoffed at the suggestion that he and his companions bore a likeness to train robbers, volunteering instead the view that they looked more like prospectors. The matter came to a quick resolution. When the officer ordered the men to come along, Dunn leaped up and ran for the bushes screaming, "It's all up, boys, we might as well fight." A gun duel between the police and Dunn, who fired from behind a wall of underbrush, ensued, ending with a bullet in Dunn's thigh and his surrender. Miner and Colquon offered no resistance. A wagon with horses was dispatched to Douglas Lake and the bound robbers returned to Quilchena where they remained overnight. The next morning, after a Seattle detective posing as a Kamloops lawyer had conducted an interview with Miner and Colquon, the police and their prizes departed for the excited town of Kamloops.

Their arrival was foreknown and a thousand local residents gathered in the rain to observe the cavalcade slowly descending the mountain road behind the town. In front of and beside the wagon rode nine yellow-clad mounted police constables while inside, huddled under a blanket, the prisoners gazed laconically ahead. The men were swiftly processed at the local jail. Colquon remained stunned, quiet, courteous and spoke in monosyllables during interrogation. The unhappy Dunn, writhing now and then with pain, was excitable and troublesome. When the officials inquired about his nationality, he pleaded ignorance, and when they sought his residency, he answered, "Anywhere, anywhere." The old man remained cool and nonchalant. "He is rather a striking-looking fellow," wrote a *Province* reporter, "with grizzled hair and moustache, erect and active, and does not appear to bear within ten years of the weight of age which the prison records now credit him with. He claims to be sixty-two, looks like a man of fifty, and moves like one of thirty." The old man replied briefly and hestitatingly to all questions addressed to him, carefully weighing the effect of his answers. When asked whether or not he was truly Bill Miner, he volunteered, in the King's English, "I can't be seeing that I never heard of the man."

This was the old man's position throughout the trial, which dragged on for several weeks. The press was convinced of Edward's true identity and filled the front pages with vivid tales of Bill Miner's exploits below the border. The editorialists, anxious to lend a proper perspective to the front page screamers, and nip in the bud any sympathetic feeling among the public for the robbers, expatiated on the gravity of the crime of train robbery and the need for firm, unflinching punishment.[1]

The writers protested but the local people, center-stage in a late version of a genuine wild west drama, felt for the plight of the old man, marvelled at his courage and ability to dissemble, and expressed an intense curiosity over the trial's outcome. The people, through historical accident, had fallen host to a noble robber who had lived among them as a model citizen. Old timers, fussy ladies, gossips, ranchers and prospectors, people in slippers, fine leathers and hobnailed boots, chortled and reminisced about their genial neighbour, now revealed as a multinational outlaw. The world, it seems, had decided that George Edwards was Bill Miner, and confirmation was ensured when Warden Kelly of San Quentin Penitentiary, who had had a good opportunity to familiarize himself with the outlaw, arrived in Kamloops and, after a brief meeting in which he probed the outlaw's mind and body, confirmed his identity. Kelly shook Edward's hand the evening of his arrival from California. "I'll shake hands with you alright," the old man said, "but I don't know you."

It seemed that the only man in town insisting upon the confusion between the gentleman and the robber was the aged criminal himself. The rest of Kamloops truly believed they had in their midst a genuine, big-league, desperado and they attended the preliminary hearing, the extended trial and the shorter second trial, in droves. The heat of the dry Caribou summer invaded the small courtroom. Sweating witnesses droned on. The jurors fought fatigue, suffocation and boredom. The judge and crown

---

1 "In a country like British Columbia," the *Province* editorialized, "the opportunities for the successful commission of such crimes is so much greater than in open and unwooded districts that they must be suppressed with utmost rigour and even the most daring and unscrupulous taught that this is one of the offences on which leniency will not look anymore than it will plead for the horse-thief on the plains or the sluice box robber in the mining camp. In the pursuit and capture of the mail robber, there are no means that are not justifiable. The crime is a most detestable one, as its consequences may be most widespread and disasterous. It strikes alike at every class of society, at the poor as well as the rich, at the merchant and at the labourer, at the corporation and at the individual. In the actual commission of the crime, there is nothing romantic or heroic. To climb in the darkness of the night on the buffers between cars and, at an opportune time, to crawl over the tender of an engine and hold pistols to the head of the driver and his fireman, does not require much courage. Any tramp can do the same. It has no savour of the lone highwayman of the old days holding up, in open day, the stage filled with passengers and in the care of an armed guard. The modern train robbery is a sordid and base crime calculated to cause much misery and distress and it should be stamped out with ruthless severity."

counsel, which included the province's Attorney General and his deputy MacLean, imbibed quarts of ice water and, between bouts of interrogation, gazed wistfully out of the courtroom windows towards the cool prospect of the North Thompson River. Lewis Colquon remained quiet and troubled throughout. Shorty Dunn giggled and laughed hysterically, then sat dejectedly, head in hands, for long unbroken intervals. During a noon-hour recess of the second trial, he broke down and complained so bitterly about the prospective ills of confinement that a doctor was summoned to minister to the hysterical accused. The old man, more worn and haggard than at the hour of his committal, often leaned back expressionless in the prisoners box, his long, thin fingers drumming on the front ledge. When an important point came up, he straightened up, glanced fiercely at counsel and sternly surveyed the faces of the jury men. Miner took his trial cooly and seriously. He knew, after all, that what remained of his cruel and frantic life was entirely at stake.

The first trial lasted three days and the prosecution presented a tight case. Mounties, Indian trackers, constables, special constables and volunteers told and retold their story of the chase and capture. The trainmen – engineers, firemen and mail clerks – recounted the minutae of the holdup and their conviction that the goggled old man who led the operation was George Edwards, who really was Bill Miner. But the first jury, or at least one member of that body remained unconvinced and, after an entire night's deliberation, the foreman announced, in the mid-morning of May 31, that there was no hope of the twelve men coming to an agreement as to the guilt of the suspects. It was rumoured that eleven jurymen pressed for conviction but the twelfth, Foreman Morrill himself, who often expressed the opinion that no poor man should be sent to prison, held out for acquittal.

The prosecution did not share Morrill's views. Justice P. A. E. Irving discharged the jury and ordered a re-trial where the earlier evidence was resubmitted in bulk. There was no hope this time for the fatigued suspects, represented by a fatigued counsel, arguing their case before a fatigued judge. The trial moved quickly, before a packed, sweating courtroom filled with a large contingent of attentive women. The decision was a foregone conclusion.

In the morning of Saturday, June 1, after a half hour deliberation, the jury entered a verdict of guilty and Justice Irving, who
expressed his agreement with the decision, sentenced Lewis
Colquon to twenty-five years and Shorty Dunn and George
Edwards to life imprisonment. The old man, like his colleagues,
reacted to the verdict without emotion or comment. The prisoners
were handcuffed and driven in a rig before scattered crowds of
onlookers, from the courthouse to the jail. The next morning they
were shackled, rewarded for their good behaviour with several
cigars, and afforded a brief opportunity to part amiably with
their jailers and admirers. The old man left in good humour,
shaking hands with a Mr. and Mrs. Duck – who testified for the
prosecution – and assuring them that he bore no ill-will. "I'll call
and see you if I ever get the chance," he closed, before joining his
friends in a ride to the railway station. Along the route to New
Westminster – at Westminster junction, Mission and Saperton –
large crowds gathered and waited to glimpse the shackled outlaws. At Mission, a voice in the crowd shouted to Miner: "Hello
Bill, here you are again," which prompted the old man to com-
plain to one of his guards, "At Kamloops I was called Mr.
Edwards, but down here even the dogs seem to take me for Bill
Miner."

It seems that the prison authorities and convict population also
took the old man for Bill Miner, and treated him accordingly.
Among branch-plant criminals, he was the revered elder states-
man whose illustrious career spanned the entire west for over half
a century. There was no man in the New Westminster penitentiary who knew so well the folkways of prison life and, evidently,
the variety of ways of getting there. To the authorities, Miner
became "old Bill," a wizened outlaw, leather-skinned, with deli-
cate feet and a gentle soul, doing a final penance under their
paternal custody. The prison authorities, apprized of the old
man's apparent decrepitude, his toothlessness, chronic eczema
and aching feet, did not see him as a high risk escape possibility.
Some were even convinced that, after a half century of demoniac
outlawry, he stood on the brink of reformation and was preparing
to give himself, tattoos and all, to Christ. Deputy Warden D. D.
Bourke's daughter, a pretty, Christian lady who dedicated her life

to the hard task of making badmen good, took a special interest in reforming the old man who, after a year in jail, had become, in her eyes, a model prisoner. Miss Bourke brought Miner religious works, which he perused with obvious sympathy, chatted with him about eternals, and concluded that the notorious robber was rapidly overcoming his ugly inclinations to confound the law, and God's will. "Why only last week," she remarked in early August 1907, "Bill said he was resigned to his fate and was satisfied, did not care to get away, and would do everything to merit a happier home in the other world." Deputy Warden Bourke, who ran the prison during the absence, due to illness, of Warden J. C. Whyte, shared his daughter's view. When the old man induced a condition of eczema by rubbing dirt in several wounds in his head, Bourke gave him a special dispensation to grow his hair and moustache long, in contravention of prison regulations. And when Miner complained of trouble with his sore feet while employed in the shoe shop, and asked to be relocated in the open air, the warden responded by moving him to the brick yard.

Miner was pleased with his new locale which afforded him a ready entry into Miss Bourke's other world. In the late afternoon of Thursday, August 8, the old man was employed shuttling bricks between the yard and a large drying kiln which stood directly below the lookout house on the west wall of the prison yard. On duty in the towerhouse above was guard Alex McNeill, armed with several rifles. His location immediately above the drying kiln obstructed the view below. With McNeill inside, Miner proceeded to dig and smash his way under the board fence adjoining the kiln. The old man did not work alone. Taking turns with him were three younger men: J. W. Clark, a twenty-one-year-old Nanaimo forger and labourer; Albert F. McLuskey, a twenty-nine-year-old burglar and labourer; and Walter John Woods, a young Victorian sentenced in December 1906 to three years for stealing. The operation proceeded quickly, in full view of several other prisoners, including Shorty Dunn, who remained silent. In a few minutes, the men were in the yard outside the fence where, using a hatchet, they freed a bolted ladder and escaped over the prison wall.

It was all very simple and, for the officials involved, terribly embarrassing. When prison officials rushed to the home of Warden Whyte and told him of the escape, the ailing official burst into tears, rose in his bed, palpitated, and was finally calmed with the aid of a physician who rushed to his side. Deputy Warden Bourke was soon very busy. He wired Ottawa, muttered something about outside help to the escaped prisoners, suspended guard McNeill, and informed reporters that the old man's bad feet and decrepitude would ensure his easy capture – within twenty-four hours or, failing that, his suicide. The warden's daughter took the escape to heart. "Bill complained of trouble with his feet while he worked in the shoe shop," she bleated to a reporter, "and he asked to be given some occupation in the outer air. It was then that papa decided to place him in the brick yard. This was ten days ago and Bill said he was happy. We all felt sorry for Bill when we realized he had to spend all of his life in prison and we took much interest in him. He pretended to become highly interested in religion and asked for religious works, and he had been so good lately that he was fast getting so that he could be regarded as an ideal prisoner. But my! It's different now . . . When he is brought back, he will have to demonstrate first that he is not shamming before I will do anything tending to make his life more pleasant. I think it was horrid of him to escape after we had done so much to make life easier for him."

There was, of course, a chase organized but it lacked the ardour of the search which led to the old man's capture. The prisoners, whose escape was first noted and reported by a boy swimming in a brook near the scaled wall, divided company a mile or so from the prison; the branch-plant robbers taking one route, and the old man another. The chase concentrated on Miner whose portrait and physique were accorded front page banner press treatment. "He carries a tattoo mark at the base of the thumb of his left hand," the *Province* revealed, "also a heart pierced with a dagger. A ballet girl is tattooed on his right forearm, also a star. Both wrist-joint bones are large. He has a mole in the centre of his breast, a mole under his left breast and another on his right shoulder. Another star is tattooed on the outside of the calf of his left leg. There is a discolouration on his left buttock, a scar on his left shin, a scar on his right leg at the knee on the inside, a mole on his left shoulder blade, two small scars on his neck, his face is spotted and Bill at some time in his life sat in the dentist's chair while he was equipped with a full set of false teeth.''

The chase led everywhere and nowhere. Ravines were crossed, creeks forded, thickets rifled, hills climbed by wandering teams of prison officers and police constables. A lone bloodhound was caressed, whispered to, pampered with fresh raw meat and then sent off to sniff the old man's trail. But the dog became confused, or developed indigestion, and lost the scent. Rumours flew as the days passed. An old man with sore feet was seen everywhere: at saloons in Vancouver where he drank and staggered away; in south Seattle where, dressed as a tramp, he lurked in dark alleys; near the Fraser River, where he posed as a Japanese fisherman; in Nicomen, east of Mission, where a footsore traveller presented himself at the door of Mr. George Deroche and availed himself of the host's hospitality by consuming a loaf of bread, three pounds of meat, five cups of coffee and a quart of strawberry preserves; at Ashcroft, where rancher Abel Stark put up a tramp in a barn and fed him bread, butter and apples; and, finally, in Winnipeg, Manitoba, where it was said the outlaw sauntered into a Main Street hotel and visited an old girlfriend.

Miner's ubiquity made good copy as did the marked public sympathy for the wanted robber. The editorial writers complained bitterly about the fifth column of bleeding hearts and soft heads which surfaced during the chase. They explored the motives of the sympathizers, concluding that what they lacked or suppressed in their inner selves, the outlaw possessed and displayed in abundance. "As men admire contrasts," one sermon concluded, "these foolish ones admire Miner. He is clever; they are conscious that they are not; he is possessed of a certain courage; they know they have not got it; he can conceive a plan and carry it through to completion; but these men know that they could not do such a thing to save their lives." The editorialists located a strain of anarchism among the local citizenry, a lack of respect for law and order which threatened the very foundations of civil society. "It is difficult at once to determine whether they are fittest for the lunatic asylum or the gaol," the harangue continued, "for towards one or the other of these resorts their aberrated brains appear to be tending. As a matter of fact, they are anarchists of a weak and watery sort, and probably their convictions on any subject are of a hazy and vacuous kind. They belong to that inert, half-baked section of the public that never takes the trouble to think, and that is usually controlled by what it is pleased to call its feelings."[2]

The lectures on moral economy multiplied, but the sympathy remained. It could be found on the lower mainland and in the interior; in Vancouver and New Westminster as well as in the Nicola Valley and Similkameen; among businessmen and workers, ranchers and farmers, men and women. "It is interesting to note the feelings of a majority of people," a Vancouver reporter wrote, "including prominent Vancouver businessmen, toilers with brain and brawn, men and women, heads of families. No less than twenty-five this morning when asked . . . if they had seen anything of Miner replied that they had not and that if they had, they surely would not tell the authorities and would aid Bill in his plight." One respondent felt that Miner had done "nothing wrong, simply robbed a train belonging to a corporation that has millions." "Oh, Bill Miner's not so bad," a businessman observed, "he only robs the C.P.R. once every two years but the C.P.R. robs us all every day." A similar opinion prevailed among Interior residents especially in the Nicola Valley where George Edwards had already become a legend. "Not only would nine-tenths of the people of the Nicola and Similkameen not betray Miner were he there," a Vancouver man who arrived from

2 The same editorialist continued, "The existence of such a contingent is a danger to the body politic, and indicates the necessity there is for the dissemination of correct opinion. The elementary truth that a respect for law and order lies at the foundation of the state, and that a want of it tends towards disintegration, does not seem to be properly grasped by this residuum of the population. They appear to regard the law as a distinct and alien entity with the operation of which they have no concern, but towards which they have a sort of adverse feeling of distaste. They seem to imagine that they can occupy a detached position from which they can regard the law and the criminal as two combatants engaged in a contest in which the law has the advantage, and in which the criminal, being the underdog, should get all the chances that can be given him."

Spences Bridge reported, "but they are proud of the fact that there is a wide-open welcome for him, good at any time and under any circumstances, with what amounts to practical protection from the police. He is regarded as a Robin Hood in these later days of steam railways, and indeed if all that is said about him here is true, he has some of the qualities which endeared to the public the old highway robber of Sherwood Forest."

Bill Miner in his flight from the law, enjoyed two special advantages. The people did not wish him back in jail, and were prepared to help him; and the federal authorities themselves seemed reluctant to have him back. No rewards were posted for the criminal's capture and arrest, no hordes of federal police officers were dispatched in pursuit, and no public inquiry was set up to report on the mechanics of the escape. The Miner caper was an embarrassment to the Laurier government, and a boon to its critics who alleged incompetence and corruption in the Justice Ministry. There were, in fact, several unanswered questions which the Borden Conservatives repeatedly raised in the months and years following the escape. Bourke hinted several times that outside help was enlisted to free Miner. Markings were found on the outside of the fence through which the convicts escaped, indicating that some of the demolition work had proceeded from the outside. The guards inside were remarkably slow in discovering the escape which they heard about from the young boy swimming in the nearby creek. Bourke himself was retired shortly thereafter, with full superannuation pay and despite his repeated statements about outside conniving, involving officials of the Justice Department, no public inquiry was launched. Rumours flew about mysterious bonds and equally mysterious detectives – some C.P.R. – who visited the prison before the break. One story, repeated in the press and parliament, claimed that Miner had stolen and hidden $50,000 in bonds during the 1904 C.P.R. holdup which he used as bait to buy help in escaping. Another story, emanating from a retired penitentiary official, and repeated in the House of Commons by New Westminster M.P. J. D. Taylor, insisted that no such bonds existed, except in the mind of Miner, who used the invention to lure several prison officials into collaborating with outside friends in facilitating the escape. "Bill

Miner did not escape from the prison by crawling under the fence through the hole through which it was alleged he went", the official reported. "The story of the loss of $50,000 worth of bonds or money by the C.P.R. or anyone else in the robbery, and that it had been secured by Miner, was an invention in the interest of the robber himself. No one ever lost that sum, no bonds were ever stolen. Miner's friends on the outside called on him and conducted fake negotiations for his so-called escape and the securing of the cached money. Certain persons made it possible for Miner to escape, apparently on the understanding that he would divide up the booty. These facts can easily be proven if the government makes an investigation."

But no public investigation was made by a government plainly unwilling to open a can of worms. Instead, federal officials busied themselves with expressions of regret, whines about the misdoings of American desperados, and tedious repetitions of their determination to bring the scoundrel to heal. "No more dangerous criminal, I think, was ever in the clutches of Canadian justice," the Prime Minister told the House of Commons. "It was a fact for which we took some credit that when one of these desperados came to Canada, thinking to play with impunity in this country the pranks he had been playing on the other side of the line, he was arrested, tried and convicted. It was a shock when we heard, and we heard it with a good deal of shame also, that he had subsequently been allowed to escape from the penitentiary."

The old man, of course, cared little about the government's shame. What mainly troubled him was the disposition of the final remnant of his own scarred life. Miner evidently had tired of Canadian hospitality and crossed the border into the country he knew best. His return went unnoticed and unsung until July 1909 when a lone old bandit, reported to be Bill Miner, held up a bank in Portland, Oregon and escaped with $12,000. Whether Miner visited Portland at all following his homecoming is not certain, but he did eventually drift east to Pennsylvania where he worked briefly maintaining electrical equipment in a sawmill, under the alias of George Anderson. Here Miner joined up with two young men, Charlie Hunter and James Hanford and headed south to

Bank County, Georgia where they worked at a sawmill and, in their spare moments, observed movements of the Southern Pacific Express whose line passed by their camp. They struck on the night of February 22, 1911. Carrying a red lantern, Miner flagged down train number 36 of the Southern Pacific at White Sulphur, seven miles north of Gainsville, boarded the cab with his two companions, sent the firemen up the track to explore a broken rail and entered the express car where dynamite was applied to open a large safe containing $65,000. Indisposed by his sore hands, or sore feet, or tired blood, or betrayed by weak powder, the old man failed to break the box after three explosions and had to settle for $1,500 obtained from a small strongbox. The payoff was low, considering the fervour of the chase. The state of Georgia, like the province of British Columbia was, in the matter of train robberies, virginal and the sheriffs and deputy sheriffs, posses and bloodhounds, Pinkertons and editorialists, pursued the robbers with a maniacal fervour. "Hardly anyone would believe the story at first," wrote the *Gainsville News*, "but the truth dawned at last and they are confronted with the fact, that here is a free, civilized, God-fearing and law-abiding community, a train robbery was committed that would abash the most God-forsaken Wild West country to be found. That such a daring hold-up could take place at their door was inconceivable, nevertheless it did take place and more than that, the robbers made a successful get-away." The robber's freedom was short-lived. Hunter and Hansford, who split with Miner and travelled together, were soon apprehended while two days after the robbery, a posse came upon a cabin in the woods near Dahlonga, occupied by an old man who called himself George Anderson. The old man was removed as an unlikely suspect to the county jail, where his scars, tattoos, moles and discolourations were meticulously explored by local police and Pinkerton detectives who forwarded his photograph to headquarters. The confirmation, that Anderson was Miner, despite the old man's protestations, came quickly and the trial, at the Hall County jail was conducted in early March. Hunter and Hansford credited Anderson with planning and executing the whole affair, pleaded guilty, and each received fifteen years. Anderson remained unco-operative throughout, denied that he was Miner and argued forcefully that the railways and corporations, who daily robbed the people, should be put out of business. But the jurymen were unconvinced and the old man, a rusted relic of the gilded age, was sentenced to twenty years.

Miner's stubborness did not end with his exile to the Newton County Public Work Camp at Covington, Georgia. Barely seven months after committal, Miner overpowered a guard with the help of a young convict, Tom Moore, and fled into the bush around Moore's home in Burke County. Posses, sheriffs and bloodhounds took to the chase and, three weeks later, the trail led to an old freight car within sight of Moore's home. A gun battle ensued resulting in the riddling of the car by sheriff's bullets, the death of Moore, and Miner's capitulation. But the old man's return was short-lived. In late June of the following year, a night guard peered into Miner's cell and discovered it empty. Hanging neatly on the bedpost were a pair of severed shackles while on the ledge below the window were several bars, removed from their appointed place. Miner and two companions fled to the swamp country below Milledgeville, stole a boat, and headed down the flooding Oconee River which stood fourteen feet above its normal level. In their wake sped the usual battalion of searchers including a steam launch commandeered by Warden J. E. Smith, which soon found the convicts' capsized boat and, nearby, the body of one of its younger passengers. Miner, however, was not around. Following the accident, he had fled further into the marshes, slogging and staggering aimlessly along the edge of a mosquito and snake-infested swamp. Five days after his escape, the old man, exhausted and sick, was found wandering in the marshes outside of the town of McIntyre.

He was removed to the Newton County Camp and there interrogated about the details of his amazing escape by a team of lawyers including Carl Vinson who later, as chairman of the House Armed Services Committee, found it easier to pry information from generals and brigadiers. But the prison officials no longer worried about the old man whose body and constitution were broken by this final ordeal. Miner lingered on awhile, finally a model prisoner, until his death on September 2, 1913 at 9:30 in the evening.

There was, it appeared, a tasteful funeral arranged by the local undertaker, a Mr. Joseph Moore, who taught Sunday school at the prison and thought the old robber a nice person to talk to and apart from the general run of convicts. Several prominent local citizens attended the burial including the pastor of the Episcopal Church, who delivered a non-eulogistic service. Miner was buried, among the bodies of other Milledgeville inmates, in an unmarked grave on the south side of Memory Hill: the city cemetery joined with Penitentiary Square by a street called Liberty.

Notes

The Miner story is briefly surveyed in F. W. Lindsay's *Outlaws in British Columbia,* Regatta City Press, Kelowna, 1963. A fuller account is Frank Anderson's *Bill Miner, Train Robber,* Frontier Books, Calgary, 1968, which contains useful information on Miner's American prison career. Several of the most informative of the numerous shorter pieces are Colin Rickards, "Bill Miner - Fifty Years a Hold-Up Man," in *The English Westerners' Brand Book,* vol. 8, Nos., 2 and 3, January, April 1966; Cecil Clark, "Hotter Than a Sheriff's Pistol," *The Shoulder Strap,* Vol. 24, Winter 1951 and by the same author, "Thousands in Loot," *Victoria Colonist,* November 1, 1962 (Magazine section, page 6). Various clippings from *The Dawson Scrapbook,* in possession of The State Historical Society of Colorado, carry accounts of Miner's American career. The *Vancouver Daily Province* and *Victoria Colonist* contain extensive and lurid accounts of the outlaw's robberies, pursuit, capture, trial and brief residency in New Westminster.